In the golden age of Asia,

Korea was one of its lamp-bearers

and that lamp is waiting to be lighted once again

for the illumination in the East

—Rabindranath Tagore
March 28, 1929

磨牙訊敢逢愁生東海

公

跋尾橫行者誰識人中

同

甲午南至書

CENTURY OF THE TIGER

ONE HUNDRED YEARS OF KOREAN CULTURE IN AMERICA

1903–2003

EDITORS

Jenny Ryun Foster

Frank Stewart • Heinz Insu Fenkl

DESIGNED BY

Elsa Carl • Clarence Lee

Mānoa Journal

Centennial Committee of Korean Immigration to the United States

University of Hawai'i Press

MĀNOA, A SERIES EDITED BY FRANK STEWART

BOOKS ON KOREA IN THIS SERIES

Century of the Tiger
www.hawaii.edu/mjournal/text/korea02.html

The Wounded Season
www.hawaii.edu/mjournal/text/korea99.html

Seeing the Invisible
www.hawaii.edu/mjournal/text/korea96.html

ISSN 1045-7909
ISBN 0-8248-2684-1 (cloth)
ISBN 0-8248-2644-2 (pbk.)
Copyright © 2003
University of Hawai'i Press
2840 Kolowalu Street
Honolulu, Hawai'i 96822
Printed in China

For subscribers, this is *Mānoa Journal*
vol. 14, no. 2 (winter 2002–2003).

COVER AND FRONTISPIECE: courtesy of
National Museum of Korea.

PUBLISHED ON THE OCCASION OF THE
CENTENNIAL CELEBRATION OF KOREAN IMMIGRATION
TO THE UNITED STATES, 1903–2003

PRINCIPAL DONOR
First Hawaiian Foundation

MAJOR DONORS
Wesley T. Park
Alexander & Baldwin Foundation
Centennial Committee of Korean Immigration
to the United States
Center for Korean Studies of the University of Hawai'i
National Endowment for the Arts
Charles Engelhard Foundation
Atherton Family Foundation
Murabayashi Foundation
Hawai'i State Foundation on Culture and the Arts
Hawai'i Council for the Humanities
Mauna Kea Resorts

CONTENTS

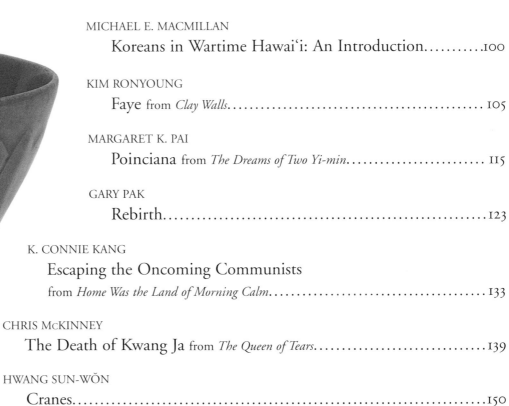

CHAPTER FOUR
WAR AND LIBERATION

CHAPTER FIVE
NEW ARRIVALS IN A CHANGED AMERICA

CELEBRATING THE TIGER

POETRY BY
Hŏ Nansŏrhŏn   Sim Hun
Ch'oe Ch'i-wŏn   Walter K. Lew
Ok-Koo Kang Grosjean   Ishle Yi Park
Kim Sowŏl   Sue Kwock Kim
Yi Sang-hwa   Naomi Long

ROCK, PINE TREE, WILLOW BOUGH: AN INTRODUCTION

In Younghill Kang's novel *The Grass Roof,* Chung-Pa leads his two best friends behind the village temple and into the dense and scary Grove of Ghosts. There, the boys make a pact: they will grow up to become the three greatest men in the world. Chung-Pa composes a song on the spot, and they sing it as they dance in a circle:

> *Our will is as strong as the rocks . . .*
> *Our minds are as enduring as the pine trees . . .*
> *And our hearts are as green as willow boughs . . .*
> *Though hard the path, heavy the task, long long the day,*
> *We will march on!*

This scene takes place just as the Korean American saga begins, near the turn of the twentieth century. The Japanese will soon invade Korea and attempt to destroy its national identity, and the first wave of Korean immigrants will leave their homeland for America.

The spirit of the boys' song—an anthem of strength, endurance, and optimism—echoes throughout the prose and poems in *Century of the Tiger: One Hundred Years of Korean Culture in America 1903–2003.*

Today, Korean Americans are one of the most successful minorities in the United States, making significant contributions in the arts, politics, law, and business. And yet, Korean Americans are also among the least visible and least understood. There are many reasons for this. When Koreans began immigrating to America in 1903, most settled in Hawai'i—a new U.S. territory in the middle of the Pacific Ocean. Fewer than one thousand continued on to the U.S. mainland. Within two years, the Korean government, under military control of Japan, halted further immigration. The few exceptions to this ban included five hundred to seven hundred young women who, starting in about 1910, were allowed to travel to Hawai'i for the purpose of meeting their prospective husbands. However, even so-called picture brides were prevented from entering the country when the U.S. Congress passed a law in 1924 that, while intended to restrict Japanese immigration, was applied to Koreans as well; by this time, Japan had annexed Korea and made all of its citizens Japanese subjects.

For the first half of the twentieth century, the size of the Korean American population remained stable: fewer than two thousand in the continental United States and only about eight thousand in Hawai'i. Because Koreans were such a small minority and most did not want to associate with the Japanese, they blended rapidly into the non-Asian population, mastering English and readily marrying non-Koreans. In Hawai'i, they also quickly moved off the plantations and started small businesses. Struggling to survive, this tiny community was overshadowed by American, Japanese, and other cul-

Seasonal Flowers and Birds,
with Chinese Couplets
Chosŏn dynasty
Ink and colors on cotton

tures. What little was known in the United States about Koreans was predominantly dis-information from a Japanese propaganda campaign designed to convince the world that Koreans were a backwards people, grateful to Japan for making Korea part of the Japanese empire. Korea's rich cultural heritage was thus unknown or largely misunderstood in the United States.

World War II created further challenges. Korean Americans had ardently protested Japanese imperialism in Asia for decades, but since they were officially regarded by the U.S. government as Japanese citizens, they were forced to register as "enemy aliens" after 1941. This was a terrible blow to their national pride and sense of justice. Nevertheless, they saw it as their patriotic duty to help America defeat the Japanese. Thus, many Koreans loyally served in the U.S. military and in civilian roles that aided the war effort.

The fall of Japan at the end of World War II promised a new era for Korea. But in 1950, Koreans in America witnessed their mother country torn apart by a tragic civil war. During the three-year conflict, Korean Americans served as interpreters and combat soldiers, and many earned distinction for military service. War on the peninsula was on the front page every day, and when an armistice ended the fighting in 1953, the arrival of 14,000 Korean war orphans, brides of U.S. servicemen, and students had doubled the number of Koreans in America. Partly as a result of these new arrivals, Congress passed the McCarran-Walter Act, which at last allowed Korean-born immigrants to become U.S. citizens.

In 1965, Congress abolished immigration quotas based on national origin and thus initiated the second wave of large-scale Korean immigration. By 1985, the Korean American population had risen to half a million; by the 1990s, it was over one million.

Despite their increasing numbers, however, second-wave Korean immigrants still found it difficult to educate other Americans about Korean culture. To do so, they would have to overcome the often-negative images of Cold War tensions on the Korean peninsula, dictatorships, martial law, and student riots. Further complicating matters, many of the newly arrived immigrants congregated in so-called Koreatowns in Los Angeles, Chicago, New York, and other urban centers; as newcomers to America's racial complexities, they sometimes clashed with their non-Korean neighbors.

Today, the history and heritage of Korean Americans are somewhat better known, partly because writers and artists have taken on the challenge of communicating to the rest of America the energetic and unique qualities of Korean culture. In addition, American society as a whole is at last recognizing just how international and culturally diverse the nation has become. The centennial celebration is a wonderful and long-awaited opportunity to speak and listen to one another—across generations, neighborhoods, and cultures.

In *Century of the Tiger,* readers will see that, like the rocks, the pine trees, and the willow boughs of Chung-Pa's song, Koreans are strong of mind and supple of heart—able to press on undaunted into the future. They will also see, through literature and art, the history that has shaped the Korean character.

The works in this book are arranged according to the period they depict or represent. Chapter one, "Land of Morning Calm," features the writing of Younghill Kang, the first Korean American novelist. Having participated in the March first demonstration of 1919, Kang was pursued by Japanese police through China and Russia, finally immigrating to North America in his twenties. Awarded a graduate degree by Harvard University in 1927, he went on to become well known in the United States not only for his writing but also for his political activism on behalf of the Korean community. The first excerpt from Kang's novel *The Grass Roof,* printed in chapter one, depicts the cultural life of the Korean countryside before Japanese occupation. The second excerpt, "Doomsday," depicts the arrival of the occupiers.

Chapter two, "Sailing to the Garden of Mugunghwa," takes its title from the ideal of a land plentiful with *mugunghwa*—the beautiful "eternal-blooming flower" known to Americans as the Rose of Sharon—which represents the undaunted Korean spirit. This chapter presents stories of the earliest immigrants: a section of the novel *East Goes West* by Younghill Kang, an excerpt from Mary Paik Lee's memoir, *Quiet*

Odyssey, and an interview by Morris Pang with his immigrant father. Although most of the first wave of immigrants stayed in Hawai'i, this chapter includes the experiences of several who landed elsewhere or traveled beyond the islands to the U.S. mainland.

Chapter three, *"Manse!"* explores how forcefully the independence movement shaped the lives of the early Korean immigrants. Though they had scattered across the Pacific, and were from the very beginning a heterogeneous group, the loss of their mother country united Koreans everywhere; they formed organizations, raised money, trained their own soldiers, established a government-in-exile, and became adept at international diplomacy to plead their country's cause. The excerpt from K. Connie Kang's memoir, *Home Was the Land of Morning Calm,* describes the atrocities committed by the Japanese following the March 1, 1919, demonstration in Korea and the impact that the demonstration and its aftermath had on Koreans overseas. Author Kim Ronyoung, in an excerpt from her novel, *Clay Walls,* writes about the determination of Koreans on the U.S. mainland to raise money for the cause, even as they experienced financial hardships and prejudice in their adopted country. Margaret

K. Pai's autobiographical novel, *The Dreams of Two Yi-min*, recounts the anguish among Koreans in Hawai'i as the community was torn by factionalism over how best to achieve Korea's independence. The chapter closes with an excerpt from Richard E. Kim's novel *Lost Names,* depicting events in Korea as the Japanese attempted to erase the last traces of Korean culture by stripping people of even their own names.

Chapter four, "War and Liberation," recalls experiences faced by Koreans during World War II and the Korean War. The chapter includes further excerpts from the novels of Kim Ronyoung and Margaret K. Pai, describing life on the U.S. mainland and in Hawai'i in the days following the Japanese attack on Pearl Harbor. The short story "Rebirth," by Hawai'i writer Gary Pak, reflects this time of confusion and spiritual longing. An excerpt from Chris McKinney's novel *The Queen of Tears* and "Cranes," a well-known short story by Korean writer Hwang Sun-wŏn, are set in Korea along the thirty-eighth parallel during the Korean War and after the partitioning of the country.

The final chapter, "New Arrivals in a Changed America," presents work by a new generation of Korean American writers. Their diverse stories recognize that Koreans have become Americans under many different circumstances—that there has been, for them, no single immigrant experience. Heinz Insu Fenkl, in an excerpt from his forthcoming novel, *Skull Water*, writes about a young Amerasian boy who, in returning to his hometown, acquires a fuller understanding of his family's past. Chang-Rae Lee's essay "Coming Home Again" explores the tender, complicated understanding between a mother and son. The short stories by Caroline Jeong-Mee Kim and June Unjoo Yang are about characters trying to transcend the communities they were born into. In "Magdalena," a teenager who feels lonely and foreign as a Korean growing up in Massachusetts develops sympathy for an eccentric woman ostracized by her church. Yang's "Compassion" is about a youth counselor trying to shed her "rich-girl" image and become a part of inner-city life. Ha-yun Jung's story "Home Spheres" compels us to ponder, among other questions, how we know "home"—and how it might be different from "homeland." Finally, in Don Lee's comic-tragic story "The Lone Night Cantina," a newly divorced Korean American woman throws herself headlong across the boundaries of identity, adopting a bold country-and-western persona in order to cope with the changes in her life.

Century of the Tiger presents the experiences of many generations of Koreans in America who came here—and continue to arrive—under a variety of circumstances. Ultimately, however, it is meant as a tribute to the first immigrants, who journeyed across the Pacific to create a new life for themselves and their children, and whose integrity established a strong and honorable foundation on which Korean Americans continue to build.

CHAPTER ONE

LAND OF
MORNING
CALM

EDWARD J. SHULTZ

KOREAN HISTORY: AN INTRODUCTION

In symbolizing a nation, national flags often reveal history. The Korean flag—with the red and blue circle at its center—does this and more: it also makes a statement about the cultural belief system of the Korean people. The divided circle connotes the dynamically opposed forces of *ŭm* and *yang* (*yin* and *yang* in Chinese) and symbolizes an ideal of unity or harmony that emerges as these opposites—light and dark, negative and positive—commingle. The harmonizing of opposing forces has been a theme in Korea's history and cultural heritage. For centuries, Koreans have sought to live in a peaceful balance among themselves and with their powerful neighbors. The nation's search for unity through opposites continues today, as North and South Korea struggle toward reunification.

Some historians locate Korea's origins as early as five thousand years ago, when the legendary king Tan'gun was born of a bear and a heavenly deity. Others place the beginnings of Korea at about 1000 B.C., when the people of the peninsula passed from a paleolithic/neolithic existence to the Bronze Age. In any event, by the beginning of the first millennium, small tribal communities appeared on the peninsula in districts ruled from walled towns. Gradually, the towns were consolidated into larger political entities, so that by the fifth century A.D., three key states—Koguryŏ in the north, Paekche in the southwest, and Silla in the southeast—dominated the Korean peninsula and southern Manchuria. China influenced the region's political and cultural values through Buddhism and Confucianism and aided these states in building stable political structures and unique legacies.

By A.D. 668, Silla had unified much of the southern two-thirds of the Korean peninsula by bringing Koguryŏ and Paekche under its control. In A.D. 936, a new kingdom defeated Silla and took the name Koryŏ, from which Westerners have derived the name Korea. The Koryŏ kingdom lasted five hundred years, until 1392, when the Yi family established Chosŏn, Korea's last kingdom.

Although Silla, Koryŏ, and Chosŏn survived for many centuries, each struggled to maintain Korea's independence amid the tides of political turbulence and warfare in East Asia. China's Sui and T'ang dynasties were the first to threaten the Koryŏ and Silla kingdoms. When the Koryŏ kingdom came to power in the early tenth century, it had to defend itself against Manchurian tribes, which repeatedly launched invasions over a forty-year period.

The Chosŏn kingdom established modern Korea's geographic boundaries, but it too encountered many foreign threats. Japanese pirate raids, followed by major invasions by Japan in 1592 and 1598, crippled the kingdom economically and socially. The Chosŏn kings repelled these threats only to be confronted by Manchu attacks in the 1630s. Again the kingdom withstood the onslaught. In the nineteenth century, Chosŏn faced imperialist threats, first by Western nations and then again by the Japanese. In

1910, the Japanese succeeded in annihilating the five-hundred-year-old Chosŏn king-dom and began a domination of Korea that lasted nearly five decades, until 1945.

Protracted conflicts and invasions of the Korean peninsula resulted in the destruction of much of the literature, art, and cultural legacy of the Silla and early Koryŏ periods. Surviving artifacts testify to the fertility of the Korean creative genius and to its earthy sense of humor and love of nature. Shamanism, Korea's earliest spiritu-al practice, stressed the need to harmonize the self with natural forces and phenomena. In the fourth century A.D., Korea was introduced to the Buddhist approach to spiritual meaning. As shamanism helped people live in harmony with nature, Buddhism assisted the individual in a spiritual and religious quest. Confucianism, introduced at roughly the same time, helped to formalize the relationships among individuals, society, and the state.

Traditional Korean society was hierarchical and divided into classes. The most aristocratic, Silla had a state under the strict control of a hereditary elite and developed a rigid caste system in which birth determined one's economic, social, and political sta-tus. Although Koryŏ retained some of these aristocratic features, it allowed for mobility

in the social order, and it inaugurated a state civil-service exami-nation in which ability was a criterion for promotion. Further modification of the social-political order occurred with the rise of the Chosŏn kingdom. During this period, a ruling class based partly on scholarship emerged: the *yangban*. The *yangban* scholar-gentry dominated Chosŏn life, and by the nineteenth century, several key *yangban* families controlled politics.

The blending of Korea's various philosophies—together with centuries of cultural contacts with its neighbors—was expressed in unique, exquisite art. The Silla dynasty, beginning in the seventh century A.D., produced jewelry and ornaments of gold, silver, and jade, as well as delicate blown-glass vessels. By about the eleventh century, Koryŏ artisans perfected celadon pot-tery so refined that it came to surpass all other pottery of its type. Architecture and stone sculpture were equally masterful thanks in part to the impetus of Buddhism in the fourteenth century.

The arts flourished at the beginning of the Chosŏn period and reached a peak in the fifteenth century under King Sejong, a ruler unequaled in Korean history. His achievements were many. One in particular stands out. By invent-ing and introducing a phonetic writing system, *han'gŭl,* King Sejong made it possible for the common people to be literate in their own language, to have access to knowl-edge of all sorts without the obstacle of having to learn Chinese ideographs. *Han'gŭl* allowed Koreans to express their ideas clearly in Korean rather than Chinese sentence structure and thought patterns. King Sejong ordered books to be printed in *han'gŭl,* and thus a vernacular literature was created. Korea was on its way to becoming a modern, unified nation.

YOUNGHILL KANG
from *The Grass Roof*

THE VALLEY OF UTOPIA

I was told by one of my aunts that I was born somewhere in northern Korea, while my mother was on a trip to China with my father. Since I cannot verify my birth place accurately, it is safe to say that I was born in that village where I was brought up, not far from Asiatic Russia and Manchuria, in a handmade house fashioned of stone, wood and clay, and covered with a grass roof that turned up slightly at the eaves like Korean women's shoes.

I know now that I was born in the year when the minds of the people were greatly perplexed. Everybody was worrying and talking about the coming war, prophesying that the Japanese would soon be over to kill all the Koreans. It was about that time when Japan was to declare war on Russia, and requested from the Korean government permission to use the roads into Manchuria, a request that was really a command, and was followed soon by military occupation.

They said that I was born on the tenth day of May, by the Korean calendar (which is about a month later than by the American), just as the sun came up and the cock crew: also that according to the Four Pillars of Destiny (the hour, day, month, and year of birth) I was born to be a wanderer all my life, with no home but the wide world. I never remember my mother, for she died a few months after I was born, but I fear she must have eaten only grass roots, and suffered every hardship, for the people were very poor just at this time. Besides the political anxiety which recalled my father from China, it had been a hard year for the crops at home, and the whole village was starving.

This village where I was born—Song-Dune-Chi, or The Village of the Pine Trees—was made up entirely of my own relatives, a clan by the name of Han, who were ruled by national ideals which had been handed down from father to son for innumerable generations. Our community had long been looked up to by others for its famous scholars and its olden-time clannish spirit, in a country for immemorial years under the iron thumb of tradition and ancestor worship, a country of which Napoleon said: "A giant is asleep. Do not wake him."

Our village was situated in a huge valley, partly poor sandy rock, and partly fertile soil, between high mountains, covered with pine and oak trees, and many high tall grasses. There were streams running down from each mountain hollow, joining the big river which murmured eternity's chant through the centre of the valley. A few miles farther on, this river passed through the marketplace where the people of my village went every five days for barter, and there it rushed into the sea. Except for the marketplace, the people were rural and isolated, and this mysterious water, constantly tumbling in, was the only far wanderer among them. My native village was the kind which all the great Oriental sages have thought Utopia in itself. The people had been happy in the same costumes, dwellings, food, and manners for over a thousand years, and were like

HŎ NANSŎRHŎN

Sending Off

Yellow gold, beautifully wrought,
the half-moon pendant was a gift
from my in-laws when I came in marriage.
I hung it on my red silk gown.
I give it to you, my love, as you
    start off today,
hoping you will look at it as a token
    of my love.
It will not be so awful if you leave
    it on the way,
just do not hand it over as a gift
    to some new love.

Translation by David R. McCann

Poems written in Chinese by Korean poets were called *hansi*, and the best of them kept a Korean sensibility despite using the language and poetic traditions of China. "Sending Off" and other *hansi* by Hŏ Nansŏrhŏn (1563–1589) continue to be admired today. The poet transforms her sorrow over her husband's leaving into a song of faithfulness and endurance. The theme of strength in the face of lost love—whether of a spouse or one's homeland—occurs again and again in Korean poetry.

the ideal state of Lao-Tze, where "though there be a neighboring state within sight, and the voices of the cocks and dogs thereof be within hearing, yet the people might grow old and die before they ever visit one another."

On the right bank of the river, bordered and interspersed by pine and weeping willow trees, was the village, and behind it, somewhat lower, the rice fields. On the left bank grew the millet and other grains, and farther over, against the opposite mountain, were to be found the deer, the hawks, the tiger cats and fabulous Dragons. I can remember in the mornings when the sun was getting up how its beams trembled on dew-shrunken foliage of the mountain, then poured down like sparkling bits of glass over the water in the valley—especially when the rice seeds were ripening in the fields. At such a time the whole world seemed to dance and glisten, for the color of the ripe rice was tawny, and lay rippling like a golden fleece under the eye. In the spring, of course, this rice would be a clear young green, the color worn by brides in my country. But at all times the rice fields were a picturesque sight, for they were kept covered by water artificially, and mirrored the changes of the elements, reflecting the bright blue of the sky, taking on the colors of the slender rain, catching the dying sun in a blurred glass, and enhancing the mystery of the Yellow Dusk, or perhaps imaging the round moon above some scholar's roof.

But life was not all Utopia to the people in my village. Sometimes the river behaved like an evil Dragon. Even if the village did not have heavy rains, there would be floods which came from the mountains, where there had been a cloudburst. The hardest time for the farmer was during the months of August and September, when all the old crops had been eaten, and the new grain had not reached fruition. Then the only food would be potatoes and fish. This cost the father of the family only a few pennies per day, but often he did not have even so much as that. Then his family had to live on grass roots and rice hulls. I remember how one farmer, after hungering many weeks during the starvation time, went away and ate too much, so that he died. This is the same fate which overtook the Chinese poet, Tu Fu, and it gave rise to a saying in the East that there is a greater danger in over-eating than in under-eating.

There is a Korean proverb: "Scatter frost upon the snow." Often the autumn floods would occur during the lean months, and then the almost empty storehouses, the cattle, dwellings, and every kind of valuable property, would be swept away by the river. The people of Han had an endless struggle for existence in spite of their beautiful surroundings amidst nature. I shall never forget a tragic picture I saw one time: an old man crying miserably, as he and his wife and children on the bank watched his house, his cattle, and all his goods being carried away on the flood. What should he do now for the winter months?

Our home was not exempt from this miserable dependence upon the elements,

but my family did not seem to mind their helpless poverty, since most of them were indulging in the mystical doctrine of Buddhism, or in the classics of Confucius, who always advocated that a man should not be ashamed of coarse food, humble clothing, and modest dwelling, but should only be ashamed of not being cultivated in the perception of beauty. The sage said: "Living on coarse rice and water, with bent arm for pillow, mirth may yet be mine. Ill-gotten wealth and honors are like to floating clouds." A man has no place in society, Confucius teaches, unless he understands aesthetics.

Many of the great men influencing my people, like Po Yi, or Chieh Chih Tuei, starved to death. Thus it was a point of honor with my family to suffer hardship, and to scorn all content except aesthetic peace. My crazy-poet uncle, the scholar of the family, cared little how his hair looked, or for dirt in his nose, but went right at it with his pen. He was a comical creature. Everything he said was poetry. If you mentioned any incident, he would quote: "Under such a situation a famous poet once said—" and then he would recite the whole poem by memory. In a few minutes he would give his own verse to fit the occasion, using the same rhymes used by the poet he had quoted. At one time he had lived at the capital, Seoul, where he had attained to high rank; and he had studied a long time in China. For him the New Year's gifts piled up, chickens, gloves, shoes, stockings, an occasional overcoat. Many respected such genius and would have died for him. My poor father, who would put days and days in working in the interests of public service which did not pay him a penny, never received these favors. Every time it rained my crazy-poet uncle wrote a poem like Li Po's. Like Confucius, he was "a man so eager that he forgot to eat, whose cares were lost in triumph, unmindful of approaching age."

My grandfather was making his own living away from us by writing poetry and selling calligraphy, and by divination. Professionally, he was a *poong-sui* (which means master of wind and water), a scientist who chooses by geomantic system the most propitious sites for burial grounds. It is a very respectable professional position, and only a great scholar of the classics would be able to master its intricacies. By scanning the horizon and by ranging over the country in the study of hills and plains, my grandfather could tell just which of the nine stars and five planets controlled the land. My grandmother one time told me that he had picked out many locations for those who were now, through the success of his efforts, famous and prosperous in society. One man, who was told by him that a certain burial ground would bring a *pak-sa* or famous doctor-of-letters to a son of the fourth generation, dug out his own great-grandfather's grave and buried the ashes into the spot indicated, being ambitious not for the fourth generation, but for himself. And later, sure enough, he became a *pak-sa* or a famous doctor-of-letters. I still do not know how to explain it, for it certainly seemed to work out. Of course one explanation is that there is a spiritual force in the mountains helpful to the vitality, energy and destiny of the people who bury their ancestors correctly.

My family has always had its wanderers. Besides my grandfather there was my prodigal-son uncle. He could write very good poetry and was full of advice for the children from the sages; especially he was fond of advice from Confucius who taught the responsibilities of family life and devotion to fathers and mothers and elder brothers. But my junior uncle did not practise what he preached. He came back home only to ask for money, mount up debts and cause trouble. Later he had children by his wife, who of course, all lived with us, but he never stayed at home, nor did any work for them. He was a small, lively man with twinkling eyes full of the wine of life, and somewhat of a dandy in his dress. I remember him best as wearing a tiny black moustache which he carefully oiled and then rearranged with his fingers in order to make it look more beautiful than it was.

My prodigal-son uncle was my grandmother's youngest and her favorite until I was born. Because for a long time I was the youngest grandson, and because I was the eldest son of the eldest son and would pray to her spirit after she was gone, my grandmother was very partial to me. I remember her picking from her own bowl the choicest bits of chicken and putting them in mine. How eagerly she would watch me eat, as if she tasted them herself! I can only remember her punishing me once. That was because of a childish indecency: I asked the servant to give me food before the hour.

In spoiling me, she was assisted by Ok-Dong-Ya, my little cousin with the beautiful smile. Ok-Dong-Ya (meaning Little-Jade-Girl) was about my own age, a daughter of the crazy poet. She would save her candies often and then give them to me with that expression my grandmother had when she gave me her chicken. But she was not just copying my grandmother. I remember Ok-Dong-Ya even then as gay, tender, womanly. She was always full of imagination. She too loved the beautiful poets and would have me recite them to her. We understood each other. She preferred me, I think, to her own brother—a fat, good-looking, sarcastic boy, some years my senior, but almost too clever. With him I always fought. His name was Eul-Choon (meaning In-the-Spring-of-the-Year). My name was Chung-Pa (meaning Green-of-Mountain). He and I often fought over our favorite poet, or the meaning of a verse of the classics.

Ewer with Scrolling Lotus
Mid–late 12th century
Stoneware with celadon glaze

The Tale of Tan'gun

Long ago, the Heavenly King's son, Hwanung, desired to live in the world of humans. His father chose for him the region around Mount T'aebaek and sent him there with three celestial ministers to assist him: Wind, Rain, and Clouds. Beside a sacred sandalwood tree atop the mountain, the Heavenly Prince established his Sacred City, brought culture to the people, and made their lives orderly.

At that time, a bear and a tiger lived in a cave near the sandalwood tree, and they prayed ardently to the divine Hwanung to transform them into human beings. Hwanung gave them a bundle of sacred mugworts and twenty cloves of garlic and said, "If you eat these and remain deep in your cave for one hundred days, you will become humans." Both animals did as they were told. After twenty-one days, the bear became a beautiful woman. But the tiger, who couldn't endure the trial any longer, ran away and remained a tiger. Unable to find a husband, the bear-woman prayed under the sandalwood tree for a child of her own. Hwanung lay with her and granted her wish. They named their son Tan'gun Wanggŏm, the Sandalwood King. When he grew up, he became the first human ruler of the kingdom he called Chosŏn (Morning Calm). Tan'gun made the city of P'yŏngyang his capital and ruled for 1,500 years. After that, he became the Mountain Spirit.

Adapted from a translation by Peter H. Lee

Sejong's Preface to the Promulgation of Han'gŭl

The speech sounds of our country's language are different from those of the Middle Kingdom (China) and are not communicable with the sounds of Chinese characters. Therefore, when my beloved ignorant people want to say something, many of them are unable to say something, many of them are unable to express their feelings in writing. Feeling compassion for this I have newly designed twenty-eight letters, only wishing to have everyone readily practice and use them conveniently every day.

King Sejong (1397–1450) was one of Korea's greatest rulers. Among other innovations of his was the creation of a council of scholars that was charged with improving all aspects of life in the country. The council's technological advances included the invention in 1443 of *han'gŭl,* a phonetic system that enabled Koreans to learn and use their native language easily. *Han'gŭl* could express new words, words unique to the Korean language, and, as the fifteenth-century scholar Sin Suk-chu said, "the sound of the wind and the crowing of roosters." King Sejong promulgated its use in a treatise, *Correct Sounds to Teach the People,* in 1446.

Calligraphy by Yoo Younghee

The livelihood of this whole family depended upon my father, who, in theory, was the master of the house, but, in fact, was the slave of everybody. He was a large, stout, heroic-looking man with a great black beard reaching halfway down his long white coat, in the style of the old-fashioned Koreans. In spite of his Homeric look, his eyes held an anxious, responsible expression. He was emotional, rather than reasoning, and had a strong sense of traditional duty. Since he was the oldest male representative of the family at home, he had to take care of his two younger brothers, and his sister before her marriage, and the brothers' wives and their children, besides raising me. He had to do everything for them, from roofing the long house with grass—an annual task—to making the children's shoes. Nor was there any division of labor. No one else felt responsible. That means, he himself was putting the roof on the house, or making the shoes for the children; no one else turned a hand.

There was a little income in the household from the salaries of my senior uncle, who in addition to his fame as a poet was a teacher of classics. The chief source for supplies was what my father made by fashioning tools of all kinds and taking them down to the sea to barter, for the whole community used very little money. The thing he made the most was a tool for gathering pine needles to cook rice with: he could do almost anything very well with his hands, and was an excellent binder of my poet uncle's books. (Always he had a deep respect for scholars, though he was not a great scholar himself.)

Sometimes during the hard months when food in the village was scarce, my father's position as head of the household was especially hard. One ghastly night of rain in flood-time the whole family sat up waiting for him to return home and bring them food. He had gone out in the night in his old straw raincoat to a particular rich man, miles away, who was reported to have poor small seeds of wheat. None but the very rich had food in the grain-house then. My father tried to get the wheat on credit, for he had nothing to trade with. The man refused to let him have the grain, not even a spoonful for my grandmother. My father went elsewhere and everywhere was refused. He could not even get a small tail of fish for my grandmother. So finally my father slipped back home and had to confess that he could get no food. The others went to bed, but he walked up and down, up and down all the long night, and he could not sleep. "It was not because I was hungry," he once told me with tears in his eyes. "I felt no hunger. But it was because I knew my mother was hungry and I had not been able to bring her food."

From the time he was only a child, my father carried the responsibility of the whole family. Although he had a living father, the geomancer, my grandfather was always away travelling, coming home just once in a while to see the family (which is how my uncles happened to be born). My grandmother was in many ways the most

Movable Type

Koreans invented movable metal type and were using it by 1234. They published the first book in 1377—long before before Gutenberg produced Europe's first printed book, in 1450. The Chinese had employed movable clay type even earlier, but clay was breakable and this method quickly fell into disuse.

In the fifteenth century, after inventing *han'gŭl*, King Sejong ordered metal type to be cast and books to be printed using the new system. These initiatives gave Koreans a vernacular literature that could at last be preserved in books to be read by everyone for ages to come.

important one in our house. I know that she was much loved by my father. She was a tiny gray-haired woman of great energy. Most Korean women are small, but she was smaller than most. I think she was pretty. But I might be prejudiced in speaking of her; since my grandmother, however plain, would still look attractive to me. She generally wore the traditional white of middle-class Korean women, and was not at all particular about her clothes. I never remember seeing her powdering her nose, nor oiling her hair like other Korean women. The wives-and-mothers-yet-to-be of Song-Dune-Chi were all told to become like her. Besides being learned in every kind of wifely detail, she was capable of the work of a man in the fields when there was sudden need. But above all, she was a true Oriental woman. The quietism of Buddha, the mysterious calm of Taoism, the ethical insight of Confucianism all helped to make her an unusually refined personality. Because of her lonely life in the long-continued absence of my grandfather, and her bewildered fear of the "foreigners" (the Japanese and the Westerners who came in ever-increasing numbers to Korea during my childhood), and because she was a woman, she was most attracted by the emotional elements of Buddhism. No one else in our house was a Buddhist. My father was a Confucian; my crazy-poet uncle was mostly a Taoist; only my grandmother loved best the stories and sayings of the pitying Buddha. Yet she usually preached to me because I was a man-child the Confucian virtues of obedience, self-sacrifice and a deep love of the classics. I remember her saying: "There is heaven above, and earth below. Amidst these two dwells man. He is the noblest creature of all that God has created. *Hé!* it is a great thing to be the Master of all. Let not your life fritter away meaninglessly. You must train yourself to be good and useful and prepare to make others happy, so always study hard the wisdom of Confucius."

My grandmother loved the great literature of the past and sound scholarship was one of her ideals. But she did not want us to be a house of scholars. She knew that the more scholars there are in a household the poorer it is. There are several reasons for this. To be a scholar you are handicapped, you have to be honest. And furthermore a scholar is not expected to work in the fields. Poets in the Orient, although much respected, make no money. Both my uncles wrote verses for all occasions, for weddings, for funerals, for births. Yet they got no money in return. Nobody thought of offering them money, but only gifts, of wine and dainties. My grandmother was just as well satisfied that my father should not be a scholar. She said that she had made one great scholar among her sons, my crazy-poet uncle, who was officially very distinguished, and that now she wanted to make one more among her grandsons and the rest must be practical.

DOOMSDAY

It may seem strange to the reader unfamiliar with Far Eastern politics that Korea, an independent nation for over forty-two centuries, should have been so helpless those first ten years of the twentieth century before the stealthy but persistent encroaching of New Japan. But Japan's strength in the East is due to rapid Westernization, especially in regard to armament. That alone, perhaps, she thoroughly learned, since the time of Perry's entrance, and is thoroughly competent to proselyte. With the vigor of a younger nation, engaged already in enormous changing, inherently imitative, it is easy for her to slough one borrowed culture and to absorb another in its place. Yes, comparatively, easy, as it was not for the older nations, China and Korea. Clinging closely to the old Confucian nature, and each in an exhausted era of their history, they were truly stunned for those first decades of world-wide intercourse.

That little Japan won over the million millions of wise, deep China first. After her victory, she began to make her demands upon Korea, during the Russo-Japanese War. She must be allowed passage for her troops through Korea, and she signed a treaty stating that she had no designs upon the Korean state as a whole. These troops were never withdrawn. They remained to shelter the swarms of low-class Japanese adventurers who followed, and to uphold them in all they mis-did. Japan moved deliberately step by step. She first seized the silent control of the incompetent and bewildered government at Seoul in 1907: hemmed in by spies and Japanese generals, the old emperor was made to abdicate to a minor son; then at last Japan spoke plainly, the 29th of August, 1910, when all treaties were annulled and Korea was publicly declared annexed…

When the news reached the grass roof in Song-Dune-Chi, my father turned a dark red, and could not even open his mouth. My uncle *pak-sa* became suddenly very old and he shriveled and fainted in his own room. My crazy-poet uncle sat staring straight ahead of him until far into the night. My first thought was a selfish and immature one.

"Now I cannot be a *pak-sa* or the prime minister of Korea."

I burst into tears. But my elders did not cry, not yet. So I ran crying out of the house. I looked up at the sky, to see if there was really a black doom up there. Were a final thunderstorm and a flood about to come which would wipe us all out? But the sky was blue and serene, and the river had only a sunny crystal foam as it whirled past. Children were standing around with scared blank faces. The village was quiet. Nobody spoke. Later on, in the afternoon, there was a general weeping, everywhere the sound of mourning, as if each house in the village were wailing for somebody dead. Some men began to drink and drink, shouting:

"The doomsday has come! We have all gone to the Hell!"

My father lurched out of the house, although he had had nothing to drink, and nothing to eat since morning.

"My poor poor children!" he cried out, and tears now streamed from his eyes. He held out his hands to us, as if we were all his eldest sons. "Now all are going to die in the ruined starvation. The time of the unending famine has come down upon us. Who knows when we may be happy again?"

And with tears running over his face, and mingling with his beard, he put up the Korean flag over our gateway and bowed down to it.

There was no supper that night. My grandmother sat up by candlelight, in the same dress she had worn in the morning. Again and again she took a cup of rice tea to my father, but he lay heavily on the mats, and he would not accept it.

In the morning, it was found that several of the young men who had been among those drunk the night before had committed suicide. Their bodies lay along the banks of the stream where the women usually did washing on this day.

A Japanese policeman came to our village, at the head of a band of pale-blue-coated Japanese, each armed with a long sword. Of course they knocked at our gate, and asked why we did not have the sun flag of Japan instead of the red and white flag of Korea betokening the male and female realm, and in accordance with the Confucian philosophy of the Book of Changes, sun and moon and all the elements used in geomancy. My father shrugged his shoulders and pretended not to understand. The small Japanese policeman then flew at my father, kicking and striking him, with menace of the sword. My grandmother saw from the window, and ran out without even stopping to put her coat over her head and screen her face from vulgar eyes.

"Don't you touch my son!" she screamed, stepping between, "because he has had nothing to eat for these two days and doesn't know what he is doing."

As soon as she came between them the policeman knocked her down. He kicked her fiercely with his Western boot. Her sons seeing it, gasped. In the eyes of Koreans to touch an old woman, the mother of sons, was a crime punishable by death. Even criminals were safe behind her skirts. My father would have strangled him, but saw that my

ANONYMOUS

Would You Go?

Would you go, would you go, would you?
Would you just go and leave me?

Oh what a time of great peace.

Then how, oh how shall I live
if you just go and leave me?

Oh what a time of great peace.

Though I might try to hold you,
still, if you are sad, might you return?

Oh what a time of great peace.

Though I must send you away,
why don't you just come back and stay?

Oh what a time of great peace.

Translation by David R. McCann

This anonymous Koryŏ folk song is in the form called *ch'angga.* Interwoven with repeated refrains, such songs were played on a musical instrument and sung by women entertainers known as *kisaeng.* Some *kisaeng* were trained to entertain at court and were highly refined dancers and poets, as well as musicians. Court *kisaeng* could become wealthy if their services were sought after. In the Confucian social structure, however, they were in the lowest class, along with butchers, slaves, prostitutes, and shamans.

grandmother had fainted with pain. He at once lifted her on his back and started off toward the market-place where there was a fairly good doctor. But her ankle was broken and she was sick for many weeks.

That night I went into my crazy-poet uncle's studio and lay down on the mat, crying miserably. By and by I heard the crazy-poet walking around and muttering in the next room. With my wet finger I made a hole in the paper door and looked through. He stood there at the outer door and just shook his fist in the face of the sky.

"Oh, stars and moon, how have you the heart to shine? Why not drop down by thunderstorm and cover all things up? And mountains, with your soul shining and rustling in the green leaves and trees and grass, can't you understand that it is over now? This national career of the people who have lived with you all these many ages, who have slept in your bosoms, whose blood you have drunk, whose muse you have been for the countless years? You spirits of water, you ghosts of the hollows, don't you see how death has just come to this people established among you for the four thousand years since the first Tan-Koon appeared on the white-headed mountain by the side of the Sacred Tree? Don't you know the soul of Korea is gone, is passing away this night, and has left us behind like the old clothes?"

I knew that my crazy-poet uncle was as if saying good-by to a ghost, just as the tall doctor had given the farewell to my grandfather's spirit on top the grass roof…Was Korea ended then? A pristine country, contemporary of Homeric times and of Golden Ages—far, far removed from the spirit of the Roman Empire and all later modernity until this day…I cried and cried myself to sleep. Outside all night I heard an unnatural day-sound—the jingle-jangle of cows which had not been put up for the night, and their astonished moos.

CHAPTER TWO

SAILING TO THE GARDEN OF MUGUNGHWA

ESTHER KWON ARINAGA

THE FIRST WAVE PIONEERS: AN INTRODUCTION

At the beginning of the twentieth century, there was an air of uncertainty about Korea's future. The great powers of Japan, China, and Russia were threatening to take over the country. In several of the provinces, a severe drought had ruined crops, causing widespread famine. In the northern provinces, particularly around P'yŏngyang, stories began to circulate about Hawai'i as a place where a person could get rich quickly and where education was free. The adventurous among the Koreans began to look with interest at the land across the Great Pacific.

It was January 13, 1903. The SS *Gaelic* eased into her berth at Honolulu Harbor, carrying the first Korean immigrants recruited to work on Hawai'i's sugar plantations. There were 56 men, 21 women, and 25 children. In the next two years more than seven thousand others, including six hundred women, would join this small band of pioneers. In 1905, the Korean government—upset about the alleged mistreatment of Korean workers in Mexico and pressured by the Japanese, who controlled Korea under a protectorate treaty—stopped workers from going abroad.

The first leg of the ocean journey was a short trip from a Korean port city to Japan, where the immigrants boarded a large ship bound for Honolulu. During the twenty-two-day ordeal from Kobe or Yokohama, people were packed like cattle into a large cargo hold; bunk beds were stacked three high. The smell of vomit permeated the ship. Until 1924, picture brides made the same journey, and though conditions had improved, the seasickness and homesickness were the same. On many of the voyages, a minister or a so-called Bible woman accompanied the immigrants, giving comfort and spiritual sustenance to the weary travelers. By the time the ships docked in Honolulu, many immigrants had been converted to Christianity.

Upon landing, the travelers were divided into groups and sent to sugar plantations on various islands. Like the Chinese and Japanese immigrants before them, the Koreans were kept together in one camp, the bachelors living in dormitories and the families in one-room apartments. Cooking was done in community kitchens. Women who had never worked before now toiled in the cane fields with the men, and did the cooking and laundry as well.

Despite their poverty, the immigrants had dreams for their children. Steeped in Confucian tradition, they felt that only education would better their sons and daughters. With foresight and great sacrifice, they sent the children who were not old enough to work in the fields to private boarding schools for Korean children. These were established first by the Methodist Mission and later by the Korean Christian Church. At the beginning, only boys were sent to these schools, but later, girls also attended them.

Dora Moon

Dora Kim Moon's life is an example of the important role played by Korean women in building the Korean community in Hawai'i.

In 1903, when Koreans were being recruited for Hawai'i's sugar plantations, she was asked by the Methodists to go on one of the early voyages and serve as a "Bible woman," or missionary. Traveling with her child on the twenty-two-day passage, Dora comforted the sick and converted many of the immigrants to Christianity. She also met a scholarly man named Hong Suk Moon, whom she married shortly after the ship arrived in Honolulu.

With several other women, she formed a prayer group that, by 1905, had become the First Korean Methodist Church.

As more Korean women began to arrive in Hawai'i as picture brides, Dora started the Korean Women's Club, which taught reading and writing, and after the March first demonstration, she supported the independence movement. She later helped form the Korean Women's Relief Society, which further aided patriots in Korea, as well as their families.

In 1931, Dora was appointed by the Methodist mission in Hawai'i to become a preacher. The following year, she started the Korean Missionary Society, which supported missionary work in Korea. By 1940, the First Korean Methodist Church had grown to more than four hundred members, and Dora held a major church office. During World War II, she rolled bandages for the American Red Cross. Until her death in 1971, at age ninety-three, she continued to serve the community.

Adapted from *Notable Women of Hawai'i*

After 1910, the Korean immigrants started to leave the plantations for Honolulu, finding jobs in laundries, tailor shops, furniture shops, and shoe-repair shops. A few opened small businesses of their own.

A high-ranking Korean official passing through Honolulu had observed the loneliness of the bachelor workers, who spent their idle time drinking, gambling, and smoking opium. At his suggestion, the Korean government approved the emigration of young women who, after exchanging pictures with potential husbands, agreed to marry the men upon their arrival in Honolulu. Unfortunately, the men often sent pictures of themselves taken many years earlier, before the sun and years of hard work had taken their toll. To the young brides of seventeen or eighteen, the first meetings with their potential husbands at the Immigration Station proved a shocking, disappointing, and sometimes frightening experience.

A large number of the picture brides whose husbands had found work in towns like Wahiawa, Hilo, and Honolulu escaped life on the plantations. And though most of the women had come from the more densely populated areas of Korea's southern provinces and were accustomed to hard work, they still found life in Hawai'i difficult. Their husbands' wages often did not cover household expenses, especially with children to feed. To supplement their incomes, the women began working in laundries, doing piecework for tailors, opening small dressmaking shops, or laundering clothes at home. With no electricity or washing machines, they had to do everything by hand.

Working outside the home and sharing mealtimes with their husbands and sons, the immigrant women were now less secluded socially than they had been in Korea. However, they continued their custom of socializing separately from men. Through their churches they established women's clubs that assisted needy families, organized religious education and social activities, and preserved traditional Korean music, dance, and holidays. Later, these clubs would become involved in community disputes over how best to support the Korean independence movement.

YOUNGHILL KANG
from *East Goes West:*
The Making of an Oriental Yankee

EAST GOES WEST

From an old, walled Korean city some thousand years old—Seoul—famous for poets and scholars, to New York. I did not come directly. But almost. A large steamer from the Orient landed me in Vancouver, Canada, and I traveled over three thousand miles across the American continent, a journey more than half as far as from Yokohama to Vancouver. At Halifax, straightway I took another liner. And this time for New York. It was in New York I felt I was destined really "to come out from the boat." The beginning of my new existence must be founded here. In Korea *to come out from the boat,* is an idiom meaning to be born, as the word *pai* for "womb" is the same as *pai* for "boat"; and there is the story of a Korean humorist who had no money, but who needed to get across a river. On landing him on the other side, the ferryman asked for his money. But the Korean humorist said to the ferryman who too had just stepped out, "You wouldn't charge your brother, would you? We both came from the same boat." And so he traveled free. My only plea for a planet-ride among the white-skinned majority of this New World is the same facetious argument. I brought little money, and no prestige, as I entered a practical country with small respect for the dark side of the moon. I got in just in time, before the law against Oriental immigration was passed.

But New York, that magic city on rock yet ungrounded, nervous, flowing, million-hued as a dream, became, throughout the years I am recording, the vast mechanical incubator of me.

It was always of New York I dreamed—not Paris nor London nor Berlin nor Munich nor Vienna nor age-buried Rome. I was eighteen, green with youth, and there was some of the mystery of nature in my simple immediate response to what was for me just a name…like the dogged moth that directs its flight by some unfathomable law. But I said to myself, "I want neither dreams nor poetry, least of all tradition, never the full moon." Korea even in her shattered state had these. And beyond them stood waiting—death. I craved swiftness, unimpeded action, fluidity, the amorphous New. Out of action rises the dream, rises the poetry. Dream without motion is the only wasteland that can sustain nothing. So I came adoring the crescent, not the full harvest moon, with winter over the horizon and its waning to a husk.

"New York at last!" I heard from the passengers around me. And the information was not needed. In unearthly white and mauve, shadow of white, the city rose, like a dream dreamed overnight, new, remorselessly new, impossibly new…and yet there in all the arrogant pride of rejoiced materialism. These young, slim, stately things a thousand houses high (or so it seemed to me, coming from an architecture that had never defied the earth), a tower of Babel each one, not one tower of Babel but many, a city of Babel towers, casually, easily strewn end up against the skies—they stood at the brink, close-crowded, the brink of America, these Giantesses, these Fates, which were not

Mugunghwa (Rose of Sharon)

The Rose of Sharon has been regarded by Koreans as a heavenly flower since ancient times. The ancient Chinese referred to Korea as "The land of gentlemen where *mugunghwa* blooms," and in the seventh century, the Silla Kingdom called itself Mugunghwa Country. In the late nineteenth century, Korea's love for the flower and identification with it increased when the line *"Mugunghwa samch'ŏlli hwaryŏ kangsan"* ("Rose of Sharon, thousand miles of beautiful mountain and river land") was written into the unofficial national anthem. At the start of the twentieth century, Korean immigrants transplanting themselves to America hoped their new home would be a utopian land—what they called a garden of *mugunghwa*. After Korea was liberated from Japan in 1945, the *mugunghwa* was adopted as the national flower. The root of the word means "immortal" or "eternal" in Korean.

built for a king nor a ghost nor any man's religion, but were materialized by those hard, cold, magic words—opportunity, enterprise, prosperity, success—just business words out of world-wide commerce from a land rich in natural resources. Buildings that sprang white from the rock. No earth clung to their skirts. They leaped like Athene from the mind synthetically; they spurned the earth. And there was no monument to the Machine Age like America.

I could not have come farther from home than this New York. Our dwellings, low, weathered, mossed, abhorring the lifeless line—the definite, the finite, the aloof—loving rondures and an upward stroke, the tilt of a roof like a boat always aware of the elements in which it is swinging—most fittingly my home was set a hemisphere apart, so far over the globe that to have gone on would have meant to go nearer not farther. How far my little grass-roofed, hill-wrapped village from this gigantic rebellion which was New York! And New York's rebellion called to me excitedly, this savagery which piled great concrete block on concrete block, topping at the last moment as in an afterthought, with crowns as delicate as pinnacled ice; this lavishness which, without prayer, pillaged coal mines and waterfalls for light, festooning the great nature-severed city with diamonds of frozen electrical phenomena—it fascinated me, the Asian man, and in it I saw not Milton's Satan, but the one of Blake.

I saw that Battery Park, if not a thing of earth, was yet a thing of dirt, as I walked about it trying to get my breath and decide what was the next step after coming from the sea. It was oddly dark and forlorn, like a little untidy room off-stage where actors might sit waiting for their cues. The shops about looked mean and low and dim. A solitary sailor stumbled past, showing neither the freedom and romance of the seas, nor the robust assurance of a native on his own shore. And the other human shadows flitting there had a stealthy and verminlike quality, a mysterious haunting corruption, suggesting the water's edge, and the meeting of foreign plague with foreign plague. I walked about the shabby little square briskly, drawing hungry lungfuls of the prowling keen March air—a Titan, he, in a titanic city—until in sudden excess of elation and aggression growing suddenly too hot with life, as if to come to grips with an opponent, I took off my long coat; and sinking down on a bench, I clapped my knee and swore the oath of battle and of triumph. The first part of a wide journey was accomplished. At least that part in space. I swore to keep on. Yes, if it took a lifetime, I must get to know the West.

Well, mine was not oath of battle in the militaristic sense. I was congenitally unmilitaristic. Inwoven in my fabric were the agricultural peace of Asia, the long centuries of peaceful living in united households, of seeking not the soul's good, but the blood's good, the blood's good of a happy, decorously branching family tree. In the old days the most excitement permitted to the individual man, if he got free from the struggle with beloved but ruthless and exacting elements, was poetry, the journey to Seoul, wine, and the moons that came with every season. His wife, usually older than himself and chosen by his mother and father, would be sure to know no poetry, but she would not begrudge him a feminine companion in Seoul, or even in some market place nearby—one of those childlike ladies who having bought—or more often inherited—the right to please by the loss of other social prestige, must live on gaiety, dancing, and fair calligraphy. But any wholehearted passion would have shivered too brutally the family tree. And I had done far worse. I had refused to marry my appointed bride. I had

repeated that I would not marry, at the ripe age of eighteen. I had said, with more pride than Adam ever got out of sinning in Eden, that *I* must choose the girl, unhelped by my forefathers or the astrologers or the mountain spirits. And this rebellion against nature and fatality I had learned from the West. Small wonder I had struggled with my father over every ounce of Western learning. I had gone against his will to mission schools, those devilish cults which preach divorce in the blood, and spiritual kinships, which foster the very distortions found, says the golden-hearted Mencius, in the cleverish man. I had studied in Japanese schools and it must be confessed, my studies had brought ever increased rebellion and dismay—to me as well as my father.

The military position of Japan—intrenched in Korea in my own lifetime—forced me into dilemma: Scylla and Charybdis. I was caught between—on the one hand, the heart-broken death of the old traditions irrevocably smashed not by me but by Japan (and yet I seemed to the elders to be conspiring with Japanese)—and on the other hand the zealous summary glibness of Japan, fast-Westernizing, using the Western incantations to realize her ancient fury of spirit, which Korea had always felt encroaching, but had snubbed in a blind disdain. Korea, a small, provincial, old-fashioned Confucian nation, hopelessly trapped by a larger, expanding one, was called to get off the earth. Death summoned. I could have renounced the scholar's dream forever (plainly scholarship had dreamed us away into ruin) and written my vengeance against Japan in martyr's blood, a blood which like that of the Tasmanians is strangely silent though to a man they wrote. Or I could take away my slip cut from the roots, and try to engraft my scholar-inherited kingdom upon the world's thought. But what I could not bear was the thought of futility, the futility of the martyr, or the death-stifled scholar back home. It was so that the individualist was born, the individualist, demanding life and more life,

Arirang
Arirang Arirang
    Ara ri yo
Arirang Ko gae ro
        No mo ganda
Na rul porigo Kashinun
    ni mun
Shimnido mot ga so
    palbyung i nanda

아리랑 아리랑 아라리오
아리랑 고개를 넘어간다
나를 버리고 가시는 님은
십리도 못가서 발병이 난다.
  2001년 새봄에
  아름다운 한글 미국 전시를
  기념하여 한국민요를 쓰다
  혜정 유영희

Calligraphy by Yoo Younghee

fulfillment, some answer to his thronging questions, some recognition of his death-wasted life, some anchor in thin air to bring him to earth though he seems cut off from the very roots of being.

And this it was—this naked individual slip—I had brought to New York.

"Dream, tall dreams," I thought. "Such are proper to man. But they must be solid, well-planned, engineered and founded on rock."

Had I not reached the arena of man's fight with death? I sat there on a park bench, savouring rebellion, dreaming the Faustian dream, without knowing of Faust, seeing myself with the Eastern scholarship in one hand, the Western in the other. And as I sat it grew colder. I had thought a little of spending the night on that bench. It appealed to me to wake up here with the dawn and find myself in New York. It would not be the first night I had slept roofless in a large city. But in the inner lining of my cap, I had four dollars, all I had left, in fact, after my long gestation by boat and by train. I decided to get myself the birthday present of a room.

"Begin tomorrow, trouble. See if I can't have some good dream. An unpleasant dream in this dark lonely park would be bad luck."

Clouds over the denser uptown regions trembled with the city's man-made whiteness, a false and livid dawn light, stolen from nature. I turned my face toward the dawn light as to a pillar of fire. And as I walked, steadily progressing toward the harsh curt lights and the Herculean noise, I wondered if the sight of a rainbow would be lost, the sound of thunder drowned here.

At last I found a hotel to my liking, neither as tall as a skyscraper—to choose such a one would not be modest the first night—and yet not a dingy one either, which would be inauspicious. The hotel had many lights inside, but not too many, not the naked glare which clashed from canyon to canyon along the outer runways of the great hive; these had a luminance more proper to honey cells and inner coffers. The fat six-foot doorman with red face seemed an imposing sentinel. Past him, I saw inside the people walking to and fro…talking mysteriously, perhaps of Michelangelo, but more likely of stocks and bonds. I tried to catch his eye. Always he looked past me, or without looking exactly at me, he would shake his head mournfully, directing his thumb toward a side door. But while he was engaged with one of the fortunate insiders who came outside, I went in. To me the gilded lamps, the marble floorway with its carpet of red, were luxurious and full of splendor. How gentlemanly, engaging, yet frankly businesslike, the sandy-colored hotel clerk, as I asked for a room, in my best high-school English which I had prepared to say before coming in!

And as I wrote my name down—Chung-Pa Han—in my unmistakably Oriental handwriting, which unconsciously dwelt on a stroke, or finished in a quirk that was not Western—I was elated that I had voted not to spend the night with the waifs and strays, but was enrolled there tangibly as a New Yorker.

I had engaged a small room for two dollars. This was half of all I had. I was satisfied. I thought I had a bargain. I had heard that all the hotels in New York cost ten and twenty dollars a night.

"They are worth that!" I thought, as the elevator boy danced up, a rich tobacco brown, well-formed and neatly mannered like his dress. He seized my big suitcase of brown cloth purchased in Seoul, Korea, a roomy bag which yet carried little besides a few books, some letters of introduction and a toothbrush.

The elevator went *zk!* and up we shot. A funny cool ziffy feeling ran into my heart. It was my first elevator. Fast climb…I thought…like going to heaven…

My room was small, white, nakedly clean, as characterless and capable as the cellophane-wrapped boxes in which American products come. The elevator boy smoothed the bed and pinched the curtains and examined the towels and looked in the wastepaper basket and picked up imaginary papers. I sat down in the chair, and crossed my legs. He stared at me dubiously. He waited. He didn't seem interested in my conversation. I asked him if he liked Shakespeare. He giggled and said coldly, "Who, suh? Me, suh? No, suh!" I know now that he was waiting for a dime. I was not sure. Besides I had nothing but bills, those four dollar bills which rested in the inner lining of my cap. I committed my first New York sin. I gave him nothing, neither then nor when I left next morning. I am sorry. I would like to go back and make it right. I have been a waiter myself. I know the importance of tips. But I would not be able to find that bell boy now. There must be fifty thousand bell boys in New York and they never stay in the same hotel long. Even the hotel may not have stayed. New York—its people, its buildings, its streets, are like a rushing river, the flood of which is changing all the time, so to be a New Yorker, one must feel like Heraclitus, that nothing is changeless but the law of change…

The bathroom was almost directly across from my room, beautiful, shining, glazed, so ordinary here, and yet a marvel of plumbing and utility. Even a prince in the old days could not have had such a tub. In Korea, the tubs were not of marble, nor machine-turned porcelain, but of humble intimate wood, and they were never used except for a grand occasion. Then all the water must come out from the well. In summer man bathed in streams, in winter from a great hollow gourd, a shell of the summer.

"But here," I thought, "a man has only to press a button. All the streams leap when he calls."

I let the water run—*shee! shee!*—as hot as I could stand it, as cold as I could stand it. I washed with soap—in my childhood, people still used an old-fashioned paste of ashes for that purpose—once more with soap, and then thoroughly with clear water. Even my hair I washed…everything…I was washing off the dirts of the Old World that was dead, as in my country people did before they set out on a Buddhist pilgrimage. Now I had washed everything. Everything but the inside. If I could, I would have washed that as thoroughly, I suppose, and left a shell. But the inner felt the echo of the outer.

In my room again, I listened at the window. That incessant hum of wheels and screech of brakes…how different from the brawling mountain streams, the remote grass-roofed villages of Korea…Korea, kingdom that was no more, taken by the little blue-clad soldiers to be a barrier against Russia, to be a continental point in Asia from which to punish Manchuria and China for their deep and stubborn resistance to the Machine Age…In sheer amazement at life, I suddenly stopped at the mirror to see if I had changed, as well as my environment. For me an unusual act. In my Korean village there were mirrors, but mostly small ones, about the size of a watch, and generally with covers. Besides, the people who had mirrors usually hid them. It was thought some kind of vice to look at one's face. Some people like my uncle, the crazy poet, never properly saw themselves.

I have read that the Koreans are a mysterious race, from the anthropologist's viewpoint. Mixtures of several blood streams must have taken place prehistorically. Many Koreans have dark brown hair, not black—mine was black, so black as to have a blackberry's shine. Many have naturally wavy hair. Mine was quite straight, as straight as pine-needles. Koreans, especially women and young men, are often ivory and rose. My face, after the sun of the long Pacific voyage, suggested copper and brass. My undertones of the skin, too, mouth and cheek, were not at all rosy, but more plum. I was a brunette Korean. Koreans are more animated and hot-tempered than the Chinese, more robust and more solid than the Japanese, and I showed these racial traits as well. At eighteen I impressed most, as being not boy, but man. I needed to shave every morning for the thick growth of hair that came overnight. My limbs retained a look of extreme plasticity, as in a growing boy, or in a Gauguin painting, but with many Koreans, even grown up, they still do. In more ways than one, I looked an alien to the Machine Age and New York. One could not tell from my outside that I had lost touch with dew and stars and ghosts.

I tried to go to sleep, to rest baptized in the roars of Manhattan traffic, as Virgil had been in the Hellenic stream. But all my old life was passing through my brain as if I had not been able to wash out the inside at all. My eyes seemed to turn back, not forward. I saw the village where I had spent my boy-

Koryŏ dynasty,
12th century
Stoneware with
celadon glaze

On the Road

Whirling east and west on a dusty
    road,
A lonely whip, a lean horse—so much
    toil!
I know it's good to return home;
But even if I did, my house would still
    be poor.

Translation by Richard J. Lynn

Prior to the invention of *han'gŭl*,
Chinese had served as the written language for many centuries. Educated
Koreans well versed in Confucian literature and history wrote thousands of
poems in Chinese. Among the most
revered poets of the Silla dynasty was
Ch'oe Ch'i-wŏn, born in A.D. 857. As a
young man, he studied in China and
became a prominent scholar, poet, and
statesman. In A.D. 885, when the Silla
dynasty was in decline, he retired to a
monastery.

hood, and where my father's father's forefather had spent his. I saw my father, responsible for the whole family, uncles and aunts and cousins every one, and I, his only son,
his vehicle through time, who had made a wide parabola from him. I saw my *pak-sa*
uncle and my poet uncle and many more…Yes, a synod of ancestors seemed coming to
visit me, watching me disapprovingly in that high Western bed, which had renounced
plain earth so literally beneath. What can you hope to find here? they said. Life, I cried.
We see no life, they said. And yet they did not scold me now. Just waited, arms in
sleeves, with the grave and patient wonder of the Asian in their eyes. And with a pang,
I saw before me my uncle's studio, through which blew in summer the pine-laden
breeze. I saw his books and the thousands of old poems in Chinese characters I knew
and loved so well. Must I leave all this behind at the portals of America?…Couldn't
they at least pass through into the world of the machines?…And against my will, a
poem came into my head, one I had heard long ago. All in one throbbing moil it
revolved, mingling in a hopeless incoherence with the foreign noises outside, of that
most spectacular city so far over the rim of the world to me and yet a greater cycle in
time than in space onward. It annoyed me that I could not quite rearrange the lines of
this poem, nor remember the rhymes perfectly.

It was written in Chinese characters, but it was a Korean poem. One, I think,
written by my crazy-poet uncle—although I am not quite sure. (Poetry writing then
was so often anonymous. Men cared for the poem, not for the fame.) It dealt with a
tragedy that had happened in our province, perhaps a hundred or more years ago, yet
still remembered and sung. A young lady of the house of Huang, or Autumn Foliage,
had been suspected of unchastity. In Korea, this was such a terrible thing that the family in which it occurred would be disgraced forever, even by rumor. The young lady did
the only thing possible in her environment. She gave orders for the building of a wood-
en coffin and said good-by. In the wooden coffin she embarked on the sea as to the
land of death. Miles away, beyond the sphere of her trouble, as if in token of true innocence, she was picked up by men of the family of Li, or Plum Blossom. She became a
daughter of the Li household and married one of the sons.

In this poem, she speaks of herself symbolically. A leaf of the family of the
Autumn Foliage floats loosely upon the sea. It is blown to rest against the branch of the
white spring plum blossoms. That leaf of the yellow foliage is carried so far away, that if
one wishes to see her, he must ride on the back of the white crane.

This poem was very short, but contained in four short lines an Asian drama of
fate which might have been entitled Hail and Farewell, or Autumn Saved by Spring, or
Distance Bridged and Unbridgeable, or many more names besides. And the images
were such that it was a poetic experience to write them in dynamic calligraphy, surren-
dering to the natural motion of leaves and scattering blossoms, of autumn and spring

and the waves. In the end I had to rise from bed and write down this poem on paper, to get it all straightened out, before I could fall asleep in my high Western bed.

My second night was not spent in a New York hotel…But of that trouble, later.
    I was up early and checked out, while the streets were still quietly rumbling. Half-past eight—it is perhaps the emptiest time. I did not know then that the people were in the subways.
    The man in the "Quick Lunch" I entered had plenty of time on his hands. He had nothing better to do than to stand on one foot and the toe of the other, and look at me quizzically, while I was eating my two doughnuts and milk. I had been inspired to order these by a previous customer, a taximan who finished so quickly that when I looked a second time he had only half a doughnut left; by the size of the last bite, I saw how he did it—half a doughnut for a bite.
    "Third breakfast this morning," he had mumbled. "First one at four, second at six…Been up all night."
    "Tough," said the quick-lunch counterman laconically. He was blonde-looking, Uneeda-cracker colored, with deep wrinkles cutting his face, so that he seemed forty-five. But I think he was about thirty-five, or he may have been ten years less. His eyes were dry, semi-humorous-looking, and in his dirty apron, he had a dry, casual ease as if, behind his counter, he would not have changed his pavement view of humanity even for the Prince of Wales.
    "Don't eat the hole!" he said to me finally, with a faint, dry grin.
    I couldn't think of anything to reply to this in English, so I just nodded and went on with my doughnut.
    "Guess he don't speak English," said the man, still regarding me like a sceptical parent, and addressing a waitress only by a rakish cock of his sandy curls. "Look at his suitcase there. The guy just came. Guess he don't speak any English yet."
    "Sure he does," she said good-humoredly. She was tall and skinny and young—about seventeen but big. Her face, long as a colt's, had a confectionery pink-and-whiteness. There was something friendly and good-natured about her.
    I took it for encouragement and began. I asked the man his name.
    "MacNeil," he said jauntily, his arms still folded, "Scotch."
    I asked him, did he know "MacFlecknoe," an English poem which I had learned in Korea.

"Who?"

And I quoted:

All human things are subject to decay:
And when Fate summons, monarchs must obey…

"Unhuh—that's fine," he said sceptically, with a wink at the girl. "And who's that other Mac, the son-of-a-bitch?"

"Yes, that's what all Mac means: son-of—"

"Well, I'll be darned if Mac means 'son-of-a-bitch'!"

By this time I felt for a piece of paper to write things down to memorize. The conversation was getting beyond me. I said if he didn't mind, I would take a few notes on what he said, to help my English.

"Yeah? Go ahead."

Without change of countenance, he moistened his thin, gray lips as he gravely took a swipe at the counter with the soiled towel over his shoulder. Nothing was too fabulous for him to accept drily in this quick-lunch world of downtown Manhattan.

"What was that you said? Not son of Mac but son-of—"

"Son-of-bitch…it's what you say here in America when you get mad."

"And mad?"

He made a fierce expression to show it.

I wrote that down.

I regarded my tutor hopefully.

"What's that?" I said, pointing to the vinegar.

"A skirt," he said. "Do you want to know that?"—indicating the salt. "'Kiss.' Ask the girl for it. Let's hear you say it. Good word to learn."

The girl broke into a young loud guffaw, not prudish nor coquettish, but evidently full of delighted appreciation for his pavement wit.

"Say, Paul, you're getting fresher every day," said she, admiringly.

I left them with reluctance, for they were touched for me with the magic of the city and its first encounter. But soon I became convinced that everyone in New York felt the same way as this dry-voiced, kidding man I had first met…the need of sustaining a role, a sort of gaminlike sophistication, harder and more polished than a diamond in the more prosperous classes, but equally present in the low, a hard shell over the soul of new-world children, essential for the pebbles rattling through subway tunnels and their sun-hid city streets.

But I was not a New Yorker yet, though fast becoming one. I set out to present a letter of introduction. It was to the head of all the YMCAs in New York, urging him to interest himself in my behalf, and I got directions by showing the address to people as I went along. By the time I reached him, New York was very busy again, and his office, high up in a skyscraper, seemed one of the busiest places to judge by the typewriters all about him *clickety-clack*ing at enormous speed.

"Ah," I thought. "Not like the missionaries, with whom it is difficult to get anything done."

When he said, after reading the letter, "Yes, and what can I do for you?" I told him I needed a job.

He said with businesslike finality, "Mr. Allen in our Harlem branch at 125th Street is the very man for you."

I waited while he did some telephoning, arranging for an interview around seven that evening. I started at once. I went on foot. That seemed to me simpler and besides I should see some more of the city.

Whom did I find to talk to on that day? I don't remember, but I know I talked. The New Yorkers were not hard at all to talk to, though they could understand me better than I could understand them. But I sat down in all the parks I came to and standing my bag beside me, rested, deliriously stretched my feet, and watched. I practised my English until I could hardly turn my tongue any more. Oh, how hard to say *r* and *th* and *w!* They had to be torn from the throat and reared high like the skyscrapers. The sounds were dry and ponderous and without juice. My own language rolls from the gullet and is inextricably mixed with moisture and nature's fire. But now with all its energy, my tongue moved between teeth and lips rigidly, to pronounce "Roman Catholic" or "Methodist Rise," as a Greek Methodist preacher gave me some lessons in a New York park. Even "Fifth Avenue" was hard for me to say, and many times I practised that because I liked to say it.

I lunched with the crowd. I ordered frankfurters and sauerkraut, not because I liked them, but because the man next to me was eating them. Already I was beginning to feel at home in New York. But my hair was too long. Somebody told me so—asking me if I wanted to look like an "Indian." I judged from his tone that an American should not. It must be cut. I wanted to make a good impression

Lotus, Fish and Birds,
Chosŏn dynasty, 19th century
Ink and color on paper

on Mr. Allen and grab that job.

I went into one of those glassed-in barber shops. The customers were wrapped up in white like Buddhist monks, only rather cleaner. I also was put to bed with a sheet. I told the barber what I wanted, saying it as well as I could by my hands, because my tongue was very tired. Here was a chance to rest, I thought. And I could not be robbed, in sight of so many people of New York. In the Orient, one goes to a barber shop as to a picture show. There is one entrance fee for everything inside.

Whenever the thin, dark barber with the sharp eyes close together said, "Do you want?" I nodded. Four or five times it was repeated, like courses of a *table-d'hôte,* and each time I said, "Yes, that too." He cut my hair, shampooed it, oiled it, perfumed it, combed it and brushed it with an Italian flourish…I was so tired after walking, that I almost went to sleep. "My, you get a lot for your money here!" I was thinking in dozing admiration. "They certainly find things to do." A Negro boy shined my shoes on my feet too.

Drowsily, I asked, "How much?" $1.60. I woke up. For a haircut, it couldn't be true! I jumped out of the chair just as I was, in my sheet. They had to show me the itemized account. Everything was there with a corresponding price. And I had thought it was according to the Oriental custom, where every luxury in the barber shop is included at the cost of one barbering, and that a very low one well within the means of everybody! There was no getting away, I had to pay the price. I had only $1.70 in the world. In less than a minute, I had only ten cents left.

ABŎJI'S STORY: AN INTERVIEW WITH MY FATHER

"Hello, Abŏji. How are you feeling tonight?"

"I am fine, son. What brings you here by my home on such a rainy night?"

"I've heard you tell interesting episodes of your experiences in Korea, China, Russia, Japan, and on a plantation in Hawaii, and I wondered if you would combine these stories together and tell me the story of your life."

Outside the rain fell in a steady downpour, sometimes increasing in intensity, sometimes decreasing, and then stopping for a little while only to start again. But we were all snug and warm inside and for the next two hours, I sat in the parlor with Abŏji while he told me his life history.

"I was born in Hamgyŏng-do, Kilchu, Korea, in 1878," he began. "I was the ninth child in a family of ten children. In comparison with our neighbors, our family was well off, for although we had no money as such, we had land, houses, cows, pigs, and chickens. You see, the possession of such goods was considered to be restricted to the wealthy. Thus, I say that we were quite well to do. Indeed we had much wealth then, especially with all the grain that we had. I can remember still how we worked in the fields all summer and then harvested the grain in such quantities that the pile would grow higher and higher, and wider and wider around the base. No, we didn't have money but we were well off.

"Many of our neighbors were not as fortunate as we were, however, and they were forced to send their sons to Russia or to Manchuria to work. Sometimes whole families went to Manchuria to live. Some of them came back and told us wonderful tales of the countries outside our village.

"Because my family could afford it, I was sent to school instead of working in the fields. I remained in school until the sixth grade. Then one night, twenty-five of us stole away from home to seek our fortunes in Russia and to see some of the wonderful things we had heard so much about.

"We stayed in Russia for about fourteen years, working as laborers at first, and as contract laborers later. We were engaged in all kinds of work—sometimes in building roads, and sometimes in building railroads. While doing the latter type of work in Vladivostok in 1902 and 1903, the Japanese and the Russians went to war. Many people died. We had to leave or take the chance of being killed. Confusion was everywhere, everybody was in a panic, all the roads and railroads were blocked, and there was no place to go. We left all we had earned and fled for our lives. Many merchants and businessmen who stayed back to try to sell their property lost their lives because of their delay. We couldn't go back to Korea because the roads were blocked. Finally, we were able to get passage on an English ship and sailed for Japan. We were safe on the ship, for the Russians and the Japanese did not dare fire upon it because of the English flag.

"We stayed in Japan for three months and then were able to get passage to Korea. When we arrived in Korea, we had no money left, and found that there were no opportunities for work of any kind and that conditions were bad. It was then that we heard of a man who was talking a lot about the opportunities in Hawaii. He said that it was a land of opportunity where everybody was rich. He promised to give us work, free houses, and adequate pay. It all looked very lucrative and so after reading the contract, which seemed quite suitable, thirteen of us signed. We were shipped to Mountain View, Hawaii.

"It was not long before we were in the cane fields and cutting away at the cane stalks. We worked in the hot sun for ten hours a day, and the pay was fifty-nine cents a day. I was not used to this kind of work and I had a difficult time. This type of work was indeed harder than the type of contract work that I did in Russia. However, I did the best I could and struggled along with the rest of the men.

"Then one day I heard of a Russian physician who lived in the vicinity of the plantation and who needed an interpreter. I could speak Russian, Japanese, and Chinese, as well as Korean, so I went to talk to him. At that time language differences were a serious handicap in interracial relations. The physician could speak only English besides his native Russian, so I interpreted Japanese, Chinese, and Korean for him. The result was that after about three days in the fields, I became an interpreter.

"After a very short period, however, the physician moved away so that I had to go back to the plantation. Fortunately, because of my experience in handling men in Russia and because I had had some schooling and could read and write well, I soon became one of the lunas.

"Oh, I had one more experience as an interpreter with the police department in Hilo. It was at the time of the Russian immigration to Hawaii. On one occasion the police station had become crowded with Russians and no one could speak to them. The Korean interpreter told the sheriff about me. I did not like the idea, because after the trial there might be hard feelings. However, the plantation boss told me to go. I went reluctantly. In the courtroom, I talked to the Russians and then interpreted what I found out to the Korean interpreter, who in turn interpreted into English from my Korean.

"Plantation camp life in those days was greatly different from the type of life we lead now in Hawaii. During those early days on the plantation, we all lived in one big camp. The married men

"**K**orea that time,
no freedom.
So much hardship.
Cannot free talking.
Somebody told me Hawaii's
a free place.
Everybody living well.
Make up my mind
to go there."

"**M**y mother felt
very sad. My father
only blamed my
mother. They fight
about my leaving.
He said, 'We don't
know where is
Hawaii. Why send
a girl there?'
I made everything ready
myself. For twenty days
I cannot look at my mother
and father straight because of
the tears coming down.
I cried to myself.
Those days girls couldn't
even go twenty miles out of
my village by themselves."

were given small houses for themselves and the single men lived in big barracks consisting of one big square sleeping room in which there was no privacy. The men were segregated racially—the Japanese occupying one building, the Chinese another, et cetera. However, everybody ate in the same place—in a big kitchen. Those who wanted to could cook their own meals, and frequently, some of the men would form a group to cook their own 'racial foods.' Everything in the camp was free except the food. The men who ate in the big kitchen paid six dollars and fifty cents a month. Food was very cheap then, one bag of rice costing only a dollar and fifty cents.

"A working day on the plantation followed the same pattern, day in and day out. The cook would get up at three o'clock in the morning and prepare breakfast and make lunches for the men, who got up at five o'clock. A train would take them to the place of work in the fields, after the lunas had gone to the boss in charge to get their assignments for the day.

"I was in charge of two hundred and fifty workers—two hundred men and fifty women. After receiving my assignment I would take my group out to the fields and begin work at six o'clock. We worked ten hours in the blazing sun and had only a half-hour for lunch. As a luna, I was responsible for my group. We worked on a contract basis because it paid more. Some of the plantations paid by the month—eighteen dollars a month. When we contracted, we would get as much as one dollar and twenty-five cents a day. My workers received between seventy-five cents to a dollar and twenty-five cents a day. The women's wages ranged from seventy-five cents to a dollar. As a luna, I was paid seventy-five dollars a month.

"When we got to the fields, I would line the workers up, with the fastest worker at the head of the line, and so on. By doing this, I got more work out of them. A good luna is always kind to his men. If he is mad all the time, the men will resent it and work poorly. I had workers of all races in my group—Hawaiians, Filipinos, Puerto Ricans, Chinese, Japanese, Portuguese, and Koreans. Every day, the Number Three Boss would inspect the camp after we left for the fields and then would come out to see how we worked. At four thirty o'clock we would quit work and walk wearily back to the train and start for the camp. On the way back, I had to record the men's time. I could tell who they were by their faces, for I knew them well. When we got back to the camp, we ate, washed, and then went directly to bed.

"During the harvesting season, we even worked on Sundays and holidays—seven days a week, ten hours a day. Otherwise we had Sunday off. Some of us went visiting while others just slept.

"I saw him for the first time at the Immigration Station. He didn't look like his picture. He was really old, old-looking. So my heart stuck. My cousin in Honolulu arranged the marriage, and I was very angry at her. I'm so disappointed, I cry for eight days and don't come out of my room. But I knew that if I don't get married, I have to go back to Korea on the next ship. So on the ninth day I came out and married him. But I don't talk to him for three months. Later on, it was all right."

Picture-bride quotations from
Montage: An Ethnic History of Women
in Hawaii

"There were three Haole bosses. They were good men. They gave us free houses and anything we needed if we were good and did not cause trouble. They did not bother us at all and most of the men liked the bosses. They all lived in big houses quite a distance away."

Thus ended Abŏji's long story about his early experiences. The rest of his story was more familiar to me: his marriage, my parents' move to Oahu in 1922, and Abŏji's purchase of a laundry there, the growth of the family, sons, daughters, and grandchildren.

As an afterthought I asked Abŏji whether he ever thought of returning to Korea some day. He replied, "At one time I wanted very much to go back to Korea, but now that I am old and I haven't seen my parents since I was eleven years old, my feelings have changed. I don't even know whether they are alive or not. Besides, I have been in Hawaii a long time and I have a family of my own here. No, I don't care very much to go back to Korea. I am too old. I think I would like to spend the rest of my life in Hawaii."

I thanked Abŏji for the story of his life. Seeing that the rain had stopped, and that it was getting rather late, I made ready to leave for my home. As I was leaving the house, I saw Abŏji staring into space—probably reminiscing. I wondered what thoughts were running through his head. Perhaps he was recalling the days spent in Hamgyŏng-do, or Vladivostok, or the ten years on the plantation here in Hawaii.

Plantation identification tags were called pŏnho, the Korean word for numbers. Shape indicated the worker's ethnicity.

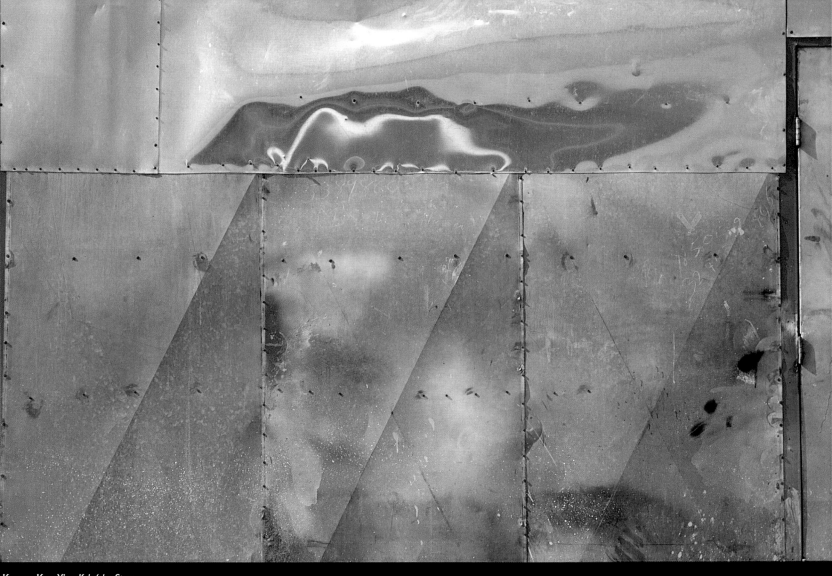

MARY PAIK LEE
     from *Quiet Odyssey:*
     A Pioneer Korean Woman
     in America

Oahu and Riverside

Life in Hawaii was not much different from that in Korea because all the people I came in contact with were Orientals. I don't remember seeing white people, at least not face to face. There was a small group of Koreans on Oahu, where we lived, and a small church. Father preached there sometimes when he was not working on the plantations. He must have done hoeing or weeding: since he had not had any farming experience, he could not do specialized work such as picking. Mother wanted to work as well, but Father would not allow her to. He said, "Even if we have to starve, I don't want you working out in the fields."

When I asked Father years later if we had eaten bananas in Hawaii, he replied that although a big bunch of bananas sold for five cents, he could not afford to buy any. Since we had arrived with only the clothes on our backs and our bedding, we never had enough money left over to buy bananas. We lived in a grass hut, slept on the ground, and had to start from scratch to get every household item. Fortunately, the weather was warm, so we didn't need much clothing, but we never had enough money for a normal way of life.

While we were living in Hawaii, Mother didn't have much housework to do in the grass hut, so she had time to talk to us about why we were the only ones in our family to have left Korea. She told me that I had begged Grandmother to come with us, but she wouldn't leave her school. Grandmother had said that her students were depending on her to teach and guide them. She was certainly a very remarkable woman, with much courage in the face of danger. It is women like her who get things started in spite of opposition, and who accomplish what seem like impossibilities. I'm glad she lived to see her dream come true. She loved all of her students as though they were her own children, and she wouldn't desert them in their time of need. Uncle said the same thing about the young boys in his high school. Also, he had a wife and several children of his own to care for. Of course, Grandfather would not leave without Grandmother. So only my father had no obligations to anyone except his own wife and two children.

Mother told me there had been a lot of discussion for several days before the final decision was made for my parents, my brother, and me to leave Korea to find a better life elsewhere. Father was reluctant to leave, but his parents insisted, saying that his presence would not help them. They knew what would happen to them in the near future. They were prepared to face great hardship or worse, but they wanted at least one member of their family to survive and live a better life somewhere else. Such strong, quiet courage in ordinary people in the face of danger is really something to admire and remember always.

My second brother, Paik Daw Sun, was born on October 6, 1905, in Hawaii. Father was desperate, always writing to friends in other places, trying to find a better place to live. Finally, he heard from friends in Riverside, California, who urged him to join them: they said the prospects for the future were better in America; that a man's wages were ten to fifteen cents an hour for ten hours of work a day. After his year in Hawaii was up, Father borrowed enough money from friends to pay for our passage to America on board the SS *China*.

We landed in San Francisco on December 3, 1906. As we walked down the gang-plank, a group of young white men were standing around, waiting to see what kind of creatures were disembarking. We must have been a very queer-looking group. They laughed at us and spit in our faces; one man kicked up Mother's skirt and called us names we couldn't understand. Of course, their actions and attitudes left no doubt about their feelings toward us. I was so upset. I asked Father why we had come to a place where we were not wanted. He replied that we deserved what we got because that was the same kind of treatment that Koreans had given to the first American missionar-

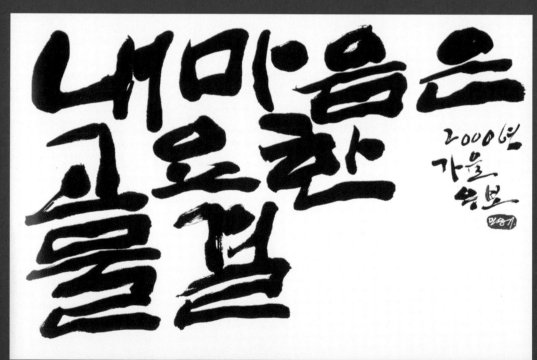

from **My Mind**

Poem by Kim Kwangsup

My mind
resembles
calm
lake–water

Calligraphy by Min Seungkee

ies in Korea: the children had thrown rocks at them, calling them "white devils" because of their blue eyes and yellow or red hair. He explained that anything new and strange causes some fear at first, so ridicule and violence often result. He said the missionaries just lowered their heads and paid no attention to their tormentors. They showed by their actions and good works that they were just as good as or even better than those who laughed at them. He said that is exactly what we must try to do here in America—study hard and learn to show Americans that we are just as good as they are. That was my first lesson in living, and I have never forgotten it.

Many old friends came with us from Hawaii. Some stayed in San Francisco, others went to Dinuba, near Fresno, but most headed for Los Angeles. We ourselves went straight to the railroad depot nearby and boarded a train for Riverside, where friends would be waiting for us. It was our first experience on a train. We were excited, but we felt lost in such a huge country. When we reached Riverside, we found friends from our village in Korea waiting to greet us.

In those days, Orientals and others were not allowed to live in town with the white people. The Japanese, Chinese, and Mexicans each had their own little settlement outside of town. My first glimpse of what was to be our camp was rows of one-room shacks, with a few water pumps here and there and little sheds for outhouses. We learned later that the shacks had been constructed for the Chinese men who had built the Southern Pacific Railroad in the 1880s.

We had reached Riverside without any plans and with very little money, not knowing what we could do for a living. After much discussion with friends, it was decided that Mother should cook for about thirty single men who worked in the citrus groves. Father did not like her to work, but it seemed to be the only way we could make a living for ourselves. She would make their breakfast at 5 A.M., pack their lunches, and cook them supper at 7 P.M. But my parents did not have the cooking utensils we needed, so Father went to the Chinese settlement and told them of our situation. He could not speak Chinese but he wrote *hanmun,* the character writing that is the same in Korean and Chinese. He asked for credit, promising to make regular payments from time to time. They trusted him and agreed to give us everything we needed to get started: big iron pots and pans, dishes, tin lunch pails, chopsticks, and so forth. They also gave us rice and groceries.

The Korean men went to the dumpyard nearby and found the materials to build a shack large enough for our dining area. They made one long table and two long benches to seat thirty men. Father made a large stove and oven with mud and straw, and he found several large wine barrels to hold the water for drinking and cooking. That was the start of our business. Mother had long, thick black hair that touched the ground. It became a nuisance in her work, so Father cut it short, leaving just enough to coil in a bun on the back of her head. It must have caused her much grief to lose her beautiful hair, but she never complained. We had already lost everything else that meant anything to us.

We lived in a small one-room shack built in the 1880s. The passing of time had made the lumber shrink, so the wind blew through the cracks in the walls. There was no pretense of making it livable—just four walls, one window, and one door—nothing else. We put mud in the cracks to keep the wind out. The water pump served several shacks. We had to heat our bath water in a bucket over an open fire outside, then pour it into a tin tub inside. There was no gas or electricity. We used kerosene lamps, and one of my chores was to trim the wicks, clean the glass tops, and keep the bowls filled with kerosene.

The Chinese men who had lived there in the 1880s must have slept on the floor. Father solved the problem of where we were going to sleep by building shelves along the four walls of our shack. Then he found some hay to put on each shelf. He put a blanket over the hay, rolled up some old clothes for a pillow—and that was a bed for a child. I used a block of wood for my pillow. It became such a habit with me that even to this day I do not like a soft pillow. My parents themselves slept on the floor.

After our shelter was taken care of, I looked around and found that all our immediate neighbors were old friends from Korea. Philip Ahn, who became a movie actor many years later, lived across from us. His father was Mr. Ahn Chang-ho. Mr. Ahn and my father, who had been boyhood friends in Korea, felt like brothers to each other and kept in touch through the years. It was good to see so many familiar faces again, and we felt happy to be there together.

Every day after school and on weekends, my older brother and I had to pile enough firewood up against the kitchen shack to last until the next day. Father found some wheels and boards at the dumpyard to make a long flatbed for carrying the wood, but we had to make several trips each day. An acre of trees grew some distance from us, where we found plenty of broken branches to gather up.

Meung's job was to keep the wine barrels filled with water so Mother could do her work. I cleaned the oil lamps, kept our shack in order, looked after my baby brother, and heated the bath water for the men at 6 P.M. so they could bathe before supper. The workers' bathhouse had just one large tub inside; I heated the water by building a fire under the floor. The men washed themselves with a hose before entering the tub.

Every Saturday Meung and I went to a slaughterhouse some distance away to get

the animal organs that the butchers threw out—pork and beef livers, hearts, kidneys, entrails, tripe—all the things they considered unfit for human consumption. We were not alone—Mexican children came there also. They needed those things to survive just as we did. The butchers stood around laughing at us as we scrambled for the choice pieces. When I told Father I didn't want to go there anymore because they were making fun of us, he said we should thank God that they did not know the value of what they threw out; otherwise, we would go hungry.

Meung started school at the Washington Irving School, not far from our settlement. When I was ready to go, Father asked a friend who spoke a little English—a Mr. Song—to take me. My first day at school was a very frightening experience. As we entered the schoolyard, several girls formed a ring around us, singing a song and dancing in a circle. When they stopped, each one came over to me and hit me in the neck, hurting and frightening me. They ran away when a tall woman came towards us. Her bright yellow hair and big blue eyes looking down at me were a fearful sight; it was my first close look at such a person. She was welcoming me to her school, but I was frightened. When she addressed me, I answered in Korean, "I don't understand you." I turned around, ran all the way home, and hid in our shack. Father laughed when he heard about my behavior. He told me there was nothing to be afraid of; now that we were living here in America, where everything is different from Korea, we would have to learn to get along with everyone.

The next day when I went to school with my brother, the girls did not dance around us; I guess the teacher must have told them not to do it. I learned later that the song they sang was:

> *Ching Chong, Chinaman,*
> *Sitting on a wall.*
> *Along came a white man,*
> *And chopped his head off.*

The last line was the signal for each girl to "chop my head off" by giving me a blow on the neck. That must have been the greeting they gave to all the Oriental kids who came to school the first day.

Because our Korean names were too difficult for them to remember, the children at school always said "Hey you!" when they wanted our attention. I told Meung that it was too late to change our names, but we should give American names to our siblings. So we started with Paik Daw Sun, who had been born in Hawaii, by calling him Ernest. When another brother was born in Riverside on August 8, 1908, we named him Stanford.

53

OK-KOO KANG GROSJEAN

The Autumn Sky

The autumn sky
and a breath of wind
soothe this unquiet mind.

I watch the leaves
of late summer falling
one by one
and suddenly the distance
between now and eternity
closes up.

I long to drop
the burden of my desires—
one by one—
the heaviest first.

Meung was only three years older than I, but he was extremely observant and considerate for his age. He told me to stop playing around and to notice how much work our mother had to do. He said that to help her, every day before school he would wash the baby's diapers, and I was to hang them on the line. After school, before going for firewood, I was to take them in, fold them, and put them away. Meanwhile he would fill the wine barrels with water from the pump. We followed this routine from then on. I was always taking care of the babies, bathing them every night, changing their diapers, and feeding them midnight bottles. He heated their bath water in a bucket outside so I could give them baths in the tin tub inside our shack.

There was one large building for community meetings in Riverside, where religious services were held on Sundays. We didn't have a minister, but several persons read the Bible and discussed it. Father preached there whenever he had time. An American lady named Mrs. Stewart, who lived in Upland, used to come to our church on Sundays. She was interested in the Korean people and brought presents for everyone at Christmastime. She gave me the first and only doll I ever had.

Meung and I had a special "gang" consisting of six members about the same age. We ran to school together, ran home for lunch, back to school, and home again. On the way to school, there was a large mulberry bush growing in the front lawn of one house. Whenever we passed, we noticed the big black berries that had fallen on the lawn. They looked so tempting that we just had to stop and see what they tasted like. They were so delicious we couldn't stop eating them. After that, every time we passed that house we helped ourselves, but we had an uneasy feeling about whether it was right or wrong to take the fruit. We childishly decided that it was all right because the berries were on the ground and weren't picked off the bush. We had a big argument about it one day. When Meung said it was wrong to take something that belonged to someone else, my girlfriend got so angry she picked up a piece of firewood and hit him on the head. When we told Father about it, he said that the berries belonged to the owner of the bush, whether they were on the bush or on the ground. That settled our arguments. From then on we looked the other way every time we passed that house.

An old Chinese peddler used to come to our place once a week with fruits and vegetables on his wagon. I told Philip Ahn to climb up the front of his wagon and talk to him while I climbed up the back and filled my apron with small potatoes, lima beans, and corn, which we roasted in hot ashes. It was our first taste of such vegetables, and they were so good. But the old man got wise to us after a while, so whenever we approached his wagon, he used the horsewhip on us.

One evening, as I was helping Mother wash the lunch pails the men brought back, I asked her what kind of work the men were doing. She told me they were picking oranges, which gave me an idea, but I didn't dare to tell her about it. After breakfast the next day, as I passed out the lunch pails, I asked some of the men why they never brought me an orange. I said I had never seen or tasted one. That evening as I took in the lunch pails, they felt a bit heavy; when I opened one I saw a beautiful orange for the first time. I was so excited I told Father about it. He must have talked to the men, because there were only a few oranges after that. It helped make the work of washing the lunch pails seem less tiring to find a few. One night some time later, when I took in the lunch pails every single one felt heavy. I got really excited, but to my surprise, each pail had a rock in it. When I asked why, the men said they were afraid I would scold them if they didn't bring something, but there were no more oranges to be picked. Everybody had a good laugh about it.

After the orange season was over, the men picked lemons and grapefruit. In the fall there was work in the walnut groves. The men would shake the walnuts from the trees with long poles, then the women and children would gather them up in sacks, take them to a clearing, and peel off the outer shells. They got paid by the sack for their labor. Between the walnut harvest and the time to prune the orange trees, the men got a short rest. When there was no work in the citrus groves, Father worked at the Riverside Cement Company on the edge of town.

Two incidents happened in Riverside that will always remain in my memory. The first was when I told Father I needed a coat to wear to school. He said that he would see what he could do about it. He rode to town on his bicycle to buy some material, and he made a coat for me. Since we did not have a sewing machine, he had to sew it by hand one evening. It was a beautiful red coat; I was so happy to wear it. All the girls at school wanted to know where I had purchased it. They couldn't believe my father had made it himself. When I asked Mother how Father could do such a wonderful thing, she smiled and said that, among other things, Father had been an expert tailor in Korea. He had studied to be a minister and had taught the Korean language to missionaries, but tailoring was how he made a living.

My second memory is equally wondrous. One evening Father woke us up in the middle of the night and said a wonderful thing was happening in the sky. Looking out the window, we saw a big star with a very long sparkling tail that seemed to stretch across the whole sky. The tail was full of small sparkling stars. It was a spectacular, awesome sight, a bit frightening to us children. We didn't understand what was going on and couldn't sleep the rest of the night, wondering what it meant and if everything would be all right the next day.

CHAPTER THREE

MANSE!

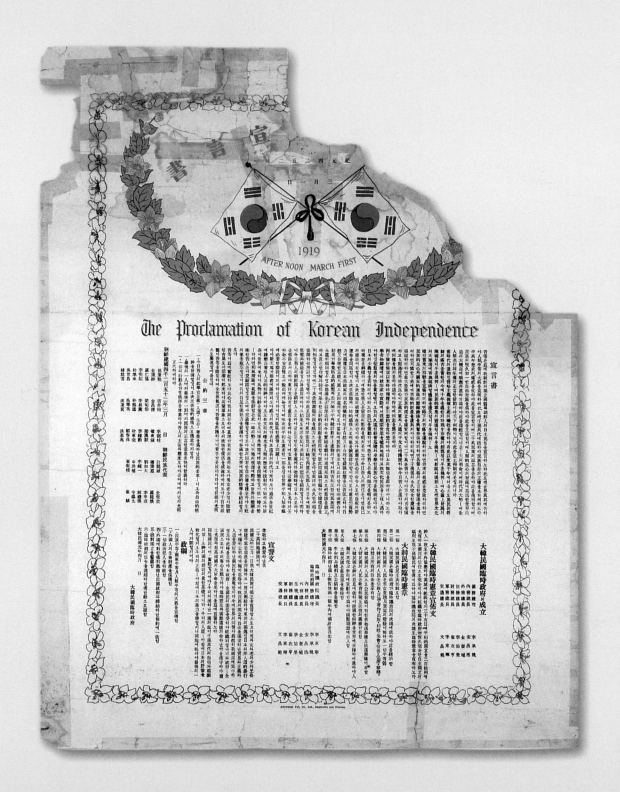

The Proclamation of Korean Independence

ESTHER KWON ARINAGA

THE STRUGGLE FOR INDEPENDENCE: AN INTRODUCTION

During the decades following World War I, disagreement over the policies of the major Christian church for Koreans in Hawai'i caused a serious and unfortunate split in the once-cohesive Korean American community. Politics, both national (Korea) and local (the Korean American community in Hawai'i), became intertwined with religion. On one issue, however, the factions did agree: the need for Korea's independence.

The Japanese annexation of Korea in 1910 affected the immigrants deeply. It saddened them that their relatives and friends lived under oppresive conditions. On March 1, 1919, more than two million Koreans in more than fifteen hundred separate gatherings in the homeland and thousands of Koreans in Hawai'i marched for Korean national freedom, simultaneously issuing a new Declaration of Independence. Japanese police forces brutally massacred the protestors in Korea, and the Japanese grip on the peninsula grew stronger.

Subsequent to this 1919 independence march, Korean women in Hawai'i organized the Korean Women's Relief Society, which pledged to assist the homeland in its struggle for freedom. Dressed in their white *chŏgori* (blouse) and *ch'ima* (skirt), the women were a colorful sight as they marched in parades and sang patriotic songs. They raised thousands of dollars by making and selling such Korean delicacies as *ttŏk* (rice cakes), *kimch'i,* and *taegu* (seasoned and dried codfish).

Despite the Japanese occupation, some of the immigrant women managed to return to Korea for visits, sometimes bringing along their children to show proudly to grandparents. These family reunions were joyful occasions, but it was painful for the women to see their country under foreign domination. Japanese was the sole language being taught in every school. Christian ministers were persecuted and imprisoned. The immigrants who had dreamed of returning to live in Korea after amassing wealth in Hawai'i began to have second thoughts.

Through Korean clubs, societies, and church groups, the immigrant women fostered a spirit of volunteerism that not only benefited the community directly, but also developed their leadership skills and a sense of community involvement. As time passed and the women secured greater economic security for Korean immigrants, they began to assist and reach out to the community at large. During World War II, for example, the women rolled bandages for the American Red Cross, promoted the sale of u.s. War Bonds, assisted USO clubs, and opened their homes to American military personnel who were far from home.

K. CONNIE KANG

from *Home Was the Land
of Morning Calm: A Saga of
a Korean-American Family*

THE RESISTANCE

On March 1, 1919, while my grandfather was in prison for the second time, there were nationwide demonstrations against the Japanese colonial rule. Organizers had taken to heart President Woodrow Wilson's doctrine of the self-determination of nations, enunciated in 1918, and they had risked their lives by rising up in an attempt to bring the world's attention to the Korean struggle for independence.

Wilson had announced it as an essential component of the post–World War I settlement to acknowledge and to respond to the rising independence aspirations among Europe's national minorities. The doctrine created independent Czechoslovakia, Yugoslavia, Poland, and Finland, among others. So Koreans greeted the American president's principle like a promise from heaven; at last the world was ready to usher in an age of justice and self-determination—even for small, powerless countries. The doctrine provided the inspiration to transform the Korean independence movement—which had been limited mostly to the activities of exiles and clandestine organizations, schools, churches—into a nationwide endeavor by Koreans to regain their country. Korean patriots meeting in Shanghai in January 1919 formed the New Korea Youth Association and sent Kyu-sik Kim as its spokesman to the peace conference in Paris. The new group also dispatched representatives to Korea, Japan, Manchuria, Siberia, and elsewhere to develop a worldwide agenda for the movement.

Two events preceded and fed the protests. In December 1918, Japanese officials, anticipating problems over Korea at the forthcoming Paris Peace Conference concluding World War I, began to circulate a petition asking Koreans to renounce any desire for independence. This document was signed by several former high Korean officials, including Wan-Yong Yi, a former cabinet member. When Japanese officials presented the petition for Kojong's seal, the deposed king turned livid and refused to approve it. The tormented monarch had not resigned himself to accepting his country's fate. Kojong and his supporters continued clandestine struggles to regain Korea even after his efforts to persuade Theodore Roosevelt and the Second Hague Conference had failed. Ultimately, these efforts cost him his life. With spies everywhere, the occupying Japanese resident-general's office kept abreast of Kojong's every move.

The last straw came with Kojong's plot to send an emissary to the Paris Peace Conference to plead Korea's case, an endeavor that Japanese officials foiled. They decided the only way to stop Kojong was to deal him the fate of his late queen. Twenty-five years earlier, the Japanese minister to Korea, Goro Miura, had directed the murder of Queen Min by using more than two dozen Japanese swordsmen and Korean hirelings, because she was forming an alliance with Russia, Japan's main rival for superiority in Korea. Now, Japanese officials plotted to eliminate Kojong. On January 21, 1919, a court herb doctor, who was threatened and then bribed by the Japanese resident-general's officials, had the emperor's favorite tea laced with poison. Japanese officials delayed announcing Kojong's death for two days, then said the king had died of apoplexy. No one believed this. Years later, in her autobiography, Princess Pang-ja, the Japanese princess who was coerced into marrying the Korean Crown Prince Ŭn Yi in Japan's scheme to unite the two countries, said her father-in-law was physically well on the eve of his death. He was in Tŏksu Palace, where he had enjoyed the evening, reminiscing with attendants about the old days. Late that night, as was his habit, he was served his favorite tea. Then he retired to his chamber, but soon violent pains attacked him and he died.

The word of foul play spread all over Korea and to Korean communities overseas. The clandestine activities of Korean patriots reached a feverish pitch. They chose the occasion of Kojong's funeral procession on March 3, 1919, to attract the world's attention to Korea's plight. Opinions ranged from capitalizing on the event to initiate peaceful marches, to using the occasion to mount an assault on Japanese officials in Korea. Ultimately, planners adopted a policy of nonviolence. Anticipating extensive police deployments on the day of the funeral, organizers moved up the date to March 1. The protests, though months in the planning, took Japanese officials completely by surprise.

The organizers were thirty-three young men, many of them Christians, but also Buddhists and members of the indigenous Ch'ŏndogyo Church, which preaches the equality of all people and the virtue of meekness. Shortly before two o'clock in the afternoon, they met at a restaurant in the heart of Seoul and signed a declaration of Korean independence. The declaration was then read to crowds at Pagoda Park across the street:

Left: Pak Yong-man (seated center) and the Korean Military Corporation, 1914

Right: An Ch'ang-ho (seated center) and the Korean Provisional Government, 1919

We herewith proclaim the independence of Korea and the liberty of the Korean people. We tell it to the world in witness of the equality of all nations and we pass it on to our posterity as their inherent right. We make this proclamation, having back of us five thousand years of history and twenty millions of united loyal people. We take this step to insure to our children, for all time to come, personal liberty in accord with the awakening consciousness of this new era. This is the clear leading of God, the moving principle of the present age, the whole human race's just claim. It is something that cannot be stamped out, or stifled, or gagged, or suppressed by any means . . .

Queen Min

The last queen of Korea, Empress Myŏngsŏng (1851–1895) was married to King Kojong, who reigned until 1907. Known by her subjects as Queen Min, she worked for Korean independence from the Japanese, whose presence continued to grow in the Korean peninsula. She supported Russian and Chinese interests in Korea primarily as forms of protection from Japanese occupation. Perceiving Queen Min to be a political threat, the Japanese brutally assassinated her and several of her ladies-in-waiting in 1895.

In the ensuing days and weeks spontaneous demonstrations spread across the country, with marching crowds waving Korean flags and chanting, *"Manse!"* (May Korea live ten thousand years!). The Japanese were ruthless in suppressing the peaceful protests. The demonstrations, which came to be known as the March First Independence Movement, hastened Japanese resolve to eradicate all vestiges of Korean nationalism. Thousands of Koreans were killed, arrested, imprisoned, and tortured. The March First Movement cost the lives of 7,645 Koreans and injured 45,562 more. The Japanese burned about a thousand churches, schools, and homes. In a village near Suwŏn, about twenty miles south of Seoul, the Japanese ordered all the villagers to gather inside their church for an important announcement. Then they set the church on fire and gunned down those who tried to escape.

In Tanch'on, my father, who was almost five, witnessed Japanese gendarmes in their tan-colored uniforms, caps with red bands, and tall black boots, pursuing unarmed demonstrators. "Even old people in white topcoats and horsehair hats were running away from soldiers and gendarmes, who were going after them with bayonets and rifles," he said.

Tong-nyŏl Yu, a kindergarten teacher from our hometown, was arrested for participating in the demonstrations. To punish her, Japanese policemen hung her upside down and pulled her pubic hair. The police had been keeping an eye on her for some time because she had taught her kindergarten pupils an anti-Japanese song that contained a derogatory word for Japanese—*waenom,* "little bastards"—because that mocked the short stature of most Japanese.

The brutal crackdown of the March First Movement stirred Koreans everywhere, including in America, and led to the creation of the Korean Provisional Government in Shanghai. In the United States, leaders convened a meeting of Koreans from twenty-seven organizations and from Mexico. During the three-day session, which began on April 14, 1919, in Philadelphia, the delegates issued a ten-point position paper encompassing the aims and aspirations of the Korean people, including the guarantee of basic human freedom and civil rights. They urged the League of Nations to recognize the Korean Provisional Government in Shanghai.

Just before they broke up, the delegates visited the Declaration Room in Independence Hall. Here, after reading the Korean Proclamation of Independence, they approached the old, cracked Liberty Bell. Placing their hands on the bell, and closing their eyes, they prayed for the freedom of Korea and the success of the new movement. Between 1919 and December 1920, an estimated seven thousand Koreans in the United States and Mexico donated $200,000—an enormous sum, considering that the average monthly income of a Korean immigrant laborer was $30.

My father was too young to know it then, but the March First Movement was not only connected to the absence of his father and his uncle from his life, but was the most significant mass protest Koreans had ever engaged in. Although it was crushed under the weight of Japan's occupation forces, it fed the struggle for Korean independence throughout the world. But the international community was apathetic to the bloodbath in Korea. The efforts of Western missionaries to publicize the Korean struggle for freedom failed to elicit much attention in the West. Korea was too far away and too small a country to arouse sustained interest. Tens of thousands of Koreans fled to China, Siberia, and America to foster the movement for Korean independence in exile. The Japanese responded with increased oppression.

After the March First Movement, the Japanese targeted Christians and put them under constant surveillance. They arrested pastors, elders, and church members at will and put them in prison, where they were interrogated and tortured. Often the mere suspicion of being anti-Japanese was sufficient cause for arrest and torture. With spies planted everywhere—even inside the churches—the Japanese did not run out of Koreans to mistreat.

My father, who had seen his father for less than a day before he was taken to prison the second time, grew up feeling as though he had no father. Consequently, he learned to be self-sufficient at a young age. When my grandfather was released from prison after his second eighteen-month term in 1921, he was a broken man, physically and mentally. "I could not recognize him," my father said. Once a fine orator, he hardly spoke now. He stopped all political and social activities. He saw only a handful of people who visited him at home. On occasion he would pen a piece and send it to the prestigious *Chosun Ilbo* newspaper, where he had been a regional correspondent. Otherwise, he rarely ventured outside the house—not even to church. He spent the rest of his life collecting antiques and artwork and writing calligraphy in his smoke-filled room. Many nights, members of my family would be startled awake in the middle of the night by the voice of my grandfather, singing *"Aegukka"* (the Korean national anthem) in his sleep, his voice, like a knife, piercing the stillness of night.

Jinja Kim   *Gathering of Faces*

KIM RONYOUNG
from *Clay Walls*

HAESU

The sky was just turning light as Chun pulled and Haesu pushed the crate of apples up Temple Street. They had invested in a wagon for their new business. Haesu had assured Chun that no risk was involved. If the business failed, she would sell the wagon to some child in the neighborhood.

At Sunset Boulevard Chun said, "This is as far as we go."

By the time they had finished stacking the apples, the sun had risen and shone obliquely on the skins. Haesu had polished each apple the night before. They now glowed a magnificent red. She selected one for its elongated shape, skillfully cut it into a floret, then set it atop the pyramid of apples. She stood back to examine her handiwork. *"Ibuji?"* she said, asking Chun to confirm that it was beautiful.

He nodded. "It looks like a lotus."

His poetic reference took her by surprise. Her look made Chun blush.

"Cigarettes," he blurted and dashed across the street to a drugstore.

How strange he is, Haesu thought. They have been married several months and he was as much a stranger to her as when she first learned she was betrothed to him. Her parents had arranged it; she never wanted him. She had begged them to reconsider, reminding them that his family was socially beneath theirs. They would not listen. They would never go back on their word; they could not. Chun had asked his American missionary employer to act as matchmaker and Haesu's parents could not refuse the esteemed foreign dignitary. When Chun had to leave Korea, Haesu was sent to California to marry him, committed for life to a man she did not love.

Haesu took a lemon from the pocket of her apron and cut it open. She squeezed the juice over the cut apple to keep the white from darkening.

The lotus was a Buddhist symbol of purity, a flower that bloomed even when rooted in stagnant water. Her family were Buddhists before their conversion to Christianity. So were Chun's.

He can't forget, Haesu told herself, he still thinks of home.

She looked up as a streetcar passed. A Chinese woman sitting at a window seat was staring at her.

She'll think I'm part of the American scene, Haesu thought. She couldn't help the smile that came to her face.

It was meeting night. While Clara and Mr. Yim were in the parlor unfolding wooden chairs and setting them in rows, Haesu and Chun were in their room soothing their weary bodies.

"Oooh, nothing feels as good as this," Haesu murmured, playing her toes in a warm solution of epsom salt. Chun had been soaking in a tub of hot water and now threw himself on the bed.

"You can't go to sleep," Haesu warned. "The meeting will start soon. You'll have to attend. What will everyone think?"

"They'll think I'm unpatriotic."

"Min Chang Mo is going to be the speaker. He was in Kyonggi Province after the March First Incident."

"I'm tired," Chun said, adjusting the pillow under his head.

"Who isn't?" Haesu said, adding more hot water to the pan.

It had taken them several weeks to learn that if they were to make a profit, they would have to push their wagon from one place to another. In the early morning they were at Temple and Sunset selling apples to workers leaving for work. At midmorning, they moved on to Grand Avenue to catch the shoppers at lunch. In the afternoon, they made stops in residential districts on their way home. As the day wore on, the apples showed signs of ageing and were sold at reduced prices to children returning home from school.

"If only we didn't have to walk so much," Haesu said. "If only we had a car or truck."

"It takes money. Lots of money," Chun said.

"We could drive around Bunker Hill. Sell all kinds of produce to wealthy customers."

"You wouldn't have to drive anywhere if we had a truck. I could do it all myself."

"What would I do?" Haesu wanted to know.

"Stay home like Clara. Like all *yangban*s."

"How much would it take?"

Chun shrugged his shoulders. "Maybe five hundred dollars."

"*Hmph!* Might as well be five million. We have all of fifty dollars saved up," she noted.

"Takes money. Everything takes money," Chun mumbled.

Haesu wiped her feet dry with a towel. "You had better get dressed, the people will be arriving soon." But she was too late. Chun's eyes were closed, his breathing turning into loud rasps.

At the first sound of people climbing the porch steps, Haesu quickened her movements. By the time she got downstairs, Koreans had crowded into the living room, hands outstretched, ready to grasp any hand they found in their path, cutting the air with the aspirated consonants and mellifluous vowels of their native tongue. Haesu moved through the crowd, taking grip of a dozen hands as she went, exchanging news of family and friends with her fellow countrymen.

Some of the men offered to help Mr. Yim set up more chairs. The ones who couldn't tell one end of the chair from the other chuckled with embarrassment as they

tried to figure it out. They let out a startled *"aigu!"* when the chair snapped open.

Haesu once asked Clara the English equivalent of *aigu.* Clara thought "oh my" or "my goodness" came close but were not exact translations. *Yŏbo* was another commonly used word for which Clara had searched for an English counterpart. She thought "you there" was something like it, but laughed when Haesu said "you there" to Chun and suggested she stick to *yŏbo.*

As even more Koreans arrived, *"Yŏbo!"* spanned the room. Additional chairs filled the space intended to separate the speaker from the audience. The remaining chairs were set up on the porch outside of raised windows. Latecomers made their way to the stairs leading to the second floor to sit on the steps. According to Clara, before the March First Independence Movement, Mr. Yim had to phone members and beg them to attend the meetings.

On March 1, 1919, Haesu was in Shanghai. She was booked on the SS *China* scheduled to leave for San Francisco when she heard about Korea's Declaration of Independence from Japan. She thought it a substantial reason for canceling her passage and returning home. But political escapees from Korea had dissuaded her. The situation in Korea was worse than ever, they had told her. The Declaration was purely symbolic, a nonviolent political gesture that had infuriated the Japanese, causing them to retaliate violently and intensify every atrocity they had ever committed on the Korean people. She was persuaded to give vent to her indignation from America.

Before the meeting was called to order, Haesu took her place on one of the four chairs facing the audience to take a few notes. She was the secretary, appointed by Mr. Yim for her "skillful use of the Korean language and beautiful handwriting." Her accounts of the meetings were published in the Korean newspaper.

The first paragraph extolled the attendance of conscientious Koreans. She then studied the guest speaker as he mingled with the crowd, jotting down notes for later amplification. "Tall. Sturdy physique. Delicate hands. Large expressive eyes. Well-delineated lips of an aristocrat. Honest, earnest expression. Distinguished. According to Korean standards, a fine-looking man."

Not by anyone's standard was Chun a handsome man, she thought. His angular face with eyebrows resembling birds arched in flight gave him a look of perpetual disconcertion. By her standards his teeth were too large and his eyes too small. Only his narrow high-bridged nose deserved admiration. That was all she found to admire by her standards.

Mr. Yim, Min Chang Mo, and K. Y. Yun, the treasurer, filled the seats next to hers, signaling the meeting was about to begin. After the Korean national anthem, Mr. Yim introduced the guest speaker. Haesu listened while taking notes. "Married. No children. Twenty-eight years old. Came from a family of scholars." She underlined "scholars." "Destined to be a professor but was forced to flee Korea. Wanted by the Japanese police for sedition."

Min wasted no time getting to his story. "They burned my mother and sister alive," he said bitterly. "I saw it with my own eyes." He told of being there in Kyonggi Province right after the March First demonstration when the Japanese police herded his mother and a score of villagers into a church, his mother carrying his infant sister on her back. He and others were left to witness what was to follow. He was stunned when the police set fire to the church. He was filled with anguish as the searing heat forced him back. His cries of agony matched those of his mother.

A shudder ran through Haesu; she put down her pen. Tongues clacked and murmurs of indignation rumbled through the audience. Someone yelled, "Those sons-of-bitches!" Mr. Yim called for order, asking for restraint, requesting that Min Chang Mo be allowed to resume his story. Haesu picked up her pen. "Forced to witness the murder of his mother and sister," she wrote.

"Then the Japanese police fired their guns at the pyre of human bodies," Min said. He raised his voice above the obscenities shouted by some of the men in the audience. "I too was enraged. I vowed to destroy every police station in Korea." Half the audience rose to its feet and shouted, *"Manse!"* The other half scrambled to join them.

It took both Mr. Yim and K. Y. Yun to calm everyone down. Min went on to say that there were about fourteen thousand military and civilian Japanese police in Korea. He needed more dynamite. He had come to America to collect money for more explosives.

Before the applause had subsided, K. Y. Yun began passing out mimeographed copies of the Treasurer's Report. Before everyone had received his copy, Yun proceeded to read the report aloud. He called off the names of contributors to the Independence Movement, waiting for hands to clap after the names of generous donors, then lumped together the names of donors of smaller amounts according to denomination. Haesu was mortified to discover that Chun's name was not on the list. When K. Y. Yun called for new pledges, Haesu promised fifty dollars.

Unable to sleep, Haesu tossed and turned in bed. At three o'clock in the morning, when Chun got up to go to the bathroom, she told him she had pledged the fifty dollars.

"I was going to warn you about that," he said as he left the room.

She felt miserable. The paucity of his response made her uneasy. He gave her the impression that there was more meaning to what he left unsaid, leaving her wondering where she stood in the matter. She didn't know which she wanted most, his approval or his absence.

Chun crawled back into bed without saying a word.

"I couldn't stand not contributing something," she explained. "My family always gave generously. I had to give something."

"You have to have something to give," he said.

She tried to think of some response. She knew he wasn't asleep; his body was taut and she sensed that his eyes were open.

Then she felt his hand on her, crawling over the rise and depressions of her body. When he turned toward her, she protested. "No! They'll hear."

"They're asleep," he said as he groped for the cleft where he would enter. Pressing his chest hard against her nipples and jamming his knees between her thighs, he formed a human vise. She wanted to scream herself free. Instead, she became wooden. Her lack of response only served as a goad, intensifying his determination to arouse her. But the more he tried, the more she wanted to expel him from her. It was over when he could hold back no longer. Grunting like a barnyard animal, he collapsed in a heap on top of her.

She pushed him aside and, almost immediately, he fell asleep. She lay there thinking how much she hated it, more each time than the time before. Finally, she turned on her side and pulled the covers over her shoulders, asking herself, "Who cares about the money?"

Something was going on with Chun, but Haesu did not ask any questions. One night, he took the money she had pledged to NAK and left. The next morning, when he returned, he handed the money to her. He began to go out several nights a week, often not returning until morning.

"Has he found a second job?" Mr. Yim asked.

"I don't know," Haesu replied. She found herself hoping that it was "another woman."

When she mentioned to Chun that Mr. Yim wondered if he had found a second job, Chun said, "He hasn't said anything to me."

"He probably doesn't want to appear as if he's prying," she said. "It isn't easy for anyone to ask you anything."

Chun ran his hands through his hair, scratching his scalp along the way. Then, smoothing his disheveled hair, he said, "It's time for us to move out. Tomorrow you go out and find us a place to live. I'll work by myself."

"We can't afford a place of our own," she said.

"Fifteen dollars a month." He pulled out his wallet and counted off the money. "First month's rent," he said, handing her the bills.

Haesu was about to ask where he got the money, but decided against it. Whatever fifteen dollars would provide was welcomed; keeping her fights with Chun private and her growing sense of obligation to the Yims were beginning to wear heavily on her.

At breakfast, she explained why she had not gone to work with Chun. "We've imposed upon you long enough. It's time we moved. I'll need you to go house hunting with me, Clara."

"I'd love to go with you," Clara exclaimed. Then a pained expression suddenly came over her face. "But what will I do after you move?"

Haesu laughed. "What you always do when I'm not here." She had meant to cheer her friend but Clara turned thoughtful, almost sad.

"Do you know that green crepe dress with the side bow? How do you think that would look with my white shoes?" Clara asked. In the next breath she said, "I don't know if I want to go. I hate it when everyone stares at me. They look at me as if I was some kind of freak."

"Nonsense. It's only because we don't look like other Americans," Haesu said.

"It's these eyes," Clara said, popping hers open as wide as she could.

"Don't be a child, Clara. You're a rare beauty. Your eyes are just right."

"That's easy for you to say. I'll bet no one asks you if you can see with your eyes."

"Who asks that?"

"There. I told you. Children ask me that all the time."

"Children!" Haesu scoffed. "What do they know? Wear the green dress and the white shoes. You'll look beautiful. I'll wear something special too. Come on, Clara, it will be fun."

With a sigh of resignation, Clara said, "All right. Let me know if you want to borrow anything."

Mr. Yim had sat quietly while the women made their plans. He now leaned toward his young wife, placing his hand on hers. "While you are out, if you see something you would like to buy for yourself, please do so." He turned to Haesu. "Clara has not been out of this house for months."

"I know. It's my fault. As soon as we get a truck, Chun says I won't have to work. Then Clara and I will go all over Los Angeles together. As a matter of fact, we can start today. Let's get ready, Clara."

Mr. Yim pulled a gold fob from his pocket. "I'm late for work," he declared. "Don't change your mind, Clara. You're more beautiful than any woman in this country." He put on his hat and walked out the door.

Haesu skipped every other step going up the stairs, unbuttoning her house dress as she went. Going through her limited wardrobe, she made her decisions quickly, taking everything she was going to wear from the dresser and closet and laying them on the bed. The corset was her least favorite garment. Why should she have to reshape her body to fit into a dress? The lacing around her small breasts needed little cinching. It was her hips that required the hardest pull, the part of her body that, in Korea, was hidden under a billowing *ch'ima.*

Her ecru crepe dress glided smoothly over her satin underslip. Ready to step into a pair of black pumps, she discovered her feet were bare. "Forgot again," she muttered impatiently. She sat on the bed to put on the taupe silk stockings. The fine mesh conformed to her legs as she carefully stretched it to her knees. Straightening the seams before securing the stockings to her plain pink garter, Haesu then worked her feet into her shoes.

As careful as she tried to be, she couldn't seem to avoid putting snags in her stockings. Yanking and tugging was how she had put on the padded socks she grew up with, calf-high coverings sturdier than the canoe-shaped shoes they fitted into, socks sewn with upturned toes to fill the upturned toes of shoes that historians linked with cultures of the Middle East. She never forgot to put them on.

It wasn't necessary but she put a touch of rouge on her cheeks. She was blushing with excitement. She flattened her lips against her teeth to rub lipstick over them, the way a door-to-door cosmetic saleslady had shown her. She had giggled throughout the demonstration, having had to make such funny faces while the saleslady applied the makeup. She remembered that Clara had scolded her for her lack of seriousness, scolded her *ŏnni* for being silly. That had struck Haesu as being even more amusing. She was a year older than Clara and entitled to the respect accorded older sisters. The whole event struck her as being a comic drama with everyone playing the wrong role, causing her to laugh harder than ever. She now wore makeup as a matter of course, concerned with wearing the right color and the correct amount.

She put on her wide-brimmed black straw hat, the only hat she owned, setting it carefully over her thick black hair. She decided to borrow white gloves and a white bag from Clara.

She found Clara sitting on the sofa downstairs. "I'm sorry," Haesu said. "I didn't mean to keep you waiting."

"I don't think I'll go with you," Clara said.

"But you're dressed and ready to go."

"I've changed my mind."

Haesu took Clara by the hand and pulled her to her feet. "You're going with me. You can't spend your life in this house dancing alone to Rudy Vallee records. We haven't been anywhere together for ages. Besides, who's going to help me with my English? I'd be lost without you. Now no more of this. Can I borrow your white purse and white gloves?"

"Of course. I'll get them for you," Clara said. She started for her room. "I'll get my hat too," she said as she went.

Haesu heaved a sigh of relief.

Clara's hat was deep cloche. The gray felt brim curved over her brows then ran along her cheeks to below her ears. In profile, only the tip of her nose and a bit of her lips and chin were visible.

"For someone who rarely goes out, you've managed to buy very smart clothes," Haesu said.

"Mrs. Thayer shops for me," Clara said.

"Mrs. Thayer?"

"Our landlady. You haven't met her. She only comes when we need her."

"You look lovely, Clara. If people stare at you, it's because you're so pretty."

They had walked a full block when they realized that neither of them had any idea where they were going.

"How did you find your house?" Haesu asked Clara.

"Mr. Yim was living in it when I came to marry him, remember?" Clara stopped in her tracks. "There's no point in going on; we don't know where to go."

Haesu slipped her arm under Clara's. "We're not going back. Do you think your landlady can help us?" She began walking Clara forward. "Where does she live?"

Clara saw that she had no choice but to show Haesu.

Mrs. Thayer lived only two blocks away. She was delighted to be of help, going as far as finding a newspaper and circling all the ads of rentals Haesu could afford. She brought out a map of the city of Los Angeles from her study and marked an **X** where the rentals were located. "There aren't too many rentals for fifteen dollars," she explained to Clara. "But tell your friend that I will be happy to recommend her to any landlord." She stepped back to look Clara over. "You look darling . . . both of you do. I don't see how anyone could turn you down."

Clara did not bother to translate the last sentence for Haesu.

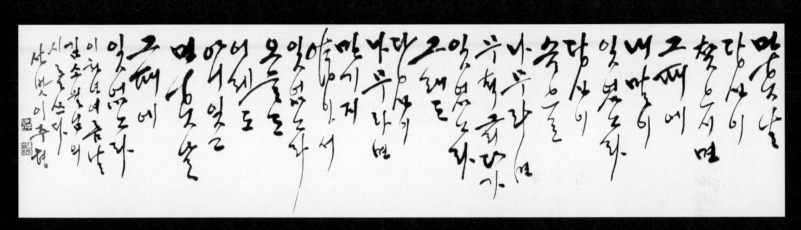

Some Day
Poem by Kim Sowŏl

If some day you come back, then I'll say, "I've forgot."

If you blame me at heart, "I've forgot after much longing."

If you still chide me, "I've forgot, I couldn't trust."

"I've forgot," not today or tomorrow, but "some day."

Calligraphy by Lee Juhyung

The first landlord did not have a chance to turn Haesu down. She screwed up her face at the musty odor in the entry and shook her head at the stained carpets. *"Aigu,"* she gasped and led Clara out the door.

The second landlord turned Haesu down from his living room window. He pulled aside the curtain, glanced at her and the newspaper in her hand, then waved no before closing the curtain.

"It must be taken," Haesu said.

Clara said nothing as she moved aside to let a woman pass. The woman scanned the newspaper in her hand then rang the doorbell to the landlord's apartment.

"Shouldn't you tell her it's been taken?" Haesu asked Clara.

Before Clara could answer, the man was at the door letting the woman in. Haesu's jaw dropped. Clara took her by the arm. "Let's go. He doesn't want 'orientals.'"

Haesu pulled away. "Why not?"

Clara shrugged her shoulders. "Some people do and some people don't. We'll have to find someone who does."

Haesu was dumbfounded. "I don't know whether to laugh or cry. Find someone who will take me? I'm not asking him to like me, I'm finding plenty of people who don't, but if I like a place and I pay what the landlord asks and I take care of his property, he can't turn me away."

"Yes he can. Don't ask me for an explanation. That's just the way it is."

Scholar's house (Ch'aekkori)
Chosŏn dynasty,
18th–19th century
Ink and color on paper (detail)

"I would certainly like to know why the Korean Declaration of Independence was modeled after the American Declaration of Independence."

"Let's go home, Haesu. I don't want to look anymore."

"No. I'm not going to do that. We're going to every place your landlady circled." Haesu opened the map. "Show me the places we've already seen." By Clara's indication, only two locations remained. "They're so close to one another," Haesu noted.

"They're in the unrestricted areas," Clara explained. "Some places are 'For Whites Only.'"

Haesu's lips opened with a smack. "All men are created equal."

"You don't have to make any speeches to me," Clara said. "But I do know one thing. Once you've made up your mind, there's no changing it." With a tilt to her head she added, "Maybe we'll find a place you like and the landlord likes you."

"We'll see," Haesu said. "We'll see."

The other apartments didn't particularly strike Haesu's fancy, but the landlord of one of them took down Mrs. Thayer's phone number and said he would let Haesu know.

Haesu omitted no detail as she told Chun what had happened. She ended her bitter account with, "I'm not going to take a place just because it's available to 'orientals.'"

Chun sighed. "You'll have to find something soon. A man came up to me today and asked if I would be interested in going into partnership with him. He wants to rent a stall at Grand Central Market."

The length of Chun's statement told her the information was significant. "Korean?" she asked.

"No. I don't know what he is. His name's Bancroft. I'm going with him the day after tomorrow to see the place. You'll have to tend the business."

"Bancroft? He asked you? We're not good enough to live in certain places and Bancroft asks you to be his partner?" Her sarcasm was mild compared to what she felt.

"He likes the way we set up our produce. He says it makes people want to buy them."

"Oh, I see. If we polish our apples nice, that's acceptable. But if we want to live in his neighborhood, that's not acceptable. It doesn't make sense to me. I think—"

Chun cut her off with a wave of his hand. "Don't waste your speech on me. I can't do anything about it."

Air escaped from her puffed up cheeks. She had plenty to say about ignorance, prejudice, and discrimination. But Chun was right, it would be wasted on him. To whom then, she wondered. All her thoughts were formed in her native language. In English, she could only utter one or two isolated words, using her hands when words failed her, exasperated that she appeared mentally deficient.

"I'm going to study English," she blurted out.

Her sudden announcement caught Chun off his guard. "English?" It took a few seconds for the information to sink in. "A roof over our heads and food in our stomachs first. English later."

"Come in, Mrs. Thayer," Haesu said. Her *th* sounded like *d* but she wanted to address the woman by name; she had not forgotten her kindness.

"I received a phone call from one of the landlords." She held an imaginary telephone receiver to her ear. "He's a robber, my dear. He will let you have the place but he's going to raise the rent. A scoundrel . . ."

"Excuse me, Mrs. Thayer." Haesu left the room to fetch Clara. "Your landlady's here. She seems upset about something."

Clara entered the parlor with her hand extended. Mrs. Thayer clasped it between her hands. "Clara dear, tell your friend that one of the landlords called." She enunciated each word carefully. "He said that Haesu could have the apartment but the rent would be twenty-five, not fifteen dollars." She let go of Clara's hand to indicate the number, folding and unfolding her fingers until she had held up the correct amount.

Clara was puzzled. "Twenty-five?"

"Yes. A thief. He's taking advantage of your friend."

Clara nodded with understanding and turned to Haesu to explain. The color rose to Haesu's face.

Mrs. Thayer quickly added, "It's okay. O-kay. I told him he could take his apartment and stuff it down the sewer." She laughed, and then realized she wasn't getting through when no one else joined her. She slowed her pace and separated each syllable. "I am going to help you. I will find a place and sublet it to you. No one can refuse to rent to me. You pay me and I pay the owner."

Clara had been following Mrs. Thayer closely. "You be landlady?"

"Sort of."

Clara understood and told Haesu the plan.

"Ask her if it's legal," Haesu said.

Mrs. Thayer's response was emphatic. "To a higher law than the one he's following. By what right does he charge you more than anyone else? Thank God we're not all like him. Yes, legal! I want to do it."

After much explanation, it was settled as Mrs. Thayer wished.

MARGARET K. PAI
from *The Dreams of Two Yi-min*

THE TRAGIC SPLIT

Returning to Hawaii, we were again passengers in the dark steerage hold of a ship. My mother was confined to her bunk for most of the fortnight journey; she said she could not bear the smells of so many people herded together in the three-tiered bunks, sweating, vomiting, and eliminating. Day after day I watched patiently over her. I wished I could go out of the crowded cabin for some fresh air but I dared not leave her.

One day she sat up and remarked, "Your father will be surprised to see how tall you've grown, Chung Sook. You and I have been away over three years."

I tried to visualize my father. I couldn't. Only the faces of my grandparents, my aunts and uncles, the servants, and our friends in Korea could I recall.

"Will *Abŏji* be at the pier when we arrive in Honolulu?" I asked.

"Of course your father will be there. He'll be so happy to see us!"

At last our ship entered Honolulu Harbor. "There's your father!" Mother cried, lifting me to the railing of the ship as it docked. She pointed to a man standing at the edge of a cluster of people. His hair was cut very short and he wore a dark suit. He waved; a quiver of nervous anticipation ran through me. I put up my hand to wave back but held it in midair, for the man standing below was a stranger.

We went down to the foot of the gangplank and waited for him. As he strode toward us he looked bigger than I had thought from my place at the ship's railing.

His face abruptly broke into a smile and his eyes lighted up with gladness. He shook hands with Mother and patted me on the back.

The Korean men and women who had come on the ship with us greeted their spouses and friends with handshakes while the Japanese people bowed low and did not touch each other. All the men on the pier wore grey or black suits, except for a few Japanese men in dark kimonos. All the women were in their native dress—bright *ch'ima* and *chŏgori* or multihued kimonos.

Father announced proudly to Mother, "*Yŏbo*, I've rented a house on Iolani Avenue. I think you will like it."

She looked pleased and asked, "How many rooms does it have?"

"Two bedrooms. A parlor, kitchen, and bathroom."

Our house was the second from the top of four identical-looking cottages built in a row on a sloping street. They were separated from each other by about five feet all around.

We had to walk with care around the colorfully wrapped gifts and many jars of food from Korea, which filled the small living room. In each bedroom was a brown chest and a high, white iron bed. When I sat on my bed it squeaked.

When I walked into the bathroom, the white toilet intrigued me, as did the wash

Parting

Poem by Kim Sowŏl

Shall I say I love her?
Then my heart yearns more.

Shall I leave, not seeing her,
But just this once more...

Ravens in the hills,
Ravens in the plain
Croak about the setting sun:
"She is setting over the hills."

The river in the south,
The river in the north;
The flowing stream
Pulls and shoves,
Flowing ever on and on.

Calligraphy by Cho Yongsun

basin that had a pipe with running water. I soon realized we did not need a maid to bring us water to wash our faces or to empty our chamber pots.

Mother stood in the kitchen a long time without saying a word. She looked lost and a little distressed. Finally, shaking her head, she muttered, "*Aigu,* I'll have to start cooking again."

Father showed her where he kept the pots and pans, and together they prepared supper. He washed the rice and set the pot on the stove, and Mother selected an assortment of *panch'an* from the jars and boxes on the living room floor. We sat on wooden stools around a small, unpainted table in the kitchen and enjoyed *kanjang* fish, strips of peppery dried fish, pickled cucumbers, and pungent "overripe" *kimch'i.*

As I was about to fall asleep the first night I overheard my father say, his voice tinged with sadness, "I wonder if our country will ever become a free nation."

Mother replied with passion, "Oh, we can't give up. We must find a way to defeat Japan."

In the next few days a stream of visitors, most of whom were members of the Korean Methodist Church, dropped in to see us. They talked about the Samil Undong, the new term coined for the famous demonstration of March 1, 1919.

"You were so brave, Mrs. Kwon," they exclaimed and heaped praises on my mother for her years of suffering and her loyalty to the cause.

While the callers knew of her past revolutionary efforts, they did not seem to share her present feelings. She was puzzled. She heard that the once-powerful Korean National Association (KNA), which was the headquarters for all independence activities, had lost its influence. Its paid membership of 2,300 at the height of the independence fervor had plummeted to about 150 supporters by 1921, the year of our return.

When she returned to Hawaii, my mother was ready to rebuild and spread the flame of patriotism the Japanese had tried to smother by imprisoning her. To her surprise and dismay she realized that not only her husband but all the Methodists had lost their passion for their country's liberation. They looked beaten and lost.

How happy Mother was to see her dear friends, the members of the Yŏngnam Puinhoe. She and I were honored guests at their first meeting after our return. The ladies were delighted with my accounts of life in Taegu and the people there.

They clapped their hands and cried, "Hee Kyung, your daughter speaks our lan-

Top: Makaweli Methodist Church, Kaua'i, 1919

Bottom: Korean National Association (Kook Min Hur), 1919

guage so beautifully!" Mother beamed.

The president, a stout woman wearing thick, dark-rimmed glasses, called the meeting to order. "Let us hear from the bravest in our society. Let us hear about her dramatic role in the Samil Undong and the days, weeks, and months she spent in prison—our own Lee Hee Kyung." The society members were proud to use their maiden names when they were together, as it was the custom in Korea for married women.

My mother gave a long and vivid account of her sojourn of the last three years. The ladies responded intermittently with *"Aigu! Aigu!"* or *"Kŭrae?"* in a questioning tone or *"Kŭrae!"* in affirmation. Several times they shouted, *"Mangha nom, mangha nom!"* Some of them, overcome with emotion, wiped away tears and blew their noses. At the end of her talk she exhorted them to waken to the cry of liberty. "Let us renew our efforts!"

The members squirmed in their chairs and looked confused. For once these women, who usually chatted and laughed incessantly when they were together, seemed to have nothing to say or laugh about.

My mother was perplexed. She asked, "Have you lost your zeal? Why are you so quiet?"

Then one woman started to explain. Pain lined her sensitive, pensive face. "We don't know how it all happened, Hee Kyung. While you were gone, Koreans here have been fighting. We've lost our leader—you remember that man we all loved so much, Pak Yong-man. He was banished by the governor and we think he has departed to Shanghai. And our Methodist church is split; half of our members have left for the church where Syngman Rhee preaches. And all the money we poured into the KNA for Korea's liberation—we don't know where it all went. There's been so much talk! And so much fighting!"

A woman interrupted, "Yes, and do you know there's even been fistfights in front of the Korean National Association building!" She gestured, flailing her arms: "The police were called. We heard that the *Advertiser* reported the news in the paper and the Americans heard about the fights. I was so ashamed."

A small, thin woman added in a conciliatory voice, "I know you must be terribly disappointed with us. This community is split in politics and in religion. We can't seem to agree on how to gain our independence or who to follow as leader."

"Yes, it's sad," agreed another lady. "Hee Kyung, you must feel that all you did was in vain. We're sorry. I wish we could think of a way to unify the factions and bring the two churches together."

"That'll never happen!" several ladies declared flatly.

All of a sudden the room turned into a hubbub of noise as everybody began talking at once, arguing, explaining, giving advice.

79

What my mother heard that day at the Yŏngnam Puinhoe was the heartbreaking story of the collision of two volatile Korean scholars who came to Hawaii to lead the Korean immigrants. They knew the immigrants loved their country so much they would be willing to die to regain it. But the philosophies of these two men were incompatible and their personalities clashed. Each man attracted hundreds of loyal supporters. By some odd, accidental strokes of luck or fate, one succeeded and the other was disgraced.

The Korean National Association, needing a bright young man to head the association, had invited Pak Yong-man, a graduate of the University of Nebraska with a degree in political science. He with a group of his friends had established the Korean Youth Army School at Kearney Farm, Nebraska. He arrived in Honolulu in 1912. The KNA was pleased with Pak's work as head of the organization and as editor of the *United Korean News.*

Initially the KNA was involved in diplomatic activities for Korea and in the education of its members' children. But after the annexation of Korea in 1910, the KNA turned more of its attention to collecting funds to relieve the plight of their countrymen under Japanese domination.

Pak was articulate and appealing. He attracted the women especially, who thought he looked dashing in a military uniform. Many women named their newborn sons after him. His lifelong ambition was to lead a military army into Korea and rout the Japanese.

In 1913 Syngman Rhee, who was a delegate from Korea to a Methodist conference in Minnesota, contacted Pak and begged him for a position in the KNA so that he could remain in the United States. Pak obliged. Upon his arrival, Rhee immediately resented working under the aegis of his friend. Rhee connived ways to showcase his own leadership qualities; he was criticized and despised by some people for the cunning, skillful methods he used to achieve his ambition—to be the Korean leader with the largest following. Only seven months after his initial connection with the KNA, Rhee started publishing a monthly called the *Pacific Magazine* in which he criticized the management of the KNA and personally attacked Pak. Hundreds of KNA members rose in protest against Pak and joined Rhee's attack. Less than two years after he was invited by Pak, Rhee succeeded in usurping his friend's position as head of the KNA.

In the meantime Pak had started to build an army of sugarcane laborers in Kahaluu, on the island of Oahu. The small band of volunteers rose early each morning and reported for training. Patriotism ran high and the men were fiercely loyal to Pak.

Three Patriots

Pak Yong-man, Syngman Rhee, and An Ch'ang-ho were three leaders in the movement to free Korea from Japanese occupation. Though they fought for the same cause, each took a different approach to achieving this goal.

Pak Yong-man believed that only military force would end Japanese occupation. After being imprisoned in Korea for anti-Japanese activities, he moved to the United States in 1904 to continue his fight for Korean independence. By 1908, he had established a small military training camp in Nebraska. He was then hired as an editor of the Korean National Association (KNA) newspaper, so he relocated to Hawai'i in 1912. At 'Āhuimanu, he built another military school, training up to three hundred soldiers at a time. Because Syngman Rhee opposed the school, it was closed in 1917, three years after it had opened. Pak then took his revolutionary activities to China, serving as an intelligence officer for the U.S. Siberian Expeditionary Forces. In 1928, the commander of the Korean Provisional Government Army accused Pak of spying for the Japanese and he was assassinated in Beijing.

Syngman Rhee had met Pak in 1903, while both were imprisoned in Korea, and the two had sworn allegiance to the independence movement. Opposed to a militant stance, Rhee sought to secure Korea's sovereignty through diplomacy and education. He came to the United States in 1905 to earn his doctorate from Princeton University, then moved to Hawai'i in 1913 to teach in the Chungang hagwŏn language school and work in the Methodist Church. During this time, he decided to open his own school, the Korean Girls' Seminary, to provide girls with an education.

After the March 1, 1919, protest demonstration, Rhee helped establish the Korean Provisional Government and formed the Korean Commission in Washington, D.C., to serve as the diplomatic arm of the Provisional Government. Through this organization, he lobbied the League of Nations to recognize Korea as an independent country and raised funds to strengthen the independence movement in America. In 1948, the Republic of Korea was formed and Rhee was elected its first president. Two years later, the Korean War broke out and Rhee led the South through three years of civil conflict. In 1960, he resigned, and later he returned to Hawai'i, where he died.

An Ch'ang-ho worked toward what he called "self-renewal": strengthening Korean industry and education before committing to armed revolt. In 1907, two years after Korea became a Japanese protectorate, he formed the New People's Association (Sinminhoe) in Seoul. This underground society built over fourteen schools and several businesses, including a ceramics factory and a cigarette company. After Japanese authorities disbanded the society in 1911, An moved to California and led the KNA there. He was later elected president of the Central Headquarters, which governed all U.S. branches of the KNA. After March 1, 1919, he went to Shanghai to serve as an official of the Korean Provisional Government. In a 1932 incident involving a fellow patriot, the Japanese police in Shanghai cracked down on Korean independence leaders and arrested An. He spent four years in prison. In 1937 he was imprisoned again, but was released for health reasons. He died the following year.

The trainees willingly paid for their uniforms and equipment.

This military activity was to be kept a secret. But word soon leaked out to the Japanese Consul in Hawaii. Alarmed, Consul Matsuoka called on the governor of the Territory of Hawaii, Lucius E. Pinkham, and pointed to the danger of the Koreans being trained to bear arms. Obviously, the consul gave no hint of his own fear that a Korean army could pose a threat to Japan's rule in Korea.

Heeding the consul's warning, Governor Pinkham ordered Pak to halt all military exercises. By 1916 Pak's dream of a military force to take to Korea came to an end in Hawaii. He was banished to Shanghai. However, few people were aware of the governor's action until years later; while Pak was the head of the KNA, he had been traveling back and forth to Shanghai, where the Korean Provisional Government in exile was established.

After he was ousted from the KNA, Pak started his own political group and called it Tongniptan (Korean Independence League). The league's purposes were to collect donations for the motherland's independence and to support those persons working for the cause. The league was organized on March 3, 1919; within a week the enrollment reached 350, and most of them, like Pak, were Methodists. Then Pak began publishing a weekly called the *Pacific Times,* to counteract Rhee's monthly publication, the *Pacific Magazine.* Syngman Rhee took up Pak's challenge and formed his own political party, the Tongjihoe (Comrade Society). The bulk of its membership was made up of members from his church, the Korean Christian Church.

His most cherished dream, Rhee said, was to educate the children of the immigrants. In fact, education was revered by all Koreans, and scholars had always been held in the highest esteem in their country.

The Methodist Board of Missions in Hawaii, which operated the Korean Compound School for Boys on Punchbowl Street, asked Rhee to serve as its principal. The Methodist Board was pleased to know that Rhee had received a doctorate from Princeton University. It was shortly after he had arrived in Hawaii in 1913 to join the KNA that he started serving at the school.

Rhee extended an invitation to Korean girls to attend the school, yet to his surprise the board strenuously objected and refused them admission. The girls, who were coming from plantation families outside of the city of Honolulu and from the outer islands, needed a place to stay. Rhee hastily decided to start a small school for them in Puunui and called the institution the Korean Girls' Seminary.

In need of money to support the new school Rhee went into the community for donations. The board reproved him for soliciting funds for a cause outside of the church domain and without its sanction. All along Rhee had been offering his services as principal at the Compound School without remuneration, as did most of the school

staff who had arrived from the U.S. mainland to serve as missionaries.

He could not tolerate the board's protests and its refusal to educate girls of Korean ancestry. Later in the year 1916, Rhee, angry and weary of the board's opposition to his beliefs and actions, resigned as principal of the Compound School.

He thought he should abandon everything that had to do with Methodists. Religion was important to him and his countrymen, but he wanted to belong to a church in no way affiliated with the strong Methodist Board of Missions in Hawaii. So he started a new church in 1916, called it the Korean Christian Church, and began recruiting members from the Korean community, most of whom were Methodists. He served both as preacher of his church and as leader of his political party.

It is debatable to this day whether the Korean community in Hawaii would have been as badly split had the Methodist Board of Missions, which was rigidly controlled by edicts from New England, not opposed Rhee's philosophy of education. That the Korean community in Hawaii was divided into two rival political parties was unfortunate; that the Korean community was divided into two rival churches was even more unfortunate.

The members of the Korean Christian Church exulted when their preacher, Syngman Rhee, returned from Washington, D.C., in 1919, where he had addressed a number of congressmen willing to listen to him on Korea's condition under colonial rule. The members of the church had further reason to gloat when Pak Yong-man was sentenced to deportation by the governor.

My mother had longed to return to the islands after her internment in prison. Upon her return, she thought she could resume her role as an activist for the cause of Korea's independence. But she found her role as a revolutionary suddenly changed. Two political parties had emerged, and the conflict between the two adversary leaders, Pak and Rhee, had produced devastating results: the permanent split of the Korean community in Hawaii, the weakening of the independence movement, and the existence of two inimical Korean churches.

Both my parents remained Methodists, loyal to their church. They also continued to support Pak by sending him funds regularly through party channels to Shanghai, where he was known to be training a military army. My mother especially favored Pak's dream of expelling the Japanese in Korea by military force. She knew too well that a peaceful statement or an assertion of independence, like the event of March 1, 1919, was futile. As to Syngman Rhee's philosophy of education, which was the theme of his religious and political preaching, my mother could not fathom how it would bring about the liberation of Korea.

RICHARD E. KIM
from *Lost Names: Scenes from
a Korean Boyhood*

Lost Names

When I arrive at the school, our teacher is already in our classroom. He is a young Japanese, a recent graduate of a college in Tokyo. He is twenty-four years old, soft-spoken, and rather gentle with the children. He is lean—in fact, so lean that we give him a nickname the moment he is assigned to our class: Chopstick. Always pale-faced and looking in poor health, he likes to recite Japanese poetry in class, though we hardly understand it.

I set about making the fire in the stove, with the help of several of my friends, who will later toss a coin to see who gets the "second place." The air in the classroom is freezing and, through my cotton socks, I can feel the icy chill of the wooden floor. It is unusual for our teacher to be in the classroom before the bell rings, so all the children are silent, hunched over their desks, rubbing their feet furtively to keep them warm. The teacher is sitting on his chair, behind the lectern on the platform, quietly looking at us. When I have the fire going at last, I shovel in some coal on top of the pine cones crackling inside the blazing stove. The stove sits in the middle of a square, tin floorboard in the center of the class. It is like a small island. I sit at a desk next to it, checking it regularly or adding more water to a tea kettle sizzling on top of it.

The bell rings, and we sit up straight, hushed.

The teacher stands up, looking at a piece of paper in his bony hand. He keeps silent for a long time, looking out the windows. It is almost like a blizzard outside—the wind roaring and howling, the snow whipping down, slanting at nearly a forty-five-degree angle. The snow is so heavy and thick that I can barely make out the other buildings across the frozen pond.

"Well," he says.

And I bid the children rise from their chairs, and, when they do, I command them to bow to our teacher. We all bow our heads to him; then we sit down.

"Today," he says, without looking at us, holding up the piece of paper in front of him, "I must have your new names. I have the new names of most of you in this class, but the principal tells me that some of you have not yet registered your names. I shall call your old names, and those who are called will be excused from the class immediately, so that they can go home and return with their new names, which have been properly registered with the proper authorities in town. Do you understand what I am saying?"

Without waiting for our reaction, and still without looking at us, he calls out several names. My name is called.

"You may be excused," he says, crunching the piece of paper into a ball in his fist. "Report back as soon as you can."

He gets down from the platform and says, "The rest of you will remain quiet and go over your homework." With that announcement, he abruptly turns away from us

and walks out of the room.

I put my shoes on outside the classroom and, brushing aside the questions from the bewildered children, I start running away from the school as fast as I can in the blinding snow and choking, icy wind, running and skidding and stumbling in the deep snow. My new name, my old name, my true name, my not-true name? I am plunging and slogging through the snow, thinking, "I am going to lose my name; I am going to lose my name; we are all going to lose our names…"

My grandmother says, "Leave the boy home. He will catch cold."

My father says, "No, Mother. I want him to come with me. I want him to see it and remember it." My father is wearing a Korean man's clothes: white pantaloon-like trousers, with the bottoms tied around his ankles, a long-sleeved white jacket, a blue vest, and a gray topcoat. My father is seldom seen in our native clothes, except when he has to attend a wedding or a funeral. He is wearing a black armband on the left sleeve of his gray topcoat. He is not wearing a hat.

"Have some hot soup before you go," says my grandmother.

"No, thank you, Mother," says my father, holding my hand. "Stay with Father and keep an eye on him."

My grandmother nods. "It is the end of the world," she mutters angrily. "Damn them! Damn them!"

"Come on," says my father to me.

Outside, by the west gate, four of my father's friends are waiting for us. They are dressed like my father—all wearing black armbands on the left sleeves of their gray top-coats. I bow to them, but no one says a word either to me or to anyone else. On the small stone bridge outside the gate, they pause for a moment, whispering among them-selves. The stream is frozen and covered thick with snow. Passers-by bow to the group. The four men—my father's friends—are the bookstore owner, an elder of our Presbyterian church, a doctor, and a farmer who also has an apple orchard. The snow is slashing down on us, and my ears are cold, even with ear muffs on. Snowflakes get inside my collar, making me shiver. We walk down the street; my father is in the mid-dle of the group, holding my hand. I slip on an icy patch and stumble, and the book-store owner helps me up and holds my hand. In the snow-covered open-air market-place, which is closed down during the winter, the wind howls even more strongly, shrieking through the electric wires and telephone poles. The snow is beating down so hard that I have to bow my head and face sideways, but the men are walking straight up, occasionally returning, in silence, the bows from the other men on the street. We go past the town hall, past the Japanese department store and shops, and through the main street, where most of the shops are—the bakery, the barber shop, the watch shop,

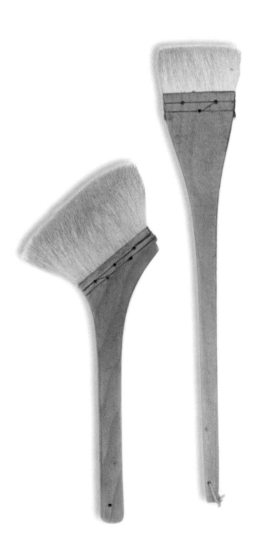

the restaurant, the clothing store, the bicycle shop, the grain store, the pharmacy, the doctor's office, the dentist's office, the hardware store, the bank, the grocery store…and the townspeople are looking out from their shops and offices—some bowing to us, some waving at us—and, as we continue down the main street, we are followed by other people, and more and more people join us as we come near the end of the main street. My father and the bookstore owner are still holding my hands, and I have to try hard to keep up with the men, though they are walking very slowly. At the end of the main street, we come to an intersection and turn to the right. It is an uphill road, and the snow-laden wind whips down from the top of the hill, almost blowing me off my feet, and I feel the men's hands tighten their grips on mine. At the top of the hill, there is a small Methodist church and, across from it, the police station. We struggle up the snow-packed hill, by the long stone wall of the police station, and enter its main gate. Inside, on the station grounds, in the deep snow, a long line of people barely moves along. We walk over the crackling snow and stand at the end of the line. We exchange bows with the people standing in line. No one says anything—me, my father, the bookstore owner, the doctor, the farmer, the elder of our church, and all those people who have preceded or followed us…

I am freezing with cold. I stamp my feet, crushing the icy snow on the ground. Without a word, the bookstore owner opens the front of his topcoat and pulls me inside and covers me up, except for my face, which is snuggled against the back of my father. My father turns, looks at me, and fixes my ear muffs. He neither says a word to me nor smiles at me. I know when to keep quiet.

The line, hardly advancing, gets longer and longer. New people are lined up even outside the station grounds.

Someone comes to us. Someone from the front of the line. He is a young Korean man. He bows to my father. "Please, sir," he says, "come and take my place."

My father shakes his head. "I will wait for my turn here. Thank you anyway."

He stands silent for a moment.

"It is all right," my father says. "Go back to your place."

He bows to my father once more and says, before he returns to the front of the line, "I am dying of shame, sir"; then, his words nearly lost in the howling snow, "I don't know what I can do."

A little while later, a Japanese policeman comes toward us. When he comes near to us, I can tell that he is an inspector. He is wearing a black cape. I see his long saber peering out of the bottom of his cape. I can hear the clank the saber makes against his black leather riding boots. He salutes my father. He has a long turned-up mustache. "It is an honor," he says to my father, "to see you in person here. You could have sent one of your servants."

YI SANG-HWA

Does Spring Come
to Stolen Fields

The land is no longer our own.
Does spring come just the same
to the stolen fields?
On the narrow path between the
    rice fields
where blue sky and green fields meet
    and touch,
winds whisper to me, urging me forward.
A lark trills in the clouds
like a young girl singing behind the hedge.
O ripening barley fields, your long hair
is heavy after the night's rain.
Lightheaded, I walk
lightly, shrugging my shoulders, almost
dancing to music, the fields are humming—
the field where violets grow, the field
where once I watched a girl planting rice,
    her hair
blue-black and shining—

I want
a scythe in my hands, I want
to stamp on this soil, soft as a
    plump breast,
I want to be working the earth and
    streaming with sweat.

What am I looking for? Soul,
my blind soul, endlessly darting
like children at play by the river,
answer me: where am I going?
Filled with the odor of grass,
    compounded
of green laughter and green sorrow,
limping along, I walk all day, as if
    possessed
by the spring devil:
for these are stolen fields, and our
    spring is stolen.

Translation by Peter H. Lee

My father is silent.

"Please come with me," says the Inspector. "I can't have you lined up out here like a common person. Please."

"I will wait for my turn, just like everyone else," says my father. "They have been here longer than I have."

"Come with me," insists the Inspector. "Please."

Afraid and, to my shame, trembling, I look up at my father.

My father looks at the Inspector and then at his friends.

Other people are watching us.

I feel the hands of the bookstore owner tighten on my shoulders.

"If you insist," says my father.

The Inspector looks down at me. "You must be freezing," he says. His white-gloved hand reaches out for my snow-covered hair.

I duck my head inside the topcoat of the bookstore owner.

"Bring the boy with you, by all means," says the Inspector.

I hear my father's boots crunching on the snow. I free myself out of the bookstore owner's hands and nearly bump into the back of my father.

He takes my hand. "Come with me."

The Inspector walks beside my father. His black cape is billowing in the wind and snow, flapping and flapping—and his saber jingling and clanking. We walk toward the front door of the granite station building. As we pass by the people in the line, they bow to my father silently. My father's head is bowed, and, without looking at the people, he goes slowly, holding my hand.

The Inspector opens the front door and holds it for us. A Korean detective inside the building quickly bows to my father. "You really didn't have to come in person, sir," he says in Korean. "I would have been glad to have registered your new name for you if I had known you were coming in person. In this cold."

We are inside the station. Other people in the line are admitted inside one at a time. The air is steamy and warm. The hallway is swarming with black-uniformed policemen, all wearing sabers. The wooden floor is slushy with melting snow.

The Inspector ushers us into a large room immediately to the right of the hallway by the door. There are two big tables, each with a policeman sitting behind. At each table, by the side of the Japanese policeman, a Korean detective sits on a chair, apparently interpreting for those Koreans who cannot understand Japanese.

The Korean detective who met us at the door brings a chair from the back of the room. He offers it to my father.

My father does not sit down.

The Inspector tells the detective to bring some tea.

Born in 1900, Yi Sang-hwa participated in the March 1, 1919, independence demonstration and in subsequent student protests. In 1923, he went to Japan to study literature. Returning to Korea a year later, he was arrested and charged with raising funds for anti-Japanese groups. He was imprisoned several more times, and in 1943 he died of cancer.

Written in 1926, "Does Spring Come to Stolen Fields" laments the occupation of Korea by the Japanese and asserts that they stole not only the land but the beauty and youthful passion of springtime itself.

One of the men sitting at one of the tables facing the Japanese policemen cannot speak Japanese and has to have the words interpreted. The man is old; he helps out in the open-air marketplace on market days, doing odd jobs.

The Japanese policeman, dipping a pen in an inkwell, does not lift his face from a large ledger on the table when he says to the Korean detective by his side, "Tell the old man we will pick out a name for him if he can't make up his mind."

The Korean detective picks up a sheet of paper and shows it to the old man, translating the policeman's words.

The old man shakes his head, looking at the paper, which contains a long list of names. "Anything," he mumbles. "It doesn't matter."

The Korean detective does not translate those words. Instead, he puts his finger on one of the names and says, "How about this one, old man?"

The old man says, "It doesn't matter which. No one's going to call me by that name anyway—or by any other name."

"Then, this will be recorded as your new name." The Korean detective tells the policeman the old man's "new" name—a Japanese name.

"All right," says the policeman. He writes the name in the ledger. "What about his family members?"

The Inspector comes back into the room, accompanied by another Japanese policeman. I know him. He is the Chief of Police.

My father exchanges bows with the Chief of Police.

The Chief of Police says, "Such inclement weather, and you honor us by being here in person. Is this your son?"

I edge nearer to my father.

The Chief of Police, a short man with bushy eyebrows and large eyes behind dark-brown tortoise-shell glasses, looks at the Inspector and says, "Well, I trust the Inspector here will take care of your matter as speedily as he can. Anything, anytime I can be of any help or service, please call on me. I am, indeed, honored by your presence here in person."

My father and he exchange bows again. The Chief of Police goes out of the room, his black leather riding boots jangling, dragging his spurs on the wet floor.

My father takes out a piece of paper from his vest pocket. He hands it to the Inspector. "I assume," he says, "this is what you want, Inspector. I hope you will be pleased."

The Inspector looks at the paper. "Yes, yes," he says. "Iwamoto...Ah—it is a very fine name, sir. It does justice to your person. It reminds me of your house by the mountain and, also, of your orchard, with all those rocky mountains around it. I will have it registered. You needn't wait for the certificate, needless to say. I will have someone bring it to your house later."

"Iwamoto…Iwamoto." I mouth the name. Our new name. My new name. "Iwa"—rock. "Moto"—root…base…foundation. "Rock-Foundation." So this is our "new" surname, our Japanese "family" name.

"Come," my father says to me.

The Korean detective leads us out, with the Inspector by my side. At the front door, which the detective holds open, the Inspector gives my father a salute. "I thank you, sir, for taking the trouble to come in person."

We step out into the cold. The snow is turning into a blizzard. The long line of people is still standing outside, hunched and huddled, rubbing their ears and faces, stamping their feet in the snow. My father pauses for a moment on the steps, one arm around my shoulders, and says:

"Look."

Afraid, bewildered, and cold, I look up at his face and see tears in his eyes.

"Take a good look at all of this," he whispers. "Remember it. Don't ever forget this day."

I look at all those people lined up, from the steps all the way to the gate and outside. I feel a tug at my hand, and I follow him down the steps. We walk by the people slowly, my father not speaking. They bow to him, some removing their hats. My father, bowing back, approaches the group of his friends still in line. In silence, they shake hands.

Then, we move on along the line of people standing in the snow. Some shake hands with my father; most of them merely bow, without words. We are outside the gate. There, too, a long line has formed and is still forming, all the way down the hill, past the gray stucco Methodist church…and I am thinking, "We lost our names; I lost my name; and these people are all going to lose their names, too, when they walk into the police station, into that half-empty large hall, when a 'new' name, a Japanese name, is entered in the big ledger with a pen dipped into a dark-blue inkwell…"

"What does our new name mean, sir?" I ask my father when we are down the hill and on the main street.

"Foundation of Rock," he says, shielding my face from the bitter-cold snow with his hand. "On this rock I will build my church…"

I do not understand him.

"It is from the Bible," he says.

By twelve o'clock, all the children in our class have new names. As soon as each class submits to the principal a complete list of all the new names, the class is sent out of the school to go to the Japanese shrine to pay its respects to the gods of the Empire and

make its report to the Emperor—to announce that we now have Japanese names. At least once a week, each class is required to go to the shrine for an hour of meditation and prayer for the victory and prosperity of the Empire. It was our class's turn the day before, and we "prayed" for the victory and safety of the German *Luftwaffe* pilots who are bombing England in—as I shall learn years later to call it—the Battle of Britain.

Every town and every village now has a shrine—a miniature copy of the "main" shrine somewhere in Japan, where all the souls of the dead soldiers, for example, are supposed to go to rest. The shrine in our town is a small, wooden structure with a gable roof and several flights of stone steps built halfway up the mountain behind our house. The shrine is tended by a middle-aged Japanese Shinto priest, a bald-headed little man with a fat wife, who happens to live in a house that is next to ours, though carefully separated from ours by a bamboo fence.

The snow is coming down hard as we struggle up the narrow, icy path in file. Whenever there is a strong wind, the heavily laden pines shower down on us swarms of little icicles and snow. My bare hands are freezing, my bare ears are numb, and my feet are wet and cold with snow that slips inside my boots. Everyone's cheeks are red and raw from the icy wind. We gasp our way up the mountain. There is a small plaza at the foot of the stone steps, and the wind at the clearing is unbearable. The lashing, biting wind shrieks and whines all around us. The town below is invisible—lost in the blizzard, smothered by the raging snow. At the command of our teacher, I have to coax the children to gather and stand in formation. Then we kneel down in the snow, with our heads bowed. The teacher tells the priest, who has come down the steps from the shrine up above, that we are all there to report to the gods and the Emperor our new names. The priest, dressed in a purple-and-white priest's garment, wears a small sort of hat on his bald head. The teacher gives him the list of our new names. The priest reads the names one by one, slowly, bowing his head to the shrine above with each name. Then the priest chants something in a singsong voice, and, when he finishes the chanting, we all bow, now standing up. Snow clings to my pants, and my hands are wet from the snow. We look like a group of snowmen, covered as we are from top to bottom with the snow. At last we are dismissed by the priest, who goes back up the stone steps into the shrine, back to the sanctuary of his gods and the spirit of the Emperor that resides in it. Years later, when, at last, our liberation comes, we raid the shrine, which is then already wrecked and has been set on fire by the townspeople, and, there, in the inner sanctuary, we discover a small wooden box; in it, we find, wrapped in rice paper, two wooden sticks to which we have been bowing and praying all those years—the sticks from a tree on the "sacred" grounds of the "main" shrine in Japan…

Our teacher dismisses the class for the day. The children, no longer in formation, scramble down the mountain path, without a word and without a sound. The teacher

Self Portrait

Poem by Yun Dongju

All alone I visit a deserted well by a paddy—field
beyond the hill.
Then I quietly look into the water.
In the well, the moon is bright; clouds saunter; the
sky spreads; blue winds breathe;
the autumn dwells; and there is a man.
Somehow I hate the man. So I turn around to go
away.
On my way back, I feel sorry for the man.
I return to the well and look down. He remains in
his place.
I hate him again. I turn around to go away.
On the way back, I long for the man.
In the well, the moon is bright; clouds saunter; the
sky spreads; the blue winds breathe;
the autumn dwells; and the man stands there like
memory.

Calligraphy by Son Insik

wants me to come with him. I follow him down the path in silence. I skid once on the way down and roll over, plunging into a deep pile of snow. He offers his hand and helps me up on my feet. His bare hand clasps my bare hand. He leads me down the mountain on the path, which forks at the foothill, one path going toward the school and the other going into the town, past our house. He takes the path that goes by our house. He is still holding my hand. I do not know how to disengage my hand from his. I do not want to be seen letting him hold my hand, but he grips it firmly and strides toward our house. We pass the Shinto priest's Japanese-style wooden house. We are at the east gate of our house.

Someone must have seen us coming down the path and told my father, because we find my father at the gate waiting for us. He has not changed his clothes.

My father and the teacher exchange bows.

I slip away from the teacher and stand by my father.

"No school this afternoon?" says my father to no one in particular.

I shake my head.

The teacher says, in Japanese, "Too much has happened to the children today already; so I sent them home for the day."

My father simply nods his head.

"I hope you don't mind my bringing him home," says my teacher, casting a quick glance at me.

"Not at all."

A moment of silence follows, all of us standing there in the pouring snow by the gate. I am wondering if my father will invite the teacher in, but he is quiet and shows no hint of asking the young Japanese in.

Then, the teacher gestures abruptly, as if to touch my face. "I am sorry," he says.

My father gives him a slight bow of his head.

"Even the British wouldn't have thought of doing this sort of primitive thing in India," says the Japanese.

I am at a loss, trying to comprehend what he says and means.

"…Inflicting on you this humiliation," he is saying, "…unthinkable for one Asian people to another Asian people, especially we Asians who should have a greater respect for our ancestors…"

"The whole world is going mad, sir," says my father quietly, "going back into another dark age. Japan is no exception."

My teacher nods. "As one Asian to another, sir, I am deeply ashamed."

"I am ashamed, too, sir," says my father, "perhaps for a reason different from yours."

My teacher, without a word, bows to my father, turns round, and disappears into the blinding snow.

"It is a small beginning," says my father, as he has said before about my Korean teacher, who is now somewhere in Manchuria. He gives me a hug. "I am ashamed to look in your eyes," he says—another one of those mysterious things he likes to say. "Someday, your generation will have to forgive us." I don't know what he is talking about, but the scene and the atmosphere of the moment, in the roaring wind and with the snow gone berserk, make me feel dramatic.

"We will forgive you, Father," say I, magnanimously.

His arm tightens around my shoulders. "Come on," he says, leading me into the house. "We have one more place to go to. Your grandfather and I are going out to the cemetery. Would you like to come?"

I nod. I am, suddenly, too overwhelmed and awed by enigmas beyond my child's understanding to speak.

"I hope our ancestors will be as forgiving as you are," he says. "It is a time of mourning."

And, only then, do I understand the meaning of the black armband on his sleeve and on those of his friends.

About four miles out of town, between our house and the orchard, the cemetery lies at the foot of a hill that gradually rises up to become a craggy, rock-strewn, barren mountain. It is what the townspeople call a common burying ground, one that is used by poor people who cannot provide their dead with a private cemetery—with the hope that, someday, when they can afford a family burial plot, they will exhume the dead and move them to their own, private graves. My family is not poor—now; it was poor in the days of my great-grandfather and of my grandfather, when he was young, and, of course, before their time. All our known ancestors are buried in the common burying ground, where I am now plowing through the deep snow in the wailing wind; my grandfather's parents and my grandmother's parents are buried next to each other.

Twenty or thirty people are moving about the burying ground. Some are in white; some, in gray, like my father and my grandfather. All are shrouded with white snow; now, some are kneeling before graves; some, brushing the snow off gravestones; some, wandering about like lost souls...

Halfway to the graves of our ancestors, we meet my father's friend the doctor and his old mother, who are coming down the hill. No one says a word, but the old woman silently touches the sleeve of my grandfather's gray topcoat. Her gray hair is undone and down in the fashion of women in mourning. Her hair is coated with snow and her eyebrows, too. She is weeping, leaning on the arm of her son. We part in silence.

Whenever we pass people on their knees before the graves of their ancestors, we bow our heads. Some people are on their way out of the grounds, and we move past each other without words, just bowing to each other.

When we are in front of the graves of our ancestors, my father wipes the snow off the gravestones. The names chiseled on the gravestones are filled with ice, so that I can barely distinguish the outlines of the letters.

The three of us are on our knees, and, after a long moment of silence, my grandfather, his voice weak and choking with a sob, says, "We are a disgrace to our family. We bring disgrace and humiliation to your name. How can you forgive us!"

He and my father bow, lowering their faces, their tears flowing now unchecked, their foreheads and snow-covered hair touching the snow on the ground. I, too, let my face fall and touch the snow, and I shiver for a moment with the needling iciness of the snow on my forehead. And I, too, am weeping, though I am vaguely aware that I am crying because the grown-ups are crying.

My grandfather unwraps a small bundle he brought with him and takes out three wine cups and a bottle of rice wine. He fills the cups with the wine, for all of us.

We hold the cups in our hands and pour the wine over the graves, one by one, with my grandfather filling our cups with more wine before each mound. The pale liquid forms a small puddle for a second on the hard snow before it trickles down into the snow, as if someone inside the mound beneath the snow-packed earth is sipping it down.

Then, my grandfather fills our cups once more, and we hold them up high before our eyes for a moment and then drink.

My grandfather would like to be alone for a while. My father and I make a final bow to the graves and leave him.

More people are trudging in the snow, coming up to the burying ground. Here and there, I see people on their knees in front of graves, some crying aloud, some chanting, wailing mournful words. An old man in white—gasping in the freezing air and the blowing snow flurries, supported by a young woman, also in white and with her hair down and disheveled, stumbles in the knee-deep snow. He comes up to my father.

The old man stretches out his wrinkled, gnarled hand to my father, touching him. His long white beard is caked with snow. His small, bleary eyes, opaque and watery, peer out of the hollows formed by his high cheekbones.

His tremulous voice says to my father, "How can the world be so cruel to us? We are now ruined—all of us! Ruined!"

My father does not speak.

Punch'ŏng Wine Bottle
Chosŏn dynasty,
late 15th century
Stoneware with white slip
and celadon glaze

The young woman says, "Come on, Father, we must hurry home."

The old man says, "Now I lost my own name and I am as dead as—"

"Please!" the young woman begs.

And—suddenly—I am repelled by the pitiful sight of the driveling, groveling old man, whose whining muttering is lost in the bitter wind and swirling snow. Turning away from him, I stride down the path made by footsteps. I stop and turn around to see if my father is following me.

He is still with the old man, who is now clutching at the arm of my father, openly wailing, and my father stands silently, with his head bowed. The young woman, too, standing behind the back of the old man, is weeping. Beyond them, I see my grandfather on his knees before the graves.

The snow keeps falling from a darkening sky, millions and millions of wild, savage pellets swirling and whishing about insolently before they assault us with malicious force. I watch the people everywhere, all those indistinct figures engulfed in the slashing snow, frozen still, like lifeless statuettes—and I am cold, hungry, and angry, suddenly seized with indescribable fury and frustration. I am dizzy with a sweet, tantalizing temptation to stamp my feet, scratch and tear at everything I can lay my hands on, and scream out to everyone in sight to stop—*Stop! Please stop!*—stop crying and weeping and sobbing and wailing and chanting…Their pitifulness, their weakness, their self-lacerating lamentation for their ruin and their misfortune repulse me and infuriate me.

What are we doing anyway—kneeling down and bowing our heads in front of all those graves? I am gripped by the same outrage and revolt I felt at the Japanese shrine, where, whipped by the biting snow and mocked by the howling wind, I stood, like an idiot, bowing my head to the gods and the spirit of the Japanese Emperor…and I remember my father's words: "I am ashamed to look in your eyes. Someday, your generation will have to forgive us." *Stop! Stop! Stop!* I want to shout out into the howling wind and the maddening snow. How long—for how many generations—are you going to say to each other, "I am ashamed to look in your eyes"? Is that going to be the only legacy we can hand down to the next generation and the next and the next?

"Oh, we are ruined!" *Ha!* What is the matter with you all, you grown-ups! All this whining, wailing, chanting, bowing to the graves, sorrowful silence, meaningful looks, burning tears…that is not going to save you from having to cry out, "Oh, ruination!" Damn, damn, damn—like my good old grandmother would say—Damn!

And—with the kind of cruelty only a child can inflict on adults—I scream out

SIM HUN

When That Day Comes

When that day comes
Mount Samgak will rise and dance,
the waters of Han will rise up.

If that day comes before I perish,
I will soar like a crow at night
and pound the Chongno bell with my head.
The bones of my skull
will scatter, but I shall die in joy.

When that day comes at last
I'll roll and leap and shout on the
   boulevard
and if joy still stifles within my breast
I'll take a knife

and skin my body and make
a magical drum and march with it
in the vanguard. O procession!
Let me once hear that thundering
   shout,
my eyes can close then.

Translation by Peter H. Lee

Sim Hun was born in Seoul in 1904. While still a high-school student, he participated in the March 1, 1919, independence demonstration and was arrested by the Japanese police and imprisoned for four months. Later, he went to China to attend Zhijiang University. When he returned to Korea, he worked as a newspaper reporter and composed poetry. In "When That Day Comes," he mentions the great fifteenth-century Chongno bell. Located in Seoul's P'agoda Park, the bell was associated with the March first demonstration, and in this poem, Sim imagines it clanging loudly on the day that Korea at last regains its freedom. He died in 1937, eight years before Korea's liberation.

toward those frozen figures:

"I don't care about losing my name! I am just cold and *hungry!*"

And only then do I give in to a delicious sensation of self-abandonment—and I begin to cry.

My father is at my side. "We'll go home now."

With tear-filled eyes, I look up at him. "I am sorry, but…"

"Yes?"

"But—what good can all this do? What good will all this do for us?" I say defiantly, flinging my arms wide open to encompass the burying ground, with all its graves and the people. "What good will all this do to change what happened!"

To my surprise, he says quickly, "Nothing."

"Then, why do you?…"

"That's enough now," he says. "Someday, you will understand."

I am not soothed by these words, which are vague and hollow to a child's comprehension of the here and now. I do not respond to him.

He bends down, bringing his face close to mine. There is a strange smile on his face. "Today," he says, "you, too, have made a small beginning." Ah—Father—always a riddle.

"Come on," he says, extending his hand to help my grandfather onto the path. "Let us all go home now."

It is dark, and, with the coming of darkness and the night, the wind is dying down, and the snow is falling straight and calmly. The blurry figures of the people move about the burying ground like ghosts haunting the graves in the snow.

At the bottom of the hill, my father asks, "Would you like me to carry you on my back?"

I nod unabashedly and climb onto his back, nuzzling my frozen face against him, clinging to his broad shoulders.

And so, in such a way then, the three of us, the three generations of my family, bid farewell to our ancestors in their graves, which we can no longer see in the heavy snow, and join the others from the town to find our way back to our home.

Today, I lost my name. Today, we all lost our names.

February 11, 1940.

CHAPTER FOUR

WAR
AND
LIBERATION

MICHAEL E. MACMILLAN

KOREANS IN WARTIME HAWAI'I: AN INTRODUCTION

The outbreak of the Pacific war in 1941 rekindled hope among Koreans in Hawai'i that their homeland would soon be liberated and Japan would be punished for its aggression against the peninsula. But to their great surprise, Island Koreans were caught in a paradox: although well known as bitter opponents of Japan, they were, by virtue of Japan's annexation of Korea in 1910, regarded as enemy aliens and subjected to some of the same restrictions imposed on alien Japanese and Japanese Americans.

After the December 7 attack on Pearl Harbor, the martial-law regime replaced civil courts with military tribunals and controlled all aspects of daily life. Curfews were invoked and blackout regulations promulgated. Liquor, food, and drugs were controlled. Gasoline was rationed. The press and other forms of communication were censored. Rents and wages were regulated, and workers were frozen in their jobs. General Orders issued by the military governor controlled everything from traffic regulations and interisland travel to garbage collection and dogs.

For Japanese in Hawai'i, the start of the war had swift and fearful effects. Within three days, the army had detained 482 persons, most of them Japanese whose loyalty was suspect. In the months that followed, 1,875 residents of Japanese ancestry were sent to the U.S. mainland for internment. Koreans were not rounded up by the authorities, but the effects of martial law were no less real and immediate. Although the General Orders for the treatment of aliens did not mention Koreans specifically, military authorities regarded Koreans as subjects of Japan and therefore bound by the same regulations. Among other things, they were subject to restrictions on their commercial activities, real property transactions, and banking accounts. They were also required to carry nationality certificates issued to them under the Alien Registration Act of 1940. And they had to be off the streets during blackout hours, which began earlier for enemy aliens than did the curfew for the general population. In some cases, Koreans were denied permission to travel among the Islands.

A prominent physician, Y. C. Yang—later Republic of Korea ambassador to the United States—volunteered for the U.S. Army immediately after the Pearl Harbor attack and was commissioned. After he had worked for a number of days without compensation, however, the authorities realized that he was an alien and dismissed him.

A particularly embittering event occurred in March 1942, when alien Koreans employed on defense projects were required to exchange their white-bordered identification badges for black-bordered badges of the type previously issued only to persons of Japanese ancestry and used to restrict movement within defense areas. The workers protested and won a small concession: the words I AM KOREAN were stamped across the bottom of their new badges.

There was clearly a tacit understanding that for some purposes Koreans were to be distinguished from alien Japanese, but these exceptions were not stated in any published regulations. Naturally, Koreans wanted a definitive clarification of their status. To be treated as a subject of Japan was a cruel blow to their pride in their national identity and in Korea's struggle against Japanese aggression—as well as an insult to the allegiance they had shown to their adopted home.

In the absence of official recognition of this loyalty, Koreans did their best to maintain the distinction between themselves and the Japanese. Many wore special identification cards and buttons prepared by organizations such as the United Korean Committee; others wore traditional Korean-style clothing.

At the same time, leaders of the Korean community conducted a campaign to bring about a change in their status. This low-key campaign—which included letters and cables to public officials, petitions, and newspaper editorials—began immediately after the outbreak of the war and reached a climax in the spring of 1943 in a well-publicized case in which a Korean civic leader, Syung Woon Sohn, was arrested for violating the curfew regulations.

Sohn was fifty-nine years old and the owner of a North King Street shoe-repair business. He had come to Hawai'i in 1905 and been active in Korean independence activities in the Islands. At the time of his arrest, he was president of the Hawai'i chapter of the Tongjihoe, an organization formed in the 1920s to support Syngman Rhee. Sohn's wife had served as superintendent of the Korean Christian Institute, with which Rhee was associated, and as an officer of Tongjihoe. She was also known as an intimate friend of Rhee's.

On the evening of March 28, 1943, Sohn's car stalled in the 1600 block of Liliha Street, preventing him from reaching his home on Kilohana Street in Kalihi Valley before the beginning of blackout at 7:45 P.M. He was arrested by two Honolulu policemen—one of them a Japanese American—at 8:15 P.M., charged with violating the regulations prohibiting enemy aliens from being outside during blackout, and released on $50 bail.

When the case came before the provost court on April 30, Sohn's attorney, Willson C. Moore, argued that Sohn deserved to be treated as a "friendly alien"—a designation separate from that given to the Japanese—because he had left Korea on a Korean passport before the Japanese annexation. Moore further argued that the annexation had been an illegal seizure of the country and that Sohn had made himself known as an enemy of Japan through his participation in Korean patriotic organizations. He had remained an alien only because American law denied him the privilege of naturalization. Moore also cited the status of Koreans on the mainland as precedent for more lenient treatment of Sohn. The provost judge, Lieutenant Colonel Moe D. Baroff, expressed sympathy but maintained that he was bound by the General Orders of the military government and had no choice but to

Young Oak Kim

During World War II, the U.S. army created the 100th Infantry Battalion / 442nd Regimental Combat Team, comprising Japanese American soldiers. As a young officer, Young Oak Kim, a second-generation Korean American, led elements of the battalion in combat and became the most decorated soldier in the 442nd, receiving a Silver Star, a Bronze Star, three Purple Hearts, and the French Croix de Guerre, among other medals. During the Korean War, the army asked Kim to return to active duty because of his fluency in Korean; he agreed, provided he would be assigned to a combat unit rather than serve as a translator. Major Kim commanded the 1st Battalion, 31st Infantry Regiment, and 7th Infantry Division in Korea. In 1972, he retired as a colonel. He subsequently joined with the Japanese American community to help found the Go for Broke Educational Foundation as a tribute to the Japanese American units of World War II.

Moses Lee

Moses Lee was an extraordinary patriot who fought under three flags: the Korean, Chinese, and American. He was born in the United States to Korean parents who had immigrated to Hawai'i in the early 1900s. His father knew Kim Ku, the premier of the Korean Provisional Government in Shanghai, and promised Kim that he would send one of his seven sons to fight for the government. To fulfill that promise, Lee volunteered in 1933 and traveled to China at the age of twenty-one. There, he trained under Kim and served as an officer in General Chiang Kai Shek's army. After contracting malaria in 1938 he was sent back to Hawai'i to recover. Afterwards, he joined the U.S. army, becoming a paratrooper and fighting in World War II. During the Korean War, he fought on the front line under the American flag.

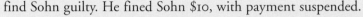

find Sohn guilty. He fined Sohn $10, with payment suspended.

Sohn petitioned General Delos C. Emmons for a review of his conviction, but Emmons was not persuaded by the petition, which included twelve pages of case-law citations, and declined to reverse the provost court's decision.

The matter might have remained a local issue but for Sohn's close link with Rhee, then the principal lobbyist for Korean interests in Washington. Sohn's wife, Nodie K. Sohn, sought Rhee's intervention immediately after her husband's arrest, and Rhee responded with a promise to take the status issue of Koreans in Hawai'i to Congress. He was quickly in touch with Hawai'i's congressional delegate, Joseph R. Farrington, and officers in the War Department. He also wired Governor Ingram M. Stainback and a longtime friend, William Borthwick, the territorial tax commissioner. After Sohn was convicted, Rhee petitioned Secretary of War Henry L. Stimson. He also addressed a letter to President Roosevelt asking him to intervene in the case.

Rhee was not alone in trying to publicize the Sohn incident. Letters were also being written by Kilsoo Haan—Rhee's main rival in Washington as spokesman for the Korean cause—and, at Haan's behest, by Guy M. Gillette, a Democratic senator from Iowa whom Haan had been cultivating. Haan wrote to President Roosevelt on May 8, asking him to intervene in the Sohn case and to order a change in army policy.

The flurry of activity surrounding the Sohn case prompted the War Department's Military Intelligence Division to review the situation in June 1943, but the result was to affirm the existing policy.

The application of enemy-alien curfew regulations to Koreans—which had come to symbolize enemy-alien status itself—finally ended on December 4, 1943, when the military government promulgated General Orders No. 45. This order amended curfew restrictions, creating a specific exemption for Koreans. The change followed within days the publication of the Cairo Declaration, in which the leaders of the United States, Great Britain, and China declared their determination "that in due course Korea shall become free and independent."

Diane Chongmin Kim *Sacrifice*

KIM RONYOUNG
from *Clay Walls*

FAYE

"Faye! Have you heard?"

"Heard what?"

"The Japs bombed Pearl Harbor!"

"What? Where's Pearl Harbor?" It must be somewhere in the Far East, I thought.

"Hawaii. It means war for the United States. Everyone's talking about it. Where have you been?"

"Right here," I said, remembering I left the house before Momma had turned on the radio. "What do you mean, war?"

"Just what I said, war. A sneak attack. Typical of the *waenom,* isn't it?"

The week's Bible lesson fell on deaf ears as everyone tried to comprehend what being at war meant. Afterwards, we stood outside the church and talked about Pearl Harbor, saying things like, "Those stupid Japs," "Punks dropping bombs on the U.S.," "The Americans will sink the 'rising sun' so fast it'll be over before we know it."

We didn't notice the car slowing down along the curb where we stood. "Hey!" a man yelled from the car. We turned to see what he wanted. The brown-haired, blue-eyed man made sure his three companions were paying attention before he growled at us. "You stinkin' Japs. Go back where you came from!"

Alice and I looked at each other. "We're not Japanese," we told him.

Reverend Lim had been standing at the top of the stairs waiting to greet his parishioners. "Go away or I'll call the police," he warned the man.

The man's spit landed at our feet. "Go back where you came from!" As the driver began to speed away, the man yelled, "You fuckin' yellow monkeys!"

Reverend Lim ran down the stairs to join us. "I think you children had better get off the streets. Go straight home and stay in your house. People are in a state of shock. Go home where it is safe."

Alice decided to stay at church and wait for her parents. I hurried down the streets I had walked earlier: past the wood-framed houses with their aprons of green grass, past the picket fences that enclosed naked dormant plants, past garage-high poinsettias bursting with fiery blossoms. I ran until I heard Momma's radio from the street. As soon as I walked in the door, she shouted, "The *waenom* bombed Pearl Harbor!"

I walked over and turned down the volume of the radio. In the same loud voice she said, "The fools. They can't beat the United States. They'll get what they deserve. At last, Korea will have her independence."

The radio announcer spoke of sneak attacks, ships sinking, fires, deaths, war. He said nothing about Korean independence.

"Momma. War means we could all be killed."

"Oh no, don't you worry. They'll never touch us here. The Americans will smash them right away. The Japanese will be defeated. Now be quiet. I want to hear this," she

WALTER K. LEW

Isan Kajok Spora

Father,
Under a thin moon
They'll spit out your only son's names:
Disobedient, Failure, No Wife

And even that will not hurt you:
All you wanted for him was
Safe,
　　　Plenty of Cash,
　　　　　No Death

But it's your past too
I am searching for. Its summer, its
Winter. Father, I'm going

Out to talk with the crewcut boy
Who sat at the sunny south window
　　and read
Boy's Life and Goethe, *Segye Munhak*

In characters that shaded like
　　paulownia leaves
Thoughts of striped melons cooling
　　in the well
While the rice blew in the east fields.

I'm sneaking round to the front porch
And placing my hands on the father
You would lose in '50
In Seoul
Just like that
Though you bicycled for days north
　　and south and
Back again, calling his name
While the tank volley and mortar came
　　down.
Yes! He is

said, turning up the volume.

It wasn't long before the phone began to ring. Koreans were getting in touch with their countrymen. They talked excitedly as they cursed the Japanese, cheered for the United States, and planned their country's independence. The telephone became inadequate and meetings were called. Momma pushed aside her work to attend. She told me about them later.

"We're going to get together. United Koreans to help the United States. Men are going to volunteer for the national guard. People with money will buy bonds. And we're going to wear badges saying we're Koreans."

"Badges?"

"You don't have to worry. You're an American citizen. But we might be mistaken for Japanese."

"That's nothing new," I said.

"The war is new. We don't want people to think we're our enemy."

Momma looked puzzled when I laughed. "There's an old saying about being one's own enemy," I explained.

"So?"

"Never mind. I don't know why it struck me as being funny. It has nothing to do with this," I said.

The Christmas dance was cancelled because of the war. No one would think of dancing when innocent people were dying. As news of bombings in Europe and invasions in the South Pacific flooded the radio and newsreels, I began to care about people I had never met, some living in places I never knew existed. Patriotism became the paramount virtue in the United States. It required hating the Japanese; I had had a lot of practice. Being at war with Japan meant mainstream Americans and I were on the same side.

Momma's group began to meet again. The smell of Momma's cooking and the sound of excitable voices filled the house once more. The war had given Koreans hope for regaining their country and reasons to organize.

"There's talk about sending the Japanese who live on the West Coast to camps," Uncle Min said.

"What camps?" Momma asked.

"Somewhere away from the West Coast. The government thinks the *waenom* are spying for Japan," he said.

"Of course they are!" Uncle Lee declared. "A Japanese is always loyal to his emperor. It's in his blood."

"Does that make him patriotic?" I asked. I could not tell if Uncle Lee was praising them or damning them.

Back from the job in Manchuria he took
To pay your tuition at proud KS:

He kneels in the doorway
Lights a long pipe, smiles as he watches you
Trim a fresh kite—almost
Breathing the real world

I am putting my hand on his shoulder,
    Father
And I am dragging him back,
I am dragging every strand and wisp of his
Unmarkered, unworshiped soul back

And Father,
Most wondrous thing

Kŭrŏnde, Appa!

He is asking me to do this.

Uncle Yang laughed. "Before December seven, it made him a 'good' Japanese. After December seven, it made him a 'bad' American."

"Aeh!" Uncle Kim snapped. *"Sang nom*s before and after any date," he said, calling them eternal bastards.

Uncle Yang took out a memo pad from his pocket and read from his notes. "A picket line at San Pedro to boycott Japanese goods. We need signs and lots of people. I'll be taking a car full. How about you, Faye?"

"What do I have to do?"

"Just walk around carrying a sign that says BOYCOTT JAPAN."

"That sounds easy. Why not?" I said.

It was easy. A photographer from the *Los Angeles Times* was at the pier. He took a picture of me carrying a sign and printed it in the newspaper. Momma clipped it out and sent it to Harold, proud as if I were Joan of Arc.

Anything I did against the enemy made me a heroine. I was glad it wasn't Koreans who bombed Pearl Harbor.

I had gone to my room to read when the men arrived for the next meeting. The subject of "camps" came up immediately.

"There's talk of sending Koreans to camps with the Japanese," Uncle Min said.

"What?" Uncle Lee barked.

I put down my book to listen.

"As far as the United States government is concerned, we are part of Japan," Uncle Min said.

"They can't do that. We can't let them do that," Uncle Yang said. I knew his eyes were blinking rapidly.

"Ignorance! Plain ignorance!" Uncle Lee spewed. "What do they think we've been screaming about all these years? Why do they think we've been demanding recognition as a separate nation?"

"It won't happen." Uncle Kim's voice was calm. "K. S. Ahn is in Washington talking to congressmen," he said.

"Yes, but will they listen?" Uncle Lee said.

"They'd better. No one's going to catch me going to camp with any Japanese," Uncle Kim said.

"Catch no Korean," Uncle Min said.

"I'm staying right here," Momma said. "No one can make me go anywhere."

"We'd better get everyone to send letters to congressmen and money to Ahn," Uncle Yang said. He paused. Probably writing notes, I thought. "We'll have to distribute the names and addresses of influential congressmen and senators to all Koreans in California," he continued.

"Senators. Good idea. Ahn needs all the support he can get," Uncle Kim said.

"Where's Rhee on this? He's known in Washington. What's he doing?" Uncle Min asked.

"Who cares?" Uncle Lee said. "Ahn's our man."

I was impressed. Letters to congressmen and senators in Washington, D.C. Momma's group had a voice and the United States government was going to hear it.

Later, when the Koreans were informed they were excluded from the "relocation" program, K. S. Ahn became a hero.

Momma sighed deeply when she heard the news. "Justice, at last. No one will mistake us for Japanese. We will be moving about freely in California."

Bertha was the first to make me realize what it meant. I was surprised to see her at our door.

"I came to say goodbye and to let you know I think the whole thing stinks," she said.

"Where are you going?" I asked, holding the door open for her.

"I'm not going anywhere. You're the one. It's so dumb. Hauling everyone off to a camp because they can't tell who's spying."

Momma called from the table. *"Nu gu wat ne?"*

"It's Bertha," I answered. Bertha beckoned me out and we sat on the porch steps. "Not us. The Japanese," I explained.

"That's not you?"

"No, we're not the same." As soon as I noticed it, I blurted out, "You've had your baby!"

She ran her hand over her stomach. "Do you mean you don't have to go?"

I nodded. "When did you have it?"

She hugged me. "I'm glad. I know you ain't done nothing."

"Was it a boy or girl?" I asked.

"I don't know." She cupped her hands around my ear and whispered. "I had an abortion."

"A what?"

"You know, popped it out of the oven before it was ready." She wrinkled her brows. "I had to. I couldn't take care of it by myself."

"Oh, Bertha. Gee, I'm sorry."

"It's okay. I'll get over it. Want to know something funny? Luke wants to marry me."

"Because you got rid of the baby?"

She laughed. "You're really something. He doesn't know about the baby. It's the war. He'll be making money as a soldier; more if he gets married. 'What the shit,' he said, 'let Uncle Sam buy us some good times.'"

"Are you going to?"

She shrugged her shoulders. "At least someone would be taking care of me."

"Do you love him?"

She grabbed my arm and rocked me back and forth. "Girl, do you take me for a fool? He may go away and never come back."

I laughed as I pulled away from her. "He'll come back."

"Yeah, then what?"

"Love and happiness. *Ta-rah.*" I spread out my arms to the vocal fanfare.

"Sure. And ice cream and candy." She put her elbows on the step above us and leaned back. "I don't know what I'm going to do. Maybe I can get a job in a war plant. They can't be fussy, they'll be needing people like me."

"A job? Will they need people like me?"

"If they'll take me, they'll take you."

"*Yah!* Faye-*yah!*" Momma called.

Bertha stood up to leave. I took her hand. "Let me know about the job. I'm serious," I said. "My mom can't refuse to let me work if it means I'm helping to win the war."

"I'll let you know," she promised as she backed toward the sidewalk. "I'm sure glad you don't have to go to no concentration camp. Ain't that some confession of stupidity? They can't find the spics so they lock everyone up."

"Yeah," I said.

My arms were beginning to ache from carrying the books. I was probably taking home more than I could read: it never seemed like too many at the library.

I turned onto Normandie Avenue, a street where stores mingled easily with homes, where Momma shopped for seaweed and miso sauce, where Jane and I used to play hopscotch.

An eerie bleakness had fallen over the street, empty of shoppers and people chatting, no one bowing to anyone. Shops were boarded up and the shades of homes drawn. Starred satin flags hung in some windows, silently signifying there was an American soldier in the Japanese family.

Had they cleared out already, I wondered. Hardly any time had passed since the date was announced. Then I remembered. My books were due on the day they were to leave. Only half the day was over and the streets were deserted, sucked clean of a whole community. The cement curb bordered a cemetery of homes.

I had a sudden urge to see our house on 37th Place, to walk the street where I had lived when our family was whole.

Yukio Watashi's voice cut through the air as he told his father to hurry. Mr. Watashi was scurrying about watering the ferns that grew in the bulbous wooden Kikkoman shoyu tubs. Other members of his family were throwing their belongings onto a truck; not their truck from the nursery but one that was almost as big as Willie's semi, the kind that took me on hayrides to Santa Monica beach huddled with my friends, singing, joking, laughing.

No one on this truck was laughing. People stood jammed together. Some held on to the wooden stakes that fenced them in. Women had tied bandanas around their heads and men wore their hats low. I could not tell the Kanos from the Hiroshis.

Yukio's father put away the watering can then climbed onto the truck. The man who had given him a hand closed the tailgate. The truck started slowly, the engine straining under the weight of its cargo.

"Faye!" a voice from the crowd of passengers shouted. "Here!" A hand fluttered in the air. I searched for a face and found it. It was Jane. She was smiling. "I'll see you after the war," she yelled.

A book slipped out of my arms as I tried to wave back. I stooped to pick it up. As I looked for Jane again, the truck disappeared around the corner.

I felt sick.

"Lord, child, don't look so sad. There'll be another one coming along soon. They's not going to forget you," a colored man said as he walked by.

I couldn't think of anything to say. I nodded and walked on to 1337.

A colored woman was watering Momma's dahlias. It was too early in the year for any blossoms, but the plants had multiplied, lining the driveway from the backyard to the front.

"The dahlias must be beautiful when they're in bloom," I said.

The woman smiled at me. "Knocks your eyes out. They just keep coming. I keep dividing them and they just keep coming. Pretty soon I won't have room for anything else," she said, laughing as she returned to her watering.

Mr. Watashi's plants will die, I thought. Dust will gather in Jane's house and the *arare* will go stale. What did that have to do with winning the war, I wondered.

As soon as I got home, I told Momma about deserted Normandie Avenue and the people jammed in the truck. "It was terrible, Momma."

Mountain

Calligraphy by Yoo Kyungsik

She sighed. "Yes, but they've done worse than that to us," she said solemnly.

"Not Jane. Not Mr. Watashi."

"No, but innocent Korean victims too." She thought a moment then added, "Maybe it isn't as bad as you think. They'll be together and safe."

"Baloney."

She picked up her sewing. "Well, there's nothing we can do about it. Just be thankful we didn't have to go with them."

I had no reply to that. "Do you know what I think?" I said finally. "Some things are just plain bad with nothing good about them at all."

The war didn't end right away like Momma said it would. Harold wanted to work his way up at Song Brothers, but when the war showed no signs of ending soon, he quit his job and came home.

"I'm going to join up, Mom. Sooner or later they'll be after me. I'm going to apply for officers' training," he said.

Momma's eyes popped open. "How wonderful!" She had picked up the expression from listening to soap operas.

Harold went to the Air Force recruiting office and made all the arrangements. "I'll be a 'ninety-day wonder,'" he told us.

While Harold prepared for the entrance examination, I went around with Uncle Yang to sell war bonds. "I've picked the most beautiful girls," he would say as Alice, Lily, and I climbed into his Model A. We had parents who insisted we represent our people. We put on our Korean dresses and were driven to rallies. The master-of-ceremonies would thank us for singing our "native" songs and dancing our "native" dances then called us "good Americans." At Pershing Square, Edward G. Robinson smiled at me.

Alice was the first to drop out when she found a summer job.

"It's at the old Walt Disney studios at Silver Lake," she said. "They're making some kind of instrument for navigators in the Air Force. It's a secret."

"How can it be a secret?" I asked. She seemed to know a lot about it.

"Each person works on a single part. Only the top guys put it together and know how it works. My job is easy. There are still openings, Faye. You should apply."

I thought of asking Momma for permission then decided to apply for the job first.

"It's a secret weapon for the Air Force," I told Momma after I had been hired. "I'll be a drill-press operator. A dollar an hour to start. Alice works there." I held my breath. I had gone over the scene in my head a hundred times, imagining what she would say, rehearsing my reply.

She said nothing for a while, as if she had to think about her response. Finally, she waved her hand in the air. "Go ahead. But only because it's wartime. I didn't raise you to be a . . . a . . ."

"Drill-press operator. After school starts, I'll be working on weekends," I added, wondering if I had pushed my luck.

She kept on sewing as if she had not heard me.

Uncle Yang put up a bigger protest. "You girls showed them Korea. That's more important than being a . . . a . . ."

"Drill-press operator. I'm sorry, Uncle Yang, but I've already taken the job."

"What am I going to do? Koreans should be represented," he said.

"Call Eleanor Song. She'll find some girls. Prettier ones than Alice and me."

He could not deny it so he laughed.

The day arrived when Harold was to take the examination. I gave him the victory sign when I left for work. When I walked in the door that evening, he was home.

"How did you do?" I asked.

"Okay, I think. It didn't seem too hard."

I crossed my fingers in the air. "Come on, God, be on our side."

Momma laughed. "Don't act silly," she said.

As each day passed, we grew more and more anxious. Finally, Momma told Harold, "Call them, call them. Ask them why they're taking so long."

"I can't do that," Harold said. "You're talking about the United States of America."

"Then I'll call," she said, pushing aside her sewing.

"Never mind. I'll do it," he protested, beating her to the phone.

He was on the line a long time. Then we heard him say, "Hallelujah."

Harold smiled as he told us about it. "The guy wasn't supposed to tell me. I told him I was losing sleep. He said the letter must be tied up in the mail. They went out last week. I said, 'Jesus, what if mine got lost?' 'I see your point,' he said. He left me hanging there while he checked. When he came back, he said, 'You know a slip of the lip can sink a ship?' 'My lips are sealed,' I told him. He said, 'You can sleep now, kid. You're among the top ten percent.'"

"Wow!" I exclaimed.

"Top ten percent?" Momma sat back in her chair and laughed.

"We celebrate." She reached into the pocket of her apron and pulled out a five dollar bill. "Port wine. It's sweet." She handed the money to Harold and waved him out the door.

He was back right away with a bottle of wine and a bag of potato chips. Momma

told him to keep the change. We drank out of the crystal punch cups, refilling them until the wine was gone. Momma had to put her sewing aside. She would laugh over nothing and her stitches went out of line. I felt as if I were on fire. My cheeks had turned a flaming red. I saluted before I said anything to Harold. After a while, I could not say anything without giggling.

"Hey, wait a minute. I've just remembered something," Harold said. He went to his room and came back with the Edwards Military Academy cap perched on his head. He began marching around the room.

Momma laughed so hard I thought she was going to fall out of her chair. *"Aigu, aigu,"* she gasped, holding her sides.

"Take it easy, Mom," Harold said, pulling the cap from his head.

She finally caught her breath. "I forgot all about that hat. It's so small for you. It's just a toy." Her eyes began to glisten. "You'll have a real one now."

I had collapsed with laughter, sapped of energy. "I'm sleepy. I think I'll go to bed."

"I think I'll go out for a while," Harold said.

"It's so late," I noted.

"Never mind," Momma told me.

After Harold left, I asked her, "Why did you let him go out? It's late."

"He's not a boy anymore," she answered.

I lay in bed thinking about our celebration, about Harold, Momma, and me laughing it up. It wasn't something I would say aloud, but war had its advantages.

I was about to leave for work when the letter arrived from the Air Force. I waited to share Harold's big moment. He opened the envelope neatly with a knife. "I'm going to have this framed," he said, grinning. As he read the letter, the grin faded from his face. "It says I didn't get in," he said with a gulp.

"Maybe they've sent you the wrong letter," I offered.

"It has my name on it."

"You go to them. Tell them they made a mistake. Go right now," Momma ordered.

"Cheez, Mom, take it easy," he said.

"It has to be a mistake. The man wouldn't have lied to you," I insisted.

Harold chewed on his lower lip. "I wonder what happened."

"Go find out. Take care of it right now," Momma demanded.

"Jesus, Mom, quit pushing!" Harold snapped. He tucked the letter into his pocket. "Shit," he said under his breath and walked out of the house.

I had no desire to go to work. I kicked off my shoes and called in sick.

The senior officer told Harold, "Competition was very keen. You were close, but we had to draw the line somewhere."

The junior officer took Harold aside. "I didn't lie to you. It has nothing to do with your score. Orientals are not allowed in officers' training. I didn't know. It's nothing personal."

"Why did you let me take the exam?" Harold asked.

The junior officer shrugged. "It's your constitutional right."

Harold's voice quavered when he told us about it later. I had never seen him look so forlorn.

"Did you tell him off?" I asked.

He scoffed. "What good would that do?"

I expected Momma to explode. I wish she had. She just kept on sewing without saying a word, stopping now and then to sigh deeply. She went to bed that night and did not get up the next day. She had no cough or temperature, but I stayed home to look after her. Every time I asked, "What's wrong, Momma?" she waved me away and turned her back to me. I cooked meat and vegetables the way she had taught me, but she pushed the dish aside and ate only rice gruel and *kimch'i*. Harold wasn't eating much either. On the third day, he said, "It's killing her."

"My cooking?" I thought that would at least bring a smile.

"Naw," he growled, "figure it out." He got up from the table. "I've gotta do something," he said and left the house.

Early in the morning of the fourth day, Momma got out of bed and told me I had better go to work.

"I don't know if I want to work anymore. Even if it is wartime," I said.

"We have no choice. United States has to win the war or there's no hope for Koreans." She tied the belt to her robe tighter.

"You've lost weight," I told her.

"The Americans are better people than our enemy," she said, ignoring my comment. She poured herself a cup of coffee. "No country is perfect."

When Harold told her that he had joined the Signal Corps, she said, "Good," then cried.

John wrote to say that after Beth's graduation he was going to join the Navy.

"Don't bother to tell him what happened," Harold said.

Willie dropped us a line from Chicago. He had joined the Navy to "get out of hicktown and see the world."

I went back to work and continued to drill holes in precisely the same place on identical pieces of dull black metal.

MARGARET K. PAI
from *The Dreams of Two Yi-min*

POINCIANA

During the spring and summer the pink, gold, and rainbow shower trees came into bloom. These tall trees grew in the older residential sections of the city, especially in Makiki and Manoa. The golden showers, glistening in the sun, hung in clusters like yellow grapes. The pink shower trees were laden thick with blossoms; their branches resembled long carnation leis. And the rainbow showers took your breath away, for their masses of tiny peach and white and pink flowers crowded for a place in the sun, and their fulness even hid the green leaves of the tree.

Then there were the poinciana trees, which appeared in regal glory in the summer and lasted through fall. Many of them lined the streets in Makiki. The royal poinciana, as they were sometimes called, did not grow as large as the shower trees. But they stood proudly, spreading their branches like umbrellas decorated with fiery red and orange flowers.

One July afternoon my father came home and told us he had been strolling under poinciana trees on Wilder Avenue.

"You went walking on a hot day like this? Why?" my mother wondered. The temperature was near ninety degrees for the fourth day in a row and everybody complained of the humidity.

I recognized the odor of perspiration drying off his shirt and face—that "peculiar *man smell* of your father" as my mother referred to it. When he was inspired he usually was oblivious to fatigue and heat.

"Today I found a name—a good name!" he announced.

Mother cried, "What name? What are you talking about?"

"Poinciana! That's what I'm going to call it!" He sat down at the round kitchen table, his hands folded in front of him. He moved his lips as if talking but made no audible sounds.

Busy preparing dinner, we ignored him. Mother placed a pan on the stove and poured oil into it. I stood by to help fry the fish.

Suddenly my father jumped up. "Yes, that's what I'm going to call it!"

"Call who—what?" I asked. The oil heating in the pan started to sizzle and spatter.

He spoke in a hushed voice, one hand outstretched, palm moving away. "Can't attention to himself by dropping his chopsticks emphatically, gulping water noisily, and spooning his soup as if he were shoveling it. He cleared his throat several times.

Then he bellowed, "I don't want to see that flat-faced singer around here again!"

"Mr. Kim?" Mother's voice was hardly audible. Then she spoke, defending him, "He is giving us news about our people."

"I don't care. You're just as bad as the rest of those crazy women. You all think he's a god!"

"No we don't. What are you saying?" She tried to remain calm.

"Why do you invite him here so often? Are you in love with him?" The spoonful of soup he held in his hand suddenly was hurled in her face. My brothers, sister, and I gasped. We had never seen our parents behave this way before.

"Remember, I don't want that damn singer around here again. And I don't want you hanging around that parasite!"

All was quiet after that outburst.

Kim Soo Han remained in Honolulu a few weeks longer, giving more benefit concerts and speeches. My mother attended several of the events where he spoke. She confided in me that he rekindled the revolutionary fervor and zeal she had felt as a young woman ready to fight against Japanese aggression. "When I hear Mr. Kim I know conditions are worse now, much worse," she sighed. "So many more Koreans are reduced to poverty. The Japanese are taking from our people their land, their money, and, worst of all, their dignity. They're cutting up our beautiful country for their military needs. They're building railroads and industrializing the economy for their military purposes. They're invading and exploiting other countries, too. Oh, they're awful, terrible!"

I listened with rapt attention, not so much because I felt sorry for the suffering in Korea but because this was the first time my mother openly revealed her feelings about the plight of her people. Heretofore she was like most of the older people I knew, who did not say much to us of the younger generation about their frustration and their desire for independence. It seemed as if our immigrant parents felt apologetic and ashamed of the status of their people, of themselves who were "a people without a country." I personally had never said I was proud to be a Korean because the feeling had not been instilled in me.

Mother lamented, "The women are suffering so much. Oh, so much. In some rural areas I hear that innocent women on the way to the market are stopped by the police and taken in for questioning. These women might be the wives of men suspected to be spies or working against the imperialist government. At the station, I hear the women are stripped naked, jeered at by the officers, slapped, bruised, shamed,

and interrogated for hours about related and unrelated happenings in the community. *Aigu!*"

After the tenor's departure from the islands, I noticed the parishioners gathered each Sunday with renewed energy and unabashed vociferation for their country's imperative need for freedom. They cursed the loathsome, frenzied activities of the Japanese. The perpetrators of suffering were labeled "crazed people." The men swore at the *waenom,* the spiteful enemy. The women wept, holding hands, and decried the state of affairs in their homeland.

In the midst of this fever and furor against the enemy one of the parishioners announced his daughter was marrying a young man of Japanese ancestry. He said the couple had met at a mainland college and they were very much in love. This impending marriage provoked an uproar in the Korean community. The wedding, which was to be quiet and private, became a public issue. The handsome aunt of the bride, a staunch Christian and an influential leader in the church, was unable to dissuade the bride from "the unforgivable act of bending to serve the enemy." She refused to sanction the marriage. The church people disapproved the use of the church for the wedding ceremony. "This is a traitorous union," the vocal members in the community declared.

The wedding took place in the bride's parents' home with only a few members from the bride's and groom's families present.

My girlfriends and I were aware of the strong anti-Japanese feeling in the community, especially in regard to intermarriage. We agreed the prudent thing to do was to avoid dating Japanese boys. And even if we were invited to a dance or a movie by a Chinese or Caucasian, perhaps we should keep the relationship from turning serious. We were suddenly conscious we were a small minority among the races in Hawaii.

When I graduated from the University of Hawaii, jobs were scarce; for women, jobs were almost nonexistent. I could have ventured as a teacher to the outer islands—Maui, Kauai, or Hawaii—as did some of my friends who graduated with me. But my father was adamant that I not subject myself to "fighting in a classroom with kids who don't want to learn." He had heard the status of a public school teacher was degrading. He suggested I become an interior decorator, but neither he nor I knew where I could go for training.

The situation confused and disappointed my mother. "At least you have finished college. I am pleased for that." She added, "I guess there really are no jobs for women. Perhaps you will find something to do later. For now you can stay with us in our business."

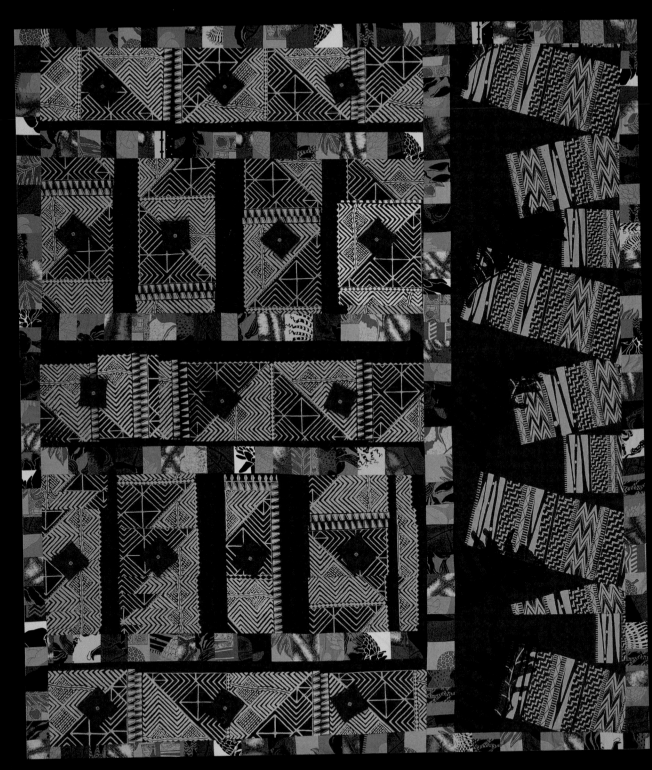

Colleen Kimura   *Quilt*

REBIRTH

They were all hiding their faces from him—these women—sitting on the two long wooden benches in the open-air garage, drawn to old lady Kiyosaki's with the promise that they would be made fertile. Of course, Herman Chung was ashamed too, ashamed of being the husband of a woman seeking the old lady's help. He contained his embarrassment by bowing his head away from the women, nudging his wife to go ahead of him and take her place at the end of one of the benches. So many things wrong with these women, he thought. If it's not their headaches, it's the pain in their backs, their periods, their too-sensitive—

"Mrs. Oda. Please come in."

A wrinkle-faced woman—her thin arms nothing more than leathery skin and blue veins encasing frail bones—called from the back door of the house, then nodded in the direction of the entrance.

Mrs. Oda rose quickly, her face pale, and scurried through the doorway with her head bent. The solid mahogany door closed behind her with a brassy snap.

"Ellie, I going," he muttered to his wife, who had taken her place at the end of a bench. The woman next to her had turned away from him. It didn't matter. He didn't want to look any of the women straight in the eye, afraid that he'd recognize one of them as the wife of a friend from work or church.

She turned to him, her face trembling and pallid. *Please don't leave me.*

"What time I pick you up?"

"I catch the bus," she said, her voice small.

"No, I pick you up."

"I catch the bus."

"Ellie—stop it. I pick you up. I come back one hour."

With that, he hurried off.

"What she tol' you?" he asked.

They were heading down Beretania Street, passing the haole church, the Congregational church with the slate-colored walls and stark-white steeple. Two children and their parents were in a far corner of the church's expansive, well-kept lawn.

"She touched me..." She pressed the area of her womb. "She said she feel something good."

"All she like is our money."

"Then why you took me there, then?"

"Nevah mind."

Ellie turned away and observed the father untangle the line of a black-and-red samurai kite. The children were watching. The mother was sitting motionless under a shadowless monkeypod tree. Up the valley, dark clouds were suspended, teasing of a hard rain.

"So what she said?"

"What you mean?"

"What she said?" Nervously, he regripped the steering wheel. "Can?"

Ellie held on to the seconds of silence as long as she could. "I tol' you. She said she feel something good."

"But what that mean?"

Ellie glanced out the window. They were now passing the Mormon temple. The statue of Jesus was extending a hand. *Give me your blessing, O Lord. Please, O Lord. Jesus's golden face soft and loving.*

"She said can?" Herman repeated.

"Yeah."

Along his side of the road, the gray and rosy marble of the Sears and Roebuck building appeared. It would be so nice to have a son, he thought. Even a daughter would be OK. Either. Or both. Could take them bicycle shopping. He took a deep breath and released, as if to assure himself that the ten dollars for the womb massage was worth spending.

"How long she said we gotta wait?"

"She nevah tell me."

"Why you nevah ask?" Fire in his tone. "Chee, why you nevah ask? We pay her dah money, might as well get our money's worth. Why you nevah ask?"

Guiltily, she turned away from him. "I nevah think."

Herman clicked his tongue with disgust. "Ten dollars, and you nevah ask her. No sense you go."

"Eh," she snapped, tossing her guilt back into his face, "it wasn't my idea." She stabbed him with her eyes. It's your stinkin' sister, she thought. And especially your damn brother-in-law.

"So what, you blaming my sister?" he said, reading her face. "Is not her fault. Is Jin Suk's fault. He dah one. Make my sister that way."

"I nevah say anything." She stared out the windshield.

Herman stopped the car at a traffic light. "But das who you blaming. You blaming my sister. Is her husband's fault."

"I not blaming anybody."

"She just speaking her mind. Sometimes she no think before she talk. Stupid, sometimes. But das 'cause Jin Suk. He dah one."

"So how come you nevah support me when she said that. You my husband. You suppose to back me up. But you nevah say nothing. Nothing. You let her talk what was her mind. So what she get five kids. So what? What…that make me one failure? You

124

married one failure?"

No sense talking. She get one-track mind now. One one-track mind.

The light changed to green. He stepped on the gas pedal. They passed the glass window of the Schumann Carriage showroom. A brand-new Cadillac was rolling out of the company parking lot onto Beretania.

"Sonavabitch haole!" Herman glared at the driver in the Caddy. "Wait 'til I pass."

The Cadillac stopped. The haole gave Herman a cursing look.

"He think he own the road!" Herman spat. "Sonavabitch."

"Watch your temper. He didn't do anything."

"What you mean he nevah do anything?" He looked into the rearview mirror and swore at the driver. "He almost hit us. What you talking about?"

"Nevah mind."

"Whose side you?"

He turned the corner, the air between them thick and ugly. A minute later, they were on their street. He drove up the driveway to their cottage, converted from a two-car garage. Before he could apologize for his outburst, Ellie got out of the car. He had brought back that sorry memory of the evening Jin Suk had entered their cottage—as if he'd owned it—and sat at their small dinner table, greedily eating their food.

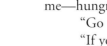

Ellie hurries to the kitchen and brings Jin Suk a plate of rice. It is all that was left in the pot and was to be her portion.

"You have some beer?" Jin Suk demands in Korean. Herman apologizes that he doesn't have any. Jin Suk grunts in disgust. "You don't even have one bottle of beer to give your eldest brother-in-law?" He glares at Ellie. "What kind of house do you keep here?"

"Where's my sister?" Herman asks in Korean.

"The bitch is in the car. Let her be. She's a pain, always complaining about money. As if I don't make enough!"

"Go get her," Ellie says to Herman in English.

"Leave her alone, that bitch. I should divorce her. All she does is make babies for me—hungry ones that I have to break my damned back every day to feed and clothe."

"Go get her," Ellie insists.

"If you want to see your bitch sister—"

"Don't say that about my sister," Herman says in Korean, his voice wavering.

"Suit yourself."

Herman rises from the table and goes outside. Ellie hears him speaking to Dora in a scolding voice, ordering her to go into the cottage. Dora is refusing him loudly.

"You see what I mean," Jin Suk tells Ellie, his mouth half-full with food and his head nodding in the direction of Dora's voice. "What a bitch," he says to himself in English. Then, spitting a bit of rice halfway to the door, he yells, "Get inside here, you bitch! Get inside here right now!"

There is quiet outside, then the sound of a car door opening and slamming. Long moments later, Herman enters the cottage, followed by Dora.

Herman watched Ellie enter the unlocked cottage, her gait strained from the weight of uncertainty and anxiety. He remembered the pain she had in her eyes when Dora had told him that if a wife was childless in Korea, it was the obligation of the husband to take on a mistress. "She cannot make babee, no good," she had said, glancing at Ellie. "In Korea, wife cannot make babee, she no good." Herman had kept eating his food, glancing up only to find Ellie in shock and near tears, then had returned to filling his mouth with rice. It was a sorry excuse for not countering his older sister's trenchant remark. However, there were days when he did think about leaving Ellie and finding another woman—a woman with a rich womb that would give him an heir, a woman whom he would rejoice with at the first buckling steps of a son. Was he to see this, ever?

He got out of the car, reluctant to enter the cottage. But perhaps Mrs. Kiyosaki was right. Perhaps they could try again tonight. Perhaps...

"Harriet Lindsey called today," Ellie said. She was inside the screen door of the cottage.

Herman was sitting on a chair outside the door and taking off his work socks. "Who's that?"

"Harriet. I used to work with her at Fort Ruger."

"The one her husband one cop?"

"Yeah."

She watched him set his work shoes to the side and air his feet, wiggling his toes in the warmth of the late-afternoon sun.

"Hard day today?" she asked.

"No. Just tired. Not enough sleep."

He got up and entered the cottage. She followed him to the kitchen sink, where he washed his hands. Then he got a glass of milk from the refrigerator and drank it all in one gulp. There was a lustiness in the way he ate and drank that appealed to Ellie—something crude but sensual. She waited until he set the empty glass in the sink.

"She told me I should see this Filipino lady," she said, looking out the kitchen window and over the small enclosed yard where they sometimes barbecued on weekends.

"Huh? Wha's this for?"

"She said this lady is good. She said right after she saw the Filipino lady, she *hāpai*. She *hāpai* five months already."

"One nada soothsayer? How many months already since we wen go the Kiyosaki lady? And what that did? We spend ten dollars for nothing."

"Harriet said this Filipino lady is good. She *hāpai*. Five months."

"I heard that. So what? You think the Filipino lady get magic?"

"I nevah say that. But why not try?"

"You still believe in dis kine magic?" Herman shook his head. He sat down at the kitchen table. "How much she charge?" he asked.

"Twenty dollars."

"Twenty dollars? How come so *pee-sah?*"

Ellie shrugged her shoulders.

"Twenty dollars," Herman mused. "Dis is one racket, these old ladies. Trying make one buck off people who need something."

He studied Ellie as she sat in the chair across from him, her head bent and her chest sunken. She's beautiful, he thought, but why she gotta have something wrong with her? He thought of his former girlfriend, whom he was supposed to marry ten years before and who was now married to his best friend. They had just had their third child, a girl.

"OK," he mumbled. "Le's go. You know how contact her?"

Ellie looked up, her eyes lit with a touch of desperate hope. "Yeah." She handed him the folded scrap of paper that was on the table. "Harriet gave me her phone number."

He read the five-digit number. "Where this stay?"

"She said she live Damon Tract."

Herman nodded. "Well, if you think going help. Call her up today. Right now."

"I did. She wants us come Saturday, daytime."

He nodded once more, then slid back his chair and went to the bathroom to shower off his filth.

A heavy rain had fallen on Puʻuloa but suddenly ceased when they came to the row of used- and new-car dealerships along Nimitz Highway. Herman drove down Lagoon Drive, a two-lane road that led to the airport, and took a right turn

OK-KOO KANG GROSJEAN

Cotton Flowers

On an early Saturday morning
an old Asian woman was
picking up empty cans
along the highway near Gilroy.

The half bent head in white kerchief
reminded me of those cotton flowers
on the parched soil
along Highway 5.

But also the young cotton blossoms
I hungrily ate
while escaping
during the Korean War.

dered what it would be like to travel on this long journey. I found out soon enough. The "freedom train" traveled all through the night, chugging away, sometimes whistling and passing what seemed like interminable expanses of farmlands and mountains.

Despite the layers of heavy clothing we wore, including coats and pants made of American blankets, the bitter wind seemed to go right through us. I wondered if we would make it to our destination without freezing to death during the night. It was too cold to talk. The only words I remember hearing from my mother were, "Don't fall asleep, you mustn't fall asleep." She said that all night long, like a lullaby, sometimes shaking me to keep me from nodding off. At times, the train stopped for what seemed like hours. I was glad when the train stopped, because the wind did not feel as vicious then. At one of those stops, I saw a small but brightly lit window far away, and I observed a piece of red cloth moving. The lighted window was conspicuous in the dark of the Korean countryside. I imagined a sorceress inside performing her rites behind the window, with a red kerchief. In the wind and cold I could almost hear her chants and gongs, and smell her incense burning. Perhaps the sorceress was working through the night to cure a sick child, or bidding a safe journey for an old woman who had died. The train would move again, and I would grit my teeth and pray that we would get to our destination without freezing.

Every now and then, the train went through tunnels. I was glad when it did, because while the train was inside the tunnel, we could get a momentary relief from the cold. I wished for more tunnels to go through, not knowing how easy it would have been for us to have been asphyxiated. Despite my mother's admonitions, I must have fallen asleep occasionally, because I only remembered parts of the long train ride. I never wished for the morning to arrive as much as then. That sentiment must have been shared by all of us huddled on the top of the train.

We greeted dawn with gratitude and relief that we were still alive. Our first stop was Gupo Station, where vendors were hawking pears as large as a child's head, which we bought and ate for breakfast. My teeth were chattering, and the juice from the pear was dripping over my red wool mittens. As I looked around, I could see that everyone on the rooftop of the train looked like soot-covered chimney sweepers. Gupo was more than four hundred miles southeast of Seoul. We had traveled two hundred miles during the night, and we had just one more stop before Pusan Station.

Besides my mother and me, our party consisted of Teacher Song's wife, her infant son, her sister-in-law, and their maid. Finally reaching Pusan, we found our way to a refugee settlement center, where we located my grandmother and aunt, who were there with Elder Kim's family. It was dinnertime and cooking fires were going when we arrived. The place was packed with refugees. Makeshift partitions of bed sheets and rags separated the living quarters of different families. The smell of people and food permeated the air. If our refugee life in Seoul was pitiful, living in the tiny rented room in Chong-no, this was a hundred times worse. Children slept, curled up in fetal positions, but their parents dozed, snoring, sitting up, leaning their weary backs against their bundles. They looked like they had been there for many days. Here and there, laundry hung on straw ropes. The prospect of living there with all those strangers depressed me.

With careful steps, so as to not run into people, we went through the rows of makeshift partitions of blankets and sheets. I spotted my grandmother's corner. Next to it was Elder Kim's family, eating dinner.

"Grandma!" I was so happy to see her. "Baby, come this way," Grandmother motioned me to come toward her. "You've made it, baby." I squeezed myself between her and my aunt. I ate rice and boiled shrimp right out of my grandmother's aluminum bowls. My first hot meal in two days, it tasted so good. Afterward, Elder Kim and my mother went out with Mrs. Song to look for a place for the night. The influx of refugees irritated the residents of Pusan. Wherever the refugees knocked, they were

turned away. Wretched and exhausted, their faces drawn with worry, the group returned late that night. We shared a small space in a corner against a wall by sleeping sitting up. On the following day, we managed to find some rooms. Teacher Song's family, my mother, and I shared one small room in a private home. My grandmother and aunt located a room in a different neighborhood. This was the start of yet another life in a strange place. I was eight years old.

Every detail of being a refugee the second time around is etched in my memory, like a video inside my head that never goes away. Even after forty-odd years, I can still taste every piece of food that my resourceful grandmother and mother provided. And the ordeal to survive: I still relive those days as if they happened only yesterday. In an eight-year-old's mind, uncluttered by other experiences, responsibilities, or preoccupations, living through a war does not go away. But so little of our hardship, and especially our life in Pusan, made any sense to me then. At least during the summer in Seoul, when I was guarding Teacher Song and Uncle Chang-Kyu, I had felt a sense of pride and accomplishment. But in Pusan, I could not figure out why I was there.

Within days after our arrival in Pusan, my grandmother, resourceful as ever, was peddling goods in a portable basket on the street. Just about everybody from Seoul—whether former schoolteachers, office workers, or well-to-do businessmen—did whatever they could to survive. The easiest thing was to put up a small stall and sell something.

Pusan was crowded and dirty. Homeless urchins in tattered clothes, with gaunt faces and lice in their hair, roamed the streets, carrying tin cans to collect leftovers. Sometimes they ran after American jeeps, which showered them with dust and dirt,

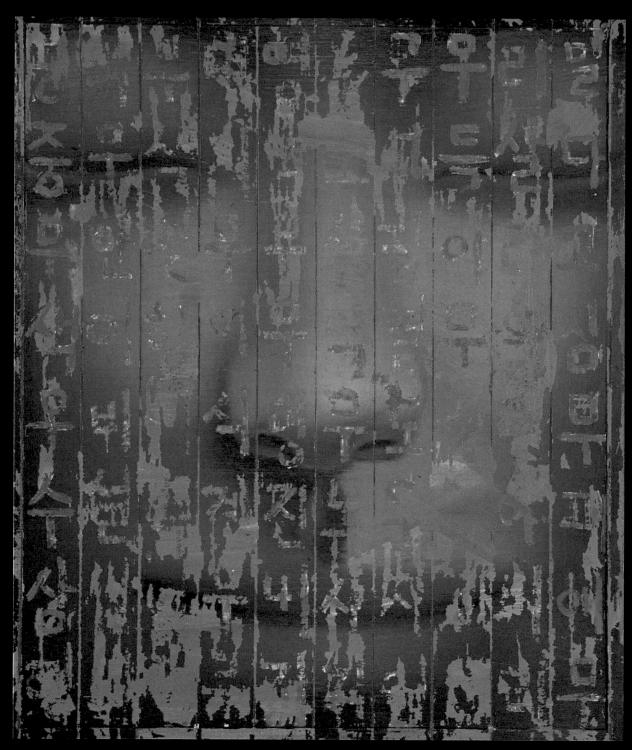

Sandra Sunnyo Lee *Self–No Self (heart sutra)*

CHRIS McKINNEY
from *The Queen of Tears*

THE DEATH OF KWANG JA

In 1952 Cho Kwang Ja walked from a village in North Korea to Seoul. She walked over a hundred miles. That summer, in the sometimes one-hundred-plus-degree heat, her skin baked to a nice, golden brown. Her tiny and bare fourteen-year-old feet developed calluses so thick that they were tougher than the bottom of most people's sandals. She stepped on sharp, jagged rocks and hardly noticed. She stepped on leftover pieces of shrapnel and didn't even feel it. Once, she stopped to sit down, and she looked at the bottoms of her feet. She smiled and pulled out the tiny shards of metal. She didn't care. She just wanted to get out of the dry, mountainous country. She wanted to see tall buildings, green mountains, and people with shoes. She wanted to get out of Communist Korea.

She wasn't a political person. If the Communists had been running Seoul, she would have embraced Communism without a second thought. She wasn't a religious person either. Despite her poor education, which left her barely literate, she sensed early in her childhood that religion was used by bigger people to get what they wanted from smaller ones. Confucianism was an example. As was Christianity. Before the white missionaries in the North were finally burnt out by the Communists, she'd seen some of these foreign holy men use their religion to get what they wanted from young girls. When Confucianism and Buddhism were outlawed by the Communists, she saw how their religions did not help the priests. Her atheism might have pushed her towards Communism had Communism not proved as useless to her as God had.

So Cho Kwang Ja was neither political nor religious. But she was ambitious. Ambition drove her over hundreds of miles of dirt roads and rocky, bald, mountainous terrain. Ambition forced her to live on nothing but dirty water and the leaves of plants she could not identify. And not only that, ambition made her smart, too. She hid whenever she came close to other humans. Villagers, soldiers, both North and South Korean, were stealthily avoided. She did a lot of her traveling by night to better her chances of not being detected by anyone. Sometimes during the day, she would sleep in the burnt-out skeletons of American or Russian tanks or shot-down planes. But most of the time, she didn't sleep. Ambition kept her awake, too.

Kwang Ja didn't even know where Seoul was, except that it was south. A missionary had once told her that the sun rose in the east and set in the west, and ambition forced her to hold on to that piece of information like it was a piece of perfect jade. So every morning she looked up at the sun and smiled when she knew which direction south was. Then she'd tell herself she'd know Seoul when she saw it. It would be big with a lot of people. It would be a place where American GIs drove around in their beautiful green jeeps, a place with riches oozing out of great buildings. As long as she kept walking south, she could never miss a place that big and magical. How naive she was.

slapped her in the face. She didn't move. She was slapped again. The few people who stopped and were actually interested were murmuring, "She's dead; she's dead."

She wanted to smile. She was proud of herself. She was really good at this. This pride suddenly melted when she felt a hand on her breast. She wasn't good enough to make her heart stop, but if she had been, she would have done it right then. She would have died. Her attempts at motionless suicide were interrupted by the laughter of a man. Knowing the ruse was over, but still refusing to open her eyes, Kwang Ja heard the laughing man say, "What we have here is an actress."

She didn't open her eyes. But she felt herself being lifted into the fancy black car. At first, the leather seat cooled her arms and hands. But then the seat and her skin grew hot, and she felt drops of sweat roll down her forehead. As the car drove on, she listened to the tread of the tires pick up tiny pebbles and hurl them against the metal of the car. She wondered if she should try to sneak a rotten grape or two into her mouth. "Look at all the refugees," the man said. "From the North, from Seoul to Pusan, now back to Seoul. Even I almost had to run to Pusan. I must go there today. Where are you from?"

Kwang Ja didn't move.

About an hour later, the car stopped. She was pulled out by what she guessed

were small female hands. She still did not open her eyes. She realized that they knew she was not dead, but she decided to feign injury just in case. The man instructed the woman to take care of her and said he would call later to give further instructions. The car door slammed shut, and Kwang Ja heard the car drive away.

She opened her eyes. It was the most beautiful thing she'd ever seen. The house was tall and made of a dark, almost reddish wood. Its roof was like those she'd seen on the burnt temples in Seoul, sloping downward from the center. Behind the house stood a mountain of pure green. It was so unlike the balding mountains of North Korea and Seoul that Kwang Ja could not believe she had traveled so far in just an hour's drive. It was as if she had flown from the sun to the moon. Then she looked at the woman holding her up. It was a familiar figure: short, slumped over, hunchbacked. It was the body of a woman who, for years, carried tremendous weight. It was a woman who was so used to bowing to men, carrying their children on her back, and holding the weight of an entire house on her shoulders that her back was permanently bent. Women like this lived in North Korea, too. It was Confucianism at its worst. Kwang Ja no longer felt as far away as she'd have liked.

She rose from the woman's arms and went up to the large wooden door. A brass ring with elaborate engravings of dragons intertwined hung from the door. She rubbed the ring, then brushed her fingers against the dragons. Behind her a voice spoke. "So you're not so sick after all."

Startled, Kwang Ja dropped the grapes. A couple bounced once, then slowly rolled toward the woman, but the rest splattered on the wooden porch. The woman stooped over to pick up the grapes. Embarrassed, Kwang Ja tried to beat her to them. The woman slapped Kwang Ja's reaching hand lightly. "I got it, I got it. You ridiculous child, you move as if it were diamonds you dropped."

Kwang Ja stood back up and wondered what diamonds were and what they tasted like.

The woman made Kwang Ja wash her bare feet before she went inside. This woman, who was dressed in simple white clothes and wore white rubber sandals, sighed when she saw the bottoms of Kwang Ja's callused feet. Then the servant's old face smiled. She led Kwang Ja into the house.

Kwang Ja saw things in this house that she had never seen before. Things like faucets, toilets, and beds were foreign to her. As were embroidered rugs, framed paintings, glass cases filled with fine china, and wooden tables that shone so much that she could see her reflection in them. But none of these things was as beautiful as the garden beyond the patio in the back. A huge glass door (another thing she'd never seen before) separated the patio from the house, but the glass was so clean that it looked like the door wasn't there. Kwang Ja almost walked through it, but the old woman pulled her back and opened the door for her.

The garden, which was about twenty yards long and ten yards wide, was separated from the mountain by a huge stone wall. It was the same kind of stone she saw as temple rubble in the city. While the vegetation of the mountain grew beautifully green, but wild, the garden was meticulously cared for. Each blade of grass seemed of equal length. Through the center of the garden ran a tiny stream where koi, fish wearing bright and diverse colors, swam above a bed of fine black gravel. Kwang Ja stepped off the patio and walked to the bridge, which was of the same wood as the house. She watched the fish, some bright orange, some white, and some wearing both colors, swim in the clear water.

Then she crossed the bridge and inspected the flower garden. Sunflowers, daisies, and roses grew out of the darkest soil she'd ever seen, while several bees buzzed around them. To the right of the garden stood an enormous ginko tree, its yellow blossoms covering every branch. A black-and-white magpie flew from one of the branches. To the left of the flower garden, several bamboo poles were staked into the ground. Vines of ripe, purple grapes wrapped themselves around the poles. Kwang Ja walked to one of these vines and pulled off a grape. She bit into it and tasted the sweet-sour juice spread on her tongue. This was what the woman meant by diamonds, she thought. Suddenly she felt like crying. This garden, this house were what Seoul was supposed to be to Kwang Ja. To her it was the heart of Seoul. Though the body, the city, might be contaminated, the heart was pure. She held in her tears, swallowed the grape, turned around to the old servant woman, and asked, "What is expected of me?"

The woman hissed. "Only that you become a lady."

Kwang Ja wasn't sure what that meant, but she did not care. She had been tempted effectively, and was willing to pay any price.

It was difficult at first. Kwang Ja had to learn how to read better, not only *han'gŭl,* women's writing, but also *hanmun,* men's writing. She had to learn all of the graces of a South Korean aristocratic woman, which meant she had to learn how to ingratiate herself with men, which was difficult considering there were no men at the house. She was forbidden to take one step outdoors so her dark skin would lighten. This meant she did not spend any time in the garden. She had to lose her northern country accent, and cover it with a more genteel one. What they wanted her to do was forget who she was and where she came from. As far as they were concerned, she was reborn during the hot summer of 1952. The Year of the Dragon. And except for not being able to eat the grapes or watch the fish outside, this was fine with her.

One of the first things Park Dong Jin, the man who had put her in the fancy black car, had done to her was have her calluses removed. Her feet were soaked in water for days, and two women scrubbed the skin off. Every day the soles of her feet were worn down to a bright red, and like a shedding snake, she left a trail of skin wherever she stepped.

She also shed her peasant clothes. She was given clothes she didn't even know how to put on. Layers of thin material of white, green, blue, and pink had to be put on a layer at a time, in a particular order. Covering these layers were the *chŏgori* and *ch'ima,* the loose, long-sleeved blouse and high-waisted, wrap-around skirt which hovered less than an inch from the ground. The material was unusually soft, unlike anything she'd ever touched before. Silk, canoe-shaped shoes finished the ensemble. Then there was her hair. The matted strands were combed out by the same two women who scrubbed her feet. For the first week, every day, she left tufts of hair in the teeth of combs. But she did not cry. She acted as if it didn't even hurt, and the two women who combed her

Refuge in the DMZ

The demilitarized zone at Korea's thirty-eighth parallel, the most heavily fortified border in the world, has become a refuge for some of Asia's most endangered species. Animals that once roamed the Korean peninsula and captured the imaginations of its people are now found only inside the 2.5-mile-wide, 155-mile-long strip that has been a virtual no-man's-land for half a century. The rare Asian black bear is thought to exist inside the zone, and there are rumors that the Korean tiger, once thought to have vanished from the peninsula, survives there. Reports also confirm that two of the world's most endangered birds, the white-naped and the red-crowned crane, have made the thirty-eighth parallel their wintering grounds.

hair believed her. Finally, after her hair was straight and silky, the servants showed her how to make the simple, long braid worn by unmarried women.

For that first year, she didn't even see Dong Jin. But she heard his name constantly. Whenever she did something good, like recite the story "The Old Man Who Became a Fish" or "The Old Woman Who Became a Goblin" flawlessly, or commit to memory Newton's laws of motion, her *sabu*, her teacher, a middle-aged man with an unusually long graying mustache, would say, "Master Park will be so proud."

Whenever she did something bad, like forget to brush her hair, her nurse, the old woman who had led her into the house, would say, "You stupid girl. If you are not careful, Master Park will throw you back out on the streets."

This Master Park for that first year was an entity she'd neither seen nor heard. To her, he became this faceless figure who held her fate in the palm of his hand. He became like that God she had learned about in the book of the white missionaries. He was a deity who could reward or punish in one stroke without even showing himself. At first, because of her atheism, Kwang Ja did not fear or believe it. But as the months rolled by and her skin lightened, her feet and hair softened, and her mind was filled, she knew she was being transformed, and she knew Master Park was the force behind it. At first she felt like a silkworm cocooning herself and changing. But then she realized she wasn't the power behind her metamorphosis. It was Master Park who cocooned her, and with this thought Kwang Ja felt more like a spider's meal than a growing butterfly or moth. She didn't know why, but she was beginning to feel fear. She did not want to be ruled by a god.

On the one-year anniversary of her rebirth, Dong Jin came to her. He quietly entered the house while Kwang Ja was on the patio, playing the *kayagŭm*. She was a quick study with everything, but she especially had a knack for playing this twelve-stringed zither, and in just a year, she could play some of the most complex compositions. Through the controlled chaos of floating notes, she heard the glass door slide open. The man she had come to know as a demigod, along with the two servants who'd scrubbed her once callus-ridden feet, walked in and stopped in front of her. And in that first instant of seeing him, her fear and her perception of him as an all-powerful being disappeared. He was definitely a man, and not an impressive-looking one at that. He was middle-aged and tall for a Korean, but his height was offset by a fat belly and bad posture. A thinning head of hair framed his round face. His eyes were small, his eyebrows bushy, and his nose was broad and flat. His mouth was unusually small, and he seemed to lack a chin. The most impressive thing about this man was the dark, Western-style suit he was wearing. Kwang Ja also noticed he was carrying a strange wooden box with him. When she stopped playing and bowed her head, she looked at his shiny black shoes, and they reminded her of his car. It seemed that Westerners were obsessed with creating shiny black things and calling them beautiful. It seemed odd to Kwang Ja that they, like their religious men, didn't seem to like bright colors.

He told her to stand up. He put his hand on her chin and turned her face, looking at each profile. She'd found out she was beautiful only the year before when she'd overheard the servants commenting on it. Without looking at the servants, he said, "Get us tea."

Kwang Ja left her *kayagǔm,* and they both walked to the other side of the patio. He told her to sit and placed the box on the table. It was a beautiful, lacquered, cherry-colored box. Dragons made of mother-of-pearl shone on the lid. As she stared at it, one of the servants obstructed her view with a kettle and two ceramic cups. They sat cross-legged at the short, wooden table, and he poured her some tea. She carefully put her right hand around the rim and gently held the bottom with her left. She took a brief sip, letting only a few drops in her mouth. Kwang Ja felt Dong Jin staring at her, and refused to look back. "Did you get the chance to taste the grapes in the garden?" he asked.

She nodded, feeling his eyes study her face.

"Who was your father?" he asked.

"I don't know. I am an orphan."

"You call yourself Cho Kwang Ja. Whose surname did you take?"

"Cho was the name of a family in the village that I went to after the missionary orphanage was abandoned."

Dong Jin poured tea in his cup. He picked it up and blew on it. The steam blew in Kwang Ja's direction, but evaporated before it hit her. "You are beautiful," he said in a deadpan manner. It was as if he were pointing at a tree and saying, "That's a tree." He sipped his tea, then continued. "There is an exotic quality to your look. An almost northern Japanese quality. Do you have Japanese blood?"

Kwang Ja jerked her head up and looked into Dong Jin's eyes. She was slipping. "No, I don't."

Dong Jin smiled. "How do you explain the shape of your eyes?"

"My eyes are the same as anyone else's. They're brown," she said, still looking directly at him, even though she knew she shouldn't be.

"So they are. But there's something different," he said. He looked like he wanted to examine her eyes with a magnifying glass. "Maybe to Westerners, Japanese, Chinese, and Koreans look alike. But I know many people of all of these nationalities. I have

Bird

Poem by Chon Sangpyong

The day beyond
the day I die
lonely in death after lonely living
birds will sing as new day dawns and petals unfold
on my soul's empty ground.

I'll be one bird
alighting on ditches and branches
when the song of loving and living
and beauty
is at its height.

Season full of emotion
week of sorrow and joy
in the gaps between knowing not knowing forgetting bird pour
out that antiquated song.

One bird sings of how
there are good things
in life
and bad things too.

Calligraphy by Lee Eunhyuk

never seen eyes like yours in any Korean woman."

Kwang Ja thought about this for a moment. Then she shrugged and looked down. "Maybe too much sun."

Dong Jin laughed. "Yes, maybe. You may be scared, but there's nothing to worry about. No one cares if you're not pure Korean. Not here. In fact, I doubt if that's what you're really scared of. You're at the age when you are supposed to be scared. The world is crazy, especially for a young woman. Do you know why I brought you here?"

Kwang Ja thought about this. She had her suspicions that he wanted to make her his concubine, but she felt it would be impolite to say so. She glanced at the box. Perhaps it contained a concubine's gift. This man, with his questions and assumptions, was angering her. Who was he to tell her what she was really scared of? "You brought me here because you feel guilty about hitting me with your fancy black car."

Dong Jin smiled. "Good guess, but no. You see, I make movies. So I brought you here because I am going to make you a star. The way to greatness is found in either creating something new or destroying something old. With you, I plan to do both."

Kwang Ja looked down. She was taught recently that matter could neither be created nor destroyed. "But I'm just a simple country girl who you accuse of being part foreign. How can I be an actress?"

"You're already an actress, child. I just want to show everyone else. From now on you'll take my name. You are a Park. You are from Pusan or Won Ju, who cares, the country is a mess and no one knows who anyone is anymore anyway. You're a distant cousin of mine whose parents have passed away. I am your guardian. We will get you another name, one that doesn't suggest a peasant upbringing, like Kwang Ja does, from a fortuneteller tomorrow. Do you accept?"

Kwang Ja sipped on her tea and let silence fill the room. She didn't want to seem too anxious. She put down the cup, sighed, and looked at him again. "I guess."

Dong Jin laughed. "You are going to be a star!"

He opened the box and pulled out a short, simple-looking knife. Its blade was covered by a silver sheath. It was obviously made by a more primitive culture. "Do you know what this is?" he asked.

"It's a knife, an old one at that."

"Has your teacher told you about the tradition of the 'silver knife'?"

Kwang Ja nodded. "Yes. In the old days, it was given to young women as both decoration and protection. A young virgin was always to wear it. But the tradition died, yes?"

Dong Jin nodded. "Yes. In fact, this knife is an artifact. It has been in my family for hundreds of years. But now I give it to you."

Kwang Ja frowned. She couldn't imagine carrying around a knife like some kind of cutthroat. "But who do I need to protect myself from?"

"We all need protection. Sometimes from strangers, mostly from acquaintances, and always from ourselves. But please, think of this as more of a symbol. It is a gift that symbolizes the fact that you are no longer the helpless girl I found in the streets. I have armed you."

Kwang Ja pulled the knife from its sheath. The silver blade drew in the light from the sun and shot it in her eyes. She tightened her grip around its hilt, and tested the blade. It was sharp. She wondered if it had ever been used. Suddenly she felt strong. Her fears disappeared. Yes, she was no longer the scared child starving in the streets of Seoul. She looked up at Dong Jin. "Thank you for the gift."

He smiled. "Keep it in the box. It's an antique. Now, let's talk about your future as an actress. You and I will go to Pusan, where you will be trained in the theater. You will also be taught more Western philosophies there..."

Kwang Ja put the sheath back on its blade and placed the knife back in the box. He was right: it was a symbol, an artifact more than an actual weapon.

"Are you listening?"

She closed the box. "Yes."

It would be years before she would open the box again. And only twice more.

The next day, in the streets of Seoul, with envious eyes focused on her, Kwang Ja and Dong Jin asked a whore/fortuneteller about a new name. She was a woman in her forties who spent her days on the streets seeing into the future, and spent nights trying to ensure that she herself would have one. Kwang Ja thought it strange that a rich man like Dong Jin would choose such a fortuneteller. But he simply said, "The ones who have lived tend to be the ones with the most vision."

The fortuneteller scribbled down what little information Kwang Ja could tell her about her heritage. The woman then threw a handful of beans onto a thin layer of sand in front of her. She carefully studied the arbitrary formation, and Kwang Ja wanted to laugh, but the whore/fortuneteller's serious manner prevented her from doing so. Suddenly, the woman looked up. "Soong Nan. Your name now will be Soong Nan. It will be a very lucky name for you."

The fact that this whore/fortuneteller was living on the street in rags told the newly named Soong Nan that she didn't know the least bit about luck. So she took the name with trepidation. The next day, Park Soong Nan went to Pusan, leaving Cho Kwang Ja buried in the fortuneteller's shallow sand.

Vase,
Koryŏ period,
early 12th century
Porcelaneous ware

HWANG SUN-WŎN

CRANES

The northern village lay snug beneath the high, bright autumn sky, near the border at the thirty-eighth parallel. White gourds lay one against the other on the dirt floor of an empty farmhouse. Any village elders who passed by extinguished their bamboo pipes first, and the children, too, turned back some distance off. Their faces were marked with fear.

As a whole, the village showed little damage from the war, but it still did not seem like the same village Sŏngsam had known as a boy.

At the foot of a chestnut grove on the hill behind the village, he stopped and climbed a chestnut tree. Somewhere far back in his mind he heard the old man with a wen shout, "You bad boy, climbing up my chestnut tree again!"

The old man must have passed away, for he was not among the few village elders Sŏngsam had met. Holding on to the trunk of the tree, Sŏngsam gazed up at the blue sky for a time. Some chestnuts fell to the ground as the dry clusters opened of their own accord.

A young man stood, his hands bound, before a farmhouse that had been converted into a Public Peace Police office. He seemed to be a stranger, so Sŏngsam went up for a closer look. He was stunned: this young man was none other than his boyhood playmate, Tŏkchae.

Sŏngsam asked the police officer who had come with him from Ch'ŏnt'ae for an explanation. The prisoner was the vice-chairman of the Farmers' Communist League and had just been flushed out of hiding in his own house, Sŏngsam learned.

Sŏngsam sat down on the dirt floor and lit a cigarette.

Tŏkchae was to be escorted to Ch'ŏngdan by one of the Peace Police.

After a time, Sŏngsam lit a new cigarette from the first and stood up.

"I'll take him with me."

Tŏkchae averted his face and refused to look at Sŏngsam. The two left the village.

Sŏngsam went on smoking, but the tobacco had no flavor. He just kept drawing the smoke in and blowing it out. Then suddenly he thought that Tŏkchae, too, must want a puff. He thought of the days when they had shared dried gourd leaves behind

sheltering walls, hidden from the adults' view. But today, how could he offer a cigarette to a fellow like this?

Once, when they were small, he went with Tŏkchae to steal some chestnuts from the old man with the wen. It was Sŏngsam's turn to climb the tree. Suddenly the old man began shouting. Sŏngsam slipped and fell to the ground. He got chestnut burrs all over his bottom, but he kept on running. Only when the two had reached a safe place where the old man could not overtake them did Sŏngsam turn his bottom to Tŏkchae. The burrs hurt so much as they were plucked out that Sŏngsam could not keep tears from welling up in his eyes. Tŏkchae produced a fistful of chestnuts from his pocket and thrust them into Sŏngsam's… Sŏngsam threw away the cigarette he had just lit, and then made up his mind not to light another while he was escorting Tŏkchae.

They reached the pass at the hill where he and Tŏkchae had cut fodder for the cows until Sŏngsam had to move to a spot near Ch'ŏnt'ae, south of the thirty-eighth parallel, two years before the liberation.

Sŏngsam felt a sudden surge of anger in spite of himself and shouted, "So how many have you killed?"

For the first time, Tŏkchae cast a quick glance at him and then looked away.

"You! How many have you killed?" he asked again.

Tŏkchae looked at him again and glared. The glare grew intense, and his mouth twitched.

"So you managed to kill quite a few, eh?" Sŏngsam felt his mind clearing itself, as if some obstruction had been removed. "If you were vice-chairman of the Communist League, why didn't you run? You must have been lying low with a secret mission."

Tŏkchae did not reply.

"Speak up. What was your mission?"

Tŏkchae kept walking. Tŏkchae was hiding something, Sŏngsam thought. He wanted to take a good look at him, but Tŏkchae kept his face averted.

Fingering the revolver at his side, Sŏngsam went on: "There's no need to make excuses. You're going to be shot anyway. Why don't you tell the truth here and now?"

"I'm not going to make any excuses. They made me vice-chairman of the League because I was a hardworking farmer, and one of the poorest. If that's a capital offense, so be it. I'm still what I used to be—the only thing I'm good at is tilling the soil." After a short pause, he added, "My old man is bedridden at home. He's been ill almost half a year." Tŏkchae's father was a widower, a poor, hardworking farmer who lived only for his son. Seven years ago his back had given out, and he had contracted a skin disease.

"Are you married?"

"Yes," Tŏkchae replied after a time.

Sandra Sunnyo Lee   *Self–No Self (gold, blue, red)*

CHAPTER FIVE

NEW ARRIVALS IN A CHANGED AMERICA

JENNY RYUN FOSTER

ONCE UPON A TIME IN AMERICA: AN INTRODUCTION

My arrival in the U.S. was without my knowledge. It happened to me. In the spring of 1974, I landed with thirty other Korean infants at Chicago's O'Hare Airport, where we were handed over to our adoptive parents. Then, like seeds blown on the breeze, each of us was carried away, scattered in all directions across the wide expanse of America.

Fate dropped me in a small industrial city in Michigan, where I grew up. As a child, I learned what it meant to be Korean very much the way one becomes aware of things in a dream. Ethnicity entered my consciousness at first only in odd and indirect ways. I hardly knew what being Korean meant, but I remember nevertheless being proud of it. It made me different from every other person in my small town: my classmates, my teachers—even my parents. Still, I never felt isolated or disadvantaged because of my differences. In fact, they allowed me to associate with everyone, of whatever race or color, and to have all the normal experiences of a small-town girl in America: a working mom, after-school rehearsals for the school play, diving practice for the swim team, a part-time job at the ice cream parlor.

And so I grew up dreaming—and living—in two worlds, and was never forced to choose between them. Slowly, though, I began to wonder what exactly it was that made me different and special. I graduated from high school and moved away to college, and it was then that my awareness changed. The large university I attended brought me in contact with people from all over the country, whose experiences were entirely different from my own small-town childhood. In learning about the great variety of family backgrounds, ethnic origins, mixed-up identities, and passionate points of view, I began to awaken to the world. Oddly, however, as a Korean I was still a singularity, and still found it difficult to learn very much about what it meant to be Korean American. I felt there was only one thing to do: go to Korea and live there.

Soon after college, I landed in Kimp'o Airport in Seoul with one suitcase and no return ticket. I was uncertain what to expect. Nevertheless, I was thrilled with the sense that this was what I was meant to do. I was meant to be standing here, making my way through customs, staring curiously at the airport's military guards—young soldiers no older than I, each carrying a rifle or machine gun, striding sternly along the linoleum walkway and among the passengers. I was meant to find a bus to Taejŏn, by using sign language and broken Korean from a phrase book. I was meant to travel for an hour and a half away from Seoul, wondering if I was on the right bus. And I was meant to encounter, at the end of that bus ride, the most wondrous, exciting, adventurous year of my life, to be welcomed warmly by Korea and the many new friends that I was destined to make.

In the Korean provinces, I found to my surprise that being American was much more important to the way I was perceived than being Korean—just the opposite situation to the one in America, where being Asian had made me stand out from the majority of Midwesterners, and being Korean had made me stand out from other Asian Americans. Whenever I had had to fill out a form in America, there was always a box to check indicating my ethnicity. The only one that seemed to fit me was ASIAN/PACIFIC ISLANDER, although at times this question would appear as "optional." I wonder if the people that ask such a question think that to be Asian/Korean is optional.

At the end of my year in Korea I recognized the irony of being an "American" in Korea and an "Asian" in America. I realized there is no easy answer to what being Korean means, or to what anyone's life and identity means. Though there were so many things that I found I didn't know, I cherished many of the simple things that I did: how to converse with a traveler underneath the setting sun at Taech'ŏn beach, the taste of *makkŏlli* (mountain wine), the beauty of cherry blossoms in the spring beside Ch'ungnam National University—like snow petals covering the walkway as far as the eye can see.

I had been given new eyes while I was away, and coming home to the United States was a shock. I thought about how insignificant one person is in our vast world, swirling with cultures and life situations that shift at the whim of gravity and time.

Before going to Korea, I had felt that I could merge and submerge into my American surroundings—alternately Korean, Asian, American. But on my return, I felt my differences were more specific. Being Korean meant having a certain cultural history that carried me back through time, a heritage made up of countless experiences, events, and people who were part of me and who continued to form who I was and would become. At the same time, I was even more aware that in this fast-paced world, one's history is difficult to hold on to and remember.

I have journeyed from Korea to the Midwest, back to Korea, and now to Hawai'i; I am still discovering who I am as well as who I am not. My passage has led me to the words on this page. My work with *Century of the Tiger* filled my mind with compelling and adventurous stories of Koreans who sailed to Hawai'i and made the U.S. their home—these stories are also part of me. I am amazed to think that my story is just one of hundreds of thousands, each different and yet somehow familiar. I am celebrating.

Grace

Calligraphy by Kwon Changryun

HEINZ INSU FENKL
for Hwang Sun-wŏn (1915–2000)
from *Skull Water*

ONE BIG WORD

I

The shadow of the 707 rippled below us like a giant black egret, flowing across the landscape, growing steadily smaller as we neared the earth, calming into a glide as the hilly contours became the flat green expanse of the rice paddies around Kimp'o Airbase. I could not imagine what power it took to keep these tons of alloy and steel in the air, to keep the airplane from simply plummeting like a stone into the fertile earth below. We were falling at more than two hundred miles an hour, and yet the landscape seemed to move lazily until the plane slowed, just before touching the runway, and then everything accelerated into a dizzying speed. The world lurched and the air grew suddenly thick with the roar of the jets, which had lulled us until that moment, and we could feel the sudden texture of the tarmac right through the landing gear, through the bottoms of our seats, as the earth ground itself into our spines. We had landed, and now the roaring jets suddenly became shrill as we lurched slightly forward in our seats and the airplane braked to a near stop. The landscape outside moved at a crawl, everything looking too large and yet oddly too small. I glanced over my little sister's head to the aisle seat and saw my mother's eyes brim with tears with the joy of being back in our homeland. Korea. 1976. Early summer in the Year of the Dragon.

2

At first, Kisu's house appeared exactly the same as when I had last seen it nearly a decade ago, six years before we had left for America. But during our first day I realized the house had aged just like Kisu's grandmother, who had grown lighter and more shriveled over those years—like a dried gourd that will rattle in the wind. It was a ramshackle house nearly a century old, built a decade before the Japanese Occupation— before the turn of the century—and since then it had sheltered four generations of Changs as the tiny village by the stream grew into Pup'yŏng. The original building was wood and whitewashed plaster, but now the roof beams were full of dry rot and the *kidung* posts were warped and tilted. When I walked across the wooden *maru* with the added weight of my years the floor creaked in spots I didn't recall and the compacted dirt of the courtyard, which had seemed as hard as baked clay when I was a child, seemed to have become softer, oddly dustlike. The black dirt floor of the dark kitchen seemed even deeper than before, though it should rightly have seemed shallower since I had grown. People from Tatagumi had been in the habit of visiting from time to time to scoop up some of the kitchen dirt to make medicine pellets, which they would cook with foul-smelling concoctions of Chinese herbs; their visits must have been frequent, or perhaps some new epidemic had coursed through Tatagumi and they had come with shovels during one of the years we had been away in the West. Just inside the gate, the slab of stone that deflected the water from the downspouts had darkened over many monsoons; when I placed my fingers in the deep pockmarks I thought it odd that they had remained the same size over those years, but then I realized that my fingers had grown both longer and thicker, and the stone had eroded deeply and quickly under the furious torrents of the monsoon rains.

For the first several months after our return to Korea, we would live in this house in Pup'yŏng in the old neighborhood of Tatagumi that still bore its Japanese name. We lived in the same rooms we had occupied once before; my mother, An-na, and I slept in the room where I had been born.

The first morning I stepped outside the front gate, I was startled by the red cock that guarded the tailor shop next door. It stood there, very alert, turning its head this way and that in its jerky rhythm, its cockscomb quivering, its wattle swaying. I expected it to shake itself like a wet dog.

The rooster clucked deep within its throat when it saw me, and it looked at me as if it were aiming its gaze, as if its eyes could peck me as hard as its knife-sharp beak. I retreated slowly, and then suddenly I felt as if I were a little boy again because there had

been a cock just like this one years ago, with the same twitchy movements, the same red, black, and orange sheen to its feathers. Perhaps this was the grandson or the great-grandson of that cock—surely, there was no way it could have survived the fights for so many years. I remembered the terror of seeing it out of the corner of my eye on those few times when I had been careless and inattentive enough for it to peck me. Those tiny, loose pieces of flesh had hung from my calf just like the rooster's wattle, with a clear and pinkish ooze before the blood began to flow. Once, my cousin Yongsu had come home with a small bag of rice from the corner store and the cock had flown at him—in a terrifying explosion of feathers—for daring to pass without feeding him. Yongsu had nearly lost an eye that time, and forever after that he and I had both remembered to toss a scrap of dried rice or a crust of old sandwich bread to distract him when we were going out. On the way home, we would call out in advance to the owner of the tailor shop, and his wife would come out, annoyed to have to leave her ironing, and hold the bird while we rushed in through the gate. Kisu's mother had joked that they had never been burglarized since the tailor started raising his fighting cocks. Once in a while, when the tailor lost or when he was fed up with a failed champion, they would share the stringy meat with Kisu's family.

I remembered seeing the tailor in his own dirt courtyard, by the water spigot, holding his precious rooster between his legs, stroking its feathers into a beautiful scarlet sheen, sharpening its claws, fitting it with the bamboo spikes it would drive like spurs into its opponent. Hyŏngbu had taken us to a single cockfight, and we had watched as the two birds circled each other and then collided in a chaos of feathers and noise. It was over in a mere instant, one strutting back and the other listing forlornly before falling on its side, surprising us with the vast amount of blood it had so suddenly spewed. Hyŏngbu had lost his bet and never took us again, and Yongsu and I had never wanted to go after that. The smell of blood and feathers mixed with the gritty cigarette smoke and the acrid sweat of the audience settled into our skin and our clothes. I could smell it in my hair all the next day, and even after I washed it out I had the queasy feeling that some tiny blood-soaked pieces of rooster fluff had gotten lodged in my scalp.

Now I simply took a few quick steps and got out of the cock's territory. It squawked at me and then turned away, its ears picking up some small sound I couldn't hear. I crossed the street and walked slowly towards the train station at the foot of the hill to Samnung. I had been planning to pay a visit to the old house on the hill where we had once lived, but just as I got to the road that cut through the neighborhood, I saw Kisu's mother leading her ninety-year-old mother out of an acupuncturist's house. The old woman was oddly dressed, probably still from the treatment, in old Japanese-style pantaloons that exposed her emaciated legs and knobby joints—a mass of veins and wrinkled flesh twisted around thin bones.

Kisu's mother was having trouble holding her mother upright, so I rushed forward and helped them back across the street, half carrying the old woman. She was so light I might have lifted her in my arms like an infant, but she was mumbling about the indignity of being outside without her proper white clothes. When we reached the gate of the house, the tailor's rooster gave us only a curious look and let us by without a challenge, twisting his neck around with a frenetic alertness as we entered the small blue door in the gate.

"What's the matter?" I asked Kisu's mother.

"Halmŏni was lucid today," she said. "She knew how sick she was, and she wanted a treatment right away."

"I almost died," said Halmŏni. "I almost died, and you kept me in that room alone all morning. What kind of daughter-in-law are you now that my son's dead?"

"Quiet, Mother. This is Kisu's friend who lives across the *maru*. He's the little girl's older brother."

Halmŏni squinted at me as she sat down on the granite stepping stone and let

ISHLE YI PARK

Ode to the
Picnic Singers, 1984

...And then at dusk the woman
climbed atop the picnic table
and belted out a Patty Kim hit,
plastic spoon a mic clutched in her
  fist!

And the kalbi spit and bubbled dark
as azalea and crushed black diamond,
meat soy-sauced and sizzling in the July
  heat waves
that hummed like the yellow frisbee
  flung

over tiny Youna Ean, kneeling among clover
  and dandelion.
Ay, the sky flapped above us like a soiled
  workshirt
on clothesline while we twisted our ankles
  over Chinese jump rope,
then flew by on flowered banana seats,
  wind teasing streamers

and the black whips of our hair, past
our brothers in visors and cut-off football
  tanks,
lost in long switch grass and dewy goose
  shit.
And our mothers raced! Piggybacking
  frilled babies

over grass to catch with their teeth
butter cookies strung on a white finish line,
to the slow butterfly thighs of their men.
Far from the dented Volvos and Hyundais

bereft in the parking lot, these husbands
  whorled and spun
in dervishes around that imported leather
  rugby ball
from Seoul, bathed in a halo of their own
  sweat
and kicked-up dirt. Our parents gathered,

her daughter-in-law remove her rubber shoes for her. "How old are you?" she said suddenly. I was about to answer her—to tell her I was seventeen, which was reckoned sixteen in the American way—when she said, "Two thousand and three hundred and forty-four years. That's a long time to be an ancestor. *Yaeya,* how many *hwan'gap* does that make? How many times does the zodiac turn in those many years, *ungh?*"

"I don't know," I said.

Kisu's mother took her by the hands and led her back to their room, and I stood there for a while, doing the calculation in my head. Each *hwan'gap* was sixty years—five turns of the lunar zodiac, which was made of twelve animal signs. Two-thousand-three-hundred-and-forty-four divided by sixty was thirty-nine, with four years left over. Thirty-nine times five was one-hundred-and-ninety-five. Four years was one third of a turn, so the zodiac had turned one-hundred-ninety-five and a quarter times in those years. I wanted to deliver the answer to Kisu's grandmother, but I knew that she was just lapsing back into her senility. The number was probably meaningless.

3

A few days after her lucid spell, Kisu's grandmother became very sick. She needed money for medical bills so our rent was a windfall for the Chang family. When the acupuncture treatments failed, they talked about taking her to a hospital the following month, but then, for no apparent reason, she suddenly got well again. She sat out on the *maru* and watched everyone in the yard as she smoked her long bamboo pipe and smacked her thin lips. All summer, through the last of the humid heat, she was healthy and lively. She even showed my little sister, An-na, the old version of the Bellflower-picking dance and she sang, with great vigor—*Toraji toraji paek toraji*—miming the picking and putting into the basket. Though she lisped and slurred because she had only two teeth, the song sounded beautiful in her high and scratchy voice. Kisu and I sat under the cherry tree and listened attentively to that song, which seemed to come from the borders of another world. With her few tufts of brittle, white hair and her shriveled skin, Halmŏni looked as if she had already been dead for a thousand years.

When the weather began to cool, Kisu's grandmother had a surge of appetite. At mealtimes we all took turns chewing her food for her and spitting it into a bowl in which Kisu's mother mixed it before spooning it out a little at a time. Soon the old woman started calling Kisu by his dead father's name and treating his mother as if she were the maid. She spent days speaking only Japanese, warning us that those who spoke Korean would get into great trouble if they were caught.

shook loose the workday, their *hangook*
   tongues
like wild geese skimming over lake.
They popped open barrel-shaped
   Budweisers
and let the foam spill over; they let the
   foam

spill over. My father tilted the can to
   baby Sarah's mouth
and laughed at her sputtering, a laughter
   so serious
I think I forgive him, his hungry
   rough cheeks waning
to the woman's hungry, rough songs. And
   Jung Yun's *uma*

sang like a torn-up hymnal. She sang
   until we dropped
the twigs and pigeon feathers from our
   hands
to sit cross-legged in the nest of our
   mothers,
she sang like a yanked-out phone cord:
   shrill,

cut, ringing, 70s pop ballad fervid
with religion so unlike our Sunday
   falsettos,
she sang and we believed in a smaller,
gruffer, chip-toothed god: she sang the
   dusk down.

And we, staring up at her knees,
rested in the blue fall of each other's
   shadows
while the *bab* and *ban chan*, paper
   plates and water coolers
were left, for once, gratefully unattended.

"It's nothing to worry about," my mother told me one night. "All of us who remember that time have the same fear and it's just coming out in Halmŏni because her mind is getting young again." Mahmi had just put An-na to bed and we were both sitting cross-legged on the floor, under the dangling bulb. Mahmi played solitaire with her small flower cards while I read a pulp novel I had shoplifted from the PX.

"What's that you're looking at?"

I showed her the cover of the latest installment in the *Doc Savage* series: the Man of Bronze in his tattered shirt and jodhpurs, his exposed torso gleaming with sweat and blood, his fists clenched, his face rugged like a slightly rough-hewn Greek god.

Mahmi looked at the illustration and turned the book over to see the back cover, holding my place open with a finger. "You're reading this because he looks like Daeri?"

"*Ungh?*" I said. I took the book back and examined it more carefully. On the color cover, Doc Savage's white-blond skullcap of hair and the creases on his face gave him a passing resemblance to my father, which I had never noticed; but the small portrait of him on the back was in black-and-white, and that older face, with its particular grimness, looked uncannily like my father when he was brooding.

"How could you not notice? It must be because you've ruined your eyes from all that reading. Let's get to sleep."

"Can I read one more chapter?"

"Let's sleep when I've finished this round, *ungh?* You should start getting up earlier." She slapped another card down on a column. It was the rain card: a man with an umbrella under black jags of what looked like seaweed, and a small toad-like thing running in the lower corner. "That look on the man's face," she said, "it's like he could stab you with his eyes."

"He knows hypno—" I hesitated because I didn't quite know the word in Korean.

"Hypnotism," said Mahmi. "Some of the old Taoists could kill you with a look or pull all your life energy out through your eyes. But any look like that is frightening enough. Did I ever tell you the dream I had after you were born?"

"The one about the snake that was so big it went all the way around the palace walls?"

"No," she said. "That was your birth dream. That was the one that said what kind of person you were going to become. I mean the other dream I had when they took me to the hospital."

"I thought I was born at home," I said.

"You were. But there were problems after."

"Problems?"

Grace Kim *Door of Hope*

CAROLINE JEONG-MEE KIM

Magdalena

A week after my sixteenth birthday, I woke up to the sound of my father shouting. At first I thought he was angry, but soon I realized he was just looking for his hat. We were going to McKinney State Park in Maine, the whole parish of the Korean Catholic Church of Lexington. I thought with embarrassment of the two bright-orange school buses the church had rented for the occasion.

I got up anyway, dragging my feet into the kitchen, where my mother was putting rows of *gim bap* into Tupperware containers. For breakfast, she gave us the uneven ends. I told her I didn't want to go.

She was unconcerned. "Why not?" she asked. My mother was a slightly chubby woman with a round, bright face. She could look cheerful even when she wasn't.

"I don't feel like it," I said. "I'm too old for it."

I sat down across from her. I had spoken in Korean, which I could still do if I didn't think about it. My parents were that way with English. They still had a terrible time pronouncing the place where we lived. Lawrence, Massachusetts. My father sounded like he was caught in a fit of sneezing when he pronounced *Massachusetts.* So we ended up speaking a third language, a strangled jumble of Korean and English that seemed to work.

"That's too bad," she said. "Everybody's going to be there."

"Who?"

"Somebody said there'll be volleyball."

"I hate volleyball."

"And there's a beach."

"There is?"

"Of course! We're going to the ocean, aren't we?"

I thought of what I looked like in my bathing suit: a skinny stick figure with a too-large head. When my parents were playful, they called me Olive Oyl; when my brother felt mean, he called me Refugee Victim. Still, I loved swimming: the feeling of being held up by nothing but salt and water. I rubbed the sleep out of my eyes. "Well, maybe I'll just check out the beach."

"Good idea," she said, as though I'd suggested something brilliant. "Now eat something or go get dressed."

My mother never liked to see me idle. Sometimes she said I was like my father, who could go off to a place in his head and live without eating. There were whole days when a curious, detached look replaced his usual worried expression and he seemed to forget who we were. This kind of dreaming she called blindness. For my mother, reality was a point of honor; her hands were always busy. She wanted me to be like her.

"Go, go," my mother said, eating and chewing behind her hand. "Hurry or we'll be late."

she was lost. Three little girls popped out of the shadow of the back seat wearing summer dresses to match their mother's: white with splashy red flowers.

A man got out and stood on the other side: middle thirties, clean-cut, the prototype of an engineer. Like Father Kwak, there was something in his hair that made it stay down and look shiny. But my eye was drawn back to the wife. She was wearing heavy blue eyeshadow that stood out like neon on her pale face and made her look strangely festive. Beneath a delicate, perspiring nose were a pair of the glossiest lips I'd ever seen outside a magazine. She was beautiful and awful at the same time. I couldn't look away. I could feel how we were all staring at her. She knew it too. Pretending not to see any of us, she stood very close to her husband, almost clinging to his side. Their three little girls, also shy, hung back on the other side of their father.

They were somehow apart from the rest of us and stood as in a portrait, refusing to come to life.

"Oh, what cute girls," my mother said. "And look at those matching dresses! Just like the mother's! Don't you think they're just too pretty?" my mother asked me, a high, false tone in her voice. "Who's that? The Shins?"

"Yes, they're new to our faith," Father Kwak said, taking his leave of us.

My mother was wearing a baggy yellow T-shirt with a large crooked pocket over one breast and equally baggy shorts. She put her yellow floppy hat on her head. "Not a very practical outfit," she said. She narrowed her eyes and gave Mrs. Shin a long look that she couldn't have seen but must have felt. Then under her breath, she said to me, "Stay away from them."

As we walked toward one of the waiting buses, I heard Father Kwak say admiringly in English, "I thought there were three daughters—not four!" then give a deep, satisfied laugh.

Our bus was divided like this: men in front, women and young children in the middle, older kids in back. I sat with Cathy, who was a year younger than I. The Shins sat in two rows behind the driver, parents in front of the children. I was curious about them and only paid half attention to Cathy, who was telling me about a boy she liked and an anonymous note she had received. It was a puzzle. But all the while, I kept trying to figure out what my mother didn't like about Mrs. Shin. It was either her tight dress or the way she had hung on her husband's arm or both. My mother had no patience for weakness, especially in women. She was always trying to toughen me up. "Speak up! Stand straight! Make the best of things!" she'd call out to me like a drill sergeant. So far, I'd tried to be a good soldier.

When we arrived at the park, Father Kwak handed Cathy and me cameras and asked us to be the official photographers. That made us shy, though we were pleased

San Toggi

산 토 끼
(San to ggi)

산	토 끼	토 끼 야	어	디	룰	가 느 냐
San	to ggi	to ggi ya	eo	di	reul	ga neu nya
산	고 개	고 개 룰	나	혼	자	넘 어 서
San	go gae	go gae reul	na	hon	ja	neom eo seo

깡 총 깡 총	뛰 면 서	어	디 룰	가 느 냐
ggang chong ggang chong	ddwi myeon seo	eo	di reul	ga neu nya
토 실 토 실	알 밤 을	주	워 —	올 테 야
to sil to sil	al bam eul	ju	weo —	ol te ya

Mountain Rabbit

Mountain rabbit, mountain rabbit,
Where are you going?
Jumping and bouncing, where are you going?

I'm going over the mountain
All by myself,
To pick up chestnuts, big and cracked chestnuts.

with the request. We took off immediately for the beach.

My mother called me back. She hung several plastic bags of food on my arms.

"What did Father Kwak talk to you about?" she asked.

"He wanted us to take pictures for the church," I said.

"Take pictures of people," she said. It was the only piece of advice she ever had regarding photography, and she gave it to me each time.

"OK, OK," I said, walking away.

"And don't lose anything!" she said. "And have fun!"

I caught up with Cathy at the picnic tables. After dumping the bags with the others, we headed down a path to the water. The beach turned out to be a narrow strip of hard, rough sand that didn't stretch very far and was scattered with strands and clumps of dried seaweed. They pinched when we stepped on them. Though it was sunny back home, it was cloudy here, and the brown water that lapped at our feet felt icy.

"So much for swimming," I said.

"Smile!" Cathy said, snapping a picture of me kicking the water.

And that's what we did all day: tell people to smile. We took pictures of boys showing off in the water, pushing each other, and doing handstands. We took pictures of the volleyball game and Mr. Paik, who got knocked hard on the head with the ball and had to sit down. All through lunch, we snapped people eating, their mouths greasy with barbecue, my father with a piece of rice on his chin.

We were a noisy bunch, and the other families that had set up camp near us gave us dirty or amused looks. Some of them stared openly, complaining within earshot that the beach seemed crowded that day. I wondered what Roger would think if he saw us here, so loud and foreign. I thought of how out of place he would feel, maybe as lonely as I felt at school sometimes. I was glad then that we weren't friends, glad that we'd gone all the way to Maine, where he couldn't possibly see me.

Coming out of the brick restroom, I saw Father Kwak and Mrs. Shin talking by the line of trees leading to the woods. Automatically, I raised the camera and took a picture. They turned to look at me in the wake of the click, for a second looking like dolls who

Bridal Robe
Colonial period,
ca. 1930–1940
Silk, damask weave,
embroidery

could only move their heads. Mrs. Shin slowly dropped her arm. I felt uneasy, so I turned away from them and said, "Thanks for the picture." But as I walked away, I saw in my mind what the camera had captured. It floated there, already developed: Mrs. Shin's white hand reaching toward Father Kwak's white collar and his face flushing with pleasure.

I forgot about it until later, when it was time to go home. We couldn't find the Shins, and their three little girls sat forlornly under a tree, waiting, while the sun sparkled down behind them. Father Kwak was sitting with my mother and some other women at one of the picnic tables, talking idly. None of the adults seemed concerned; they all looked sleepy and full, as though waiting for someone else to give the word. But Cathy and I and some of the other kids wanted to get going. We had other lives besides church—lives quicker and more confusing, which we were eager to return to.

"What's he look like again?" asked Hank.

Cathy and I were sitting with two boys our age, Hank and John, at a picnic table dotted with bird droppings. Hank was the taller one and played football for Concord High.

"Forget the guy. *Didja see her?*" John asked. He whistled through the space between his front teeth.

"Hot?"

"What's the temperature of the sun?" He paused and looked at Cathy and me. "I just love her dress," he said in a high falsetto. Then he raised an eyebrow at Hank.

"Oh, *her,*" Hank said and then, more loudly, "Yeah, buddy!" They high-fived each other.

"Whatever," Cathy said. "As if she'd let you near her." I took a picture of Cathy getting up. "Pure fantasy. Are you going to help us find them or not?"

"But we like fantasy," John said, running a palm back and forth over his close-cropped hair.

Hank and John weren't the only ones who thought Mrs. Shin was hot. I'd seen the look in Mr. Lim's eyes as he ate with his fingers across from the Shins: a wide-eyed, tak-

NAOMI LONG

A Dark Balance

for Mary

when we were born
tiger and snake
crouched in our blood

feral, amber-eyed

others never knew
from our disguise,
the disobedience

of a boneyard silence

osprey carcasses
reptilian spines
mammoth tusks

father's ruby trenches
where his mind left him

night after night
a rack of splintered faces
yankee, gook

and mother's southern moon
waning
under the roof

we bid our time—
the snowy ascents,
the mountain ranges

the long distance sight
to ten years ahead

when we'd
turn our skins inside out
and forsake each other

tiger to the forest
snake to the sea

Naomi Long
Eloise and Mary

Then she missed another week. And another. It got cold.

One Saturday in December, I came into the kitchen to find my mother on the phone with Father Kwak. She had on her false charming voice and was stacking empty glass jars while she talked. Her plan this Saturday was to make *kimch'i*. Lying about were the familiar tubs, jars of red pepper and paste, Morton's salt, and piles of wilting cabbage heads. I poured myself a glass of orange juice and turned to leave. My mother motioned with her hand for me to stay.

"That's just terrible," I heard her saying. "Of course, I'll call you right away after I've seen her . . . No, you're right to worry if you haven't been able to reach her . . . I know. This snow is terrible. No, you shouldn't come out here . . . Well, my daughter will drive me. That's what children are for . . . Yes, I promise I'll call just as soon as we get back . . . No, no, please don't thank me. I'm worried myself now . . ."

"That poor man," she said, hanging up. "I can't tell whether he's in love with her or it's really just God, but he certainly does care about her. He gave me his telephone number twice. *Twice!* And he knows I have the church directory. The poor man. He's out of his mind with worry."

"What's wrong?" I asked.

"It's that Shin woman—what's she call herself? Maggalina?"

"Magdalena," I said.

My mother rolled her eyes and said, "A name a Korean person can't even pronounce properly."

"So what's wrong with her?" I asked.

"I don't know," she said. "Father Kwak thinks she might be too sick to answer the phone. He says that when he talked to her last week, she didn't sound well. And now she's stopped answering her phone."

"Could she have gone somewhere?"

"Father Kwak says she wouldn't have the money. C'mon, let's get going. I have to finish this," she said, looking around the kitchen.

I tried to get out of it, but my mother was afraid of driving in the snow. Within minutes, we were bundled up and sitting in the car, our breath coming out in engine puffs.

"Dirty weather," my mother said. She looked at the snow angrily.

I turned on the wipers and backed out of the driveway. I asked my mother why she didn't like Mrs. Shin.

"Oh, she's so tiresome," my mother said. "I don't like people like that—people who need so much attention. People who can't take care of themselves."

I nodded.

"Those people," she said, "they make life seem so hard. They make it seem impossible. But it's not really. It doesn't have to be. You do what you can and hope for the best. If you need to change something, change it. If you can't, ignore it." She leaned back against the seat. "Don't be like your father, brooding over your life."

"I'm not like him," I said.

She looked over at me and said, "Good. I hope you're right."

"What does she do for work?" I asked.

"She's a tailor."

"She's a tailor?" For some reason, that seemed strange. I don't know what I thought her occupation would be. I guess I could never imagine her doing anything except maybe getting dressed up, sitting in front of her mirror, and putting on that everlasting blue eyeshadow. Just then I swerved to avoid a car fishtailing ahead of me, and my mother slapped her chest with one hand and grabbed my arm with the other.

"No more talking!" she said. "Concentrate!"

We found Mrs. Shin's apartment on Front Street above the tailor shop where she worked. It was in a neighborhood of sub shops and package stores close to the old shoe mills. Next to a gray metal door, we saw MAGDALENA scrawled on a small, square piece of paper held up by peeling tape. It flapped when the wind kicked up. We went through the unlocked door and up a flight of stairs to another door. The air felt warm and moist and smelled slightly sour. I knocked. No answer. My mother knocked. Silence. She called out, "Mrs. Shin! Mrs. Shin!"

I jiggled the locked knob. My mother kept banging. After a long while, we heard a kind of croaking coming from the other side. Then the sounds of the locks being undone. Half of Mrs. Shin's face peeked out. She looked like a skeleton. Her skin was so white and thin that I could make out the shape of her sockets. Underneath her chapped lips protruded the line of her teeth. Her cotton nightgown hung on two knobby shoulders, and her hair, usually sprayed and brittle, sat close to her head in wet strands. She hung on the door and weaved.

When she moved aside, my mother went in and dropped our bags on the kitchen table. Then she took off her coat and, guiding Mrs. Shin by the shoulders, turned her away from the door. "Why don't we get you to lie down?" she said. They shuffled down a short hallway and disappeared.

I shut the door and sat down at the kitchen table. From there I could see into the living room, which was empty except for a small TV on a chair and some cushions on the floor. Every blind was drawn, and the air felt old. I was a little shaken. Mrs. Shin looked so hollowed out.

I took off my coat and stood in the living room. The room didn't feel used because the walls were empty and bare, but in the corner by the door was a messy pile of shoes. They were the only things giving life to the room. When I walked down a short hallway, I heard my mother's murmuring voice coming from a room on the left. I opened a closed door to my right and entered a haze of pink. Soft pink walls, a tiny child's bed with a silky pink cover, a pink lamp on a box with the word CLOROX. Against one wall were several boxes of toys, all of them unopened and new. Other than that, there was just a child-sized vanity table. Pink, of course.

Then I saw a sheet of paper taped next to the window. It looked like a drawing. When I stepped closer, I saw a copy of Michelangelo's *God Creating Adam*. Not the whole thing, just the section showing God reaching for Adam, and Adam about to receive the touch. And amazingly—I don't know how Mrs. Shin caught the exact expression—Adam looked up at God utterly, infinitely bored. The angels surrounded God like shadows; Mrs. Shin had left them faceless.

While my mother heated up a can of Campbell's beef and barley soup, she told me to go and sit with Mrs. Shin. She seemed a little shaken too and said the woman looked much worse than she'd expected. *Dammit!* She wished she'd brought along Father Kwak's number.

Mrs. Shin's room was dark and smelled oily. The one window in the room was covered with a dark sheet. Mrs. Shin was lying on a mattress along the wall, her hair spread damp and greasy on the pillow, as if she had just emerged from the sea. Her eyes were closed. I sat down close to her head.

Her beauty, always close to garish, was now frightening. She made me angry and sad, confused as to whether I wanted to pick her up and hold her or shake her to revive her. Instead I said, *Magdalena, Magdalena,* just to hear the sound. It came out harshly from my throat, like a curse.

She turned her head and opened her eyes. *Pop,* just like a bird.

"Who are you?" she asked in Korean. Then she smiled, reached out a thin hand and touched my hair, called me Christina, the name of one of her daughters. *Beautiful, beautiful*, she said in Korean.

I was startled, but stumbled through my Korean. "*Anyunghaseo.* Me, I am . . . the daughter . . . of the Ohs . . ."

She touched her own face, her lips. "Are you me?" she asked wonderingly. "Am I dead?" Then she was suddenly suspicious, her voice growing louder and louder. She struggled to sit up. "Whore!" she called out. "Slut! Crazy mother!"

I was about to repeat what I'd just said, but the look in Mrs. Shin's round eyes stopped me. She was terrified. She looked at me as though I was an assassin come to end her days. As though I was facing her with a knife. Looking in her strangely unblinking eyes, I could almost feel the handle in my grip. It stopped us both cold.

My mother came running in. "What—," she said.

"Aaaaaaaaaaa!" Mrs. Shin screamed. Kicking out her legs, she backed away into a corner and started babbling.

"What's she saying?" I asked my mother.

"I don't know," my mother said, standing uncertainly by the door.

Mrs. Shin began to wail. Then in a flurry of skinny elbows and legs, she kicked the blankets away and crawled toward the door.

"Do something!" I said.

My mother approached Mrs. Shin. When she got close, Mrs. Shin kicked her in the knee. My mother fell, but she didn't look hurt, only stunned. I never saw her stopped by anything before. I walked toward Mrs. Shin, and she turned to kick me. I felt the beatings of a bird, then managed to back away. She screamed, screamed, screamed at us, straining harsh words through her vocal cords but in a language nobody else could understand. Then it turned into pure sound.

She screamed until her face was red, then purple, then a bright, shining white. All the while, she continued kicking at nothing, at the air, at herself. She kicked and jerked until her body gave out. Then, just as suddenly, she went limp and every sound ceased. I saw tears running down into her hairline and heard her ragged breathing whistling in and out between her cracked lips.

My mother rode in the ambulance with Mrs. Shin, who was still disoriented. After everyone left, I put on my coat and locked up the apartment. I was to meet them at the hospital. When I stepped outside, it was dark and cold, and I saw a slip of paper at my feet. MAGDALENA. I picked it up and tried to put it back, but the tape wouldn't stick anymore. No matter how many times I tried, it fluttered down again. MAGDALENA. I shivered as I watched snow drift down in the weak orange glow of the streetlamp and slowly blanket the empty, littered street. I stood there until my hands and face were numb. Then I reached down for the wet, blurred slip of paper and, filled with a fear I couldn't name, stepped out into the bitter night.

Kloe Sookhee Kang *Tracing a Stranger Self*

COMING HOME AGAIN

When my mother began using the electronic pump that fed her liquids and medication, we moved her to the family room. The bedroom she shared with my father was upstairs, and it was impossible to carry the machine up and down all day and night. The pump itself was attached to a metal stand on casters, and she pulled it along wherever she went. From anywhere in the house, you could hear the sound of the wheels clicking out a steady time over the grout lines of the slate-tiled foyer, her main thoroughfare to the bathroom and the kitchen. Sometimes you would hear her halt after only a few steps, to catch her breath or steady her balance, and whatever you were doing was instantly suspended by a pall of silence.

I was usually in the kitchen, preparing lunch or dinner, poised over the butcher block with her favorite chef's knife in my hand and her old yellow apron slung around my neck. I'd be breathless in the sudden quiet, and, having ceased my mincing and chopping, would stare blankly at the brushed sheen of the blade. Eventually, she would clear her throat or call out to say she was fine, then begin to move again, starting her rhythmic *ka-jug;* and only then could I go on with my cooking, the world of our house turning once more, wheeling through the black.

I wasn't cooking for my mother but for the rest of us. When she first moved downstairs she was still eating, though scantily, more just to taste what we were having than from any genuine desire for food. The point was simply to sit together at the kitchen table and array ourselves like a family again. My mother would gently set herself down in her customary chair near the stove. I sat across from her, my father and sister to my left and right, and crammed in the center was all the food I had made—a spicy codfish stew, say, or a casserole of gingery beef, dishes that in my youth she had prepared for us a hundred times.

It had been ten years since we'd all lived together in the house, which at fifteen I had left to attend boarding school in New Hampshire. My mother would sometimes point this out, by speaking of our present time as being "just like before Exeter," which surprised me, given how proud she always was that I was a graduate of the school.

My going to such a place was part of my mother's not so secret plan to change my character, which she worried was becoming too much like hers. I was clever and able enough, but without outside pressure I was readily given to sloth and vanity. The famous school—which none of us knew the first thing about—would prove my mettle. She was right, of course, and while I was there I would falter more than a few times, academically and otherwise. But I never thought that my leaving home then would ever be a problem for her, a private quarrel she would have even as her life waned.

Now her house was full again. My sister had just resigned from her job in New York City, and my father, who typically saw his psychiatric patients until eight or nine in the evening, was appearing in the driveway at four-thirty. I had been living at home for nearly a year and was in the final push of work on what would prove a dismal failure of a novel. When I wasn't struggling over my prose, I kept occupied with the things she usually did—the daily errands, the grocery shopping, the vacuuming and the cleaning, and, of course, all the cooking.

When I was six or seven years old, I used to watch my mother as she prepared our favorite meals. It was one of my daily pleasures. She shooed me away in the beginning, telling me that the kitchen wasn't my place, and adding, in her half-proud, half-deprecating way, that her kind of work would only serve to weaken me. "Go out and play with your friends," she'd snap in Korean, "or better yet, do your reading and homework." She knew that I had already done both, and that as the evening approached there was no place to go save her small and tidy kitchen, from which the clatter of her mixing bowls and pans would ring through the house.

I would enter the kitchen quietly and stand beside her, my chin lodging upon the point of her hip. Peering through the crook of her arm, I beheld the movements of her hands. For *kalbi,* she would take up a butchered short rib in her narrow hand, the flinty bone shaped like a section of an airplane wing and deeply embedded in gristle and flesh, and with the point of her knife cut so that the bone fell away, though not completely, leaving it connected to the meat by the barest opaque layer of tendon. Then she methodically butterflied the flesh, cutting and unfolding, repeating the action until the meat lay out on her board, glistening and ready for seasoning. She scored it diagonally,

then sifted sugar into the crevices with her pinched fingers, gently rubbing in the crystals. The sugar would tenderize as well as sweeten the meat. She did this with each rib, and then set them all aside in a large shallow bowl. She minced a half-dozen cloves of garlic, a stub of ginger-root, sliced up a few scallions, and spread it all over the meat. She wiped her hands and took out a bottle of sesame oil, and, after pausing for a moment, streamed the dark oil in two swift circles around the bowl. After adding a few splashes of soy sauce, she thrust her hands in and kneaded the flesh, careful not to dislodge the bones. I asked her why it mattered that they remain connected. "The meat needs the bone nearby," she said, "to borrow its richness." She wiped her hands clean of the marinade, except for her little finger, which she would flick with her tongue from time to time, because she knew that the flavor of a good dish developed not at once but in stages.

Whenever I cook, I find myself working just as she would, readying the ingredients—a mash of garlic, a julienne of red peppers, fantails of shrimp—and piling them in little mounds about the cutting surface. My mother never left me any recipes, but this is how I learned to make her food, each dish coming not from a list or a card but from the aromatic spread of a board.

I've always thought it was particularly cruel that the cancer was in her stomach, and that for a long time at the end she couldn't eat. The last meal I made for her was on New Year's Eve, 1990. My sister suggested that instead of a rib roast or a bird, or the usual overflow of Korean food, we make all sorts of finger dishes that our mother might fancy and pick at.

We set the meal out on the glass coffee table in the family room. I prepared a tray of smoked-salmon canapés, fried some Korean bean cakes, and made a few other dishes I thought she might enjoy. My sister supervised me, arranging the platters, and then with some pomp carried each dish in to our parents. Finally, I brought out a bottle of champagne in a bucket of ice. My mother had moved to the sofa and was sitting up, surveying the low table. "It looks pretty nice," she said. "I think I'm feeling hungry."

This made us all feel good, especially me, for I couldn't remember the last time she had felt any hunger or had eaten something I cooked. We began to eat. My mother picked up a piece of salmon toast and took a tiny corner in her mouth. She rolled it around for a moment and then pushed it out with the tip of her tongue, letting it fall back onto her plate. She swallowed hard, as if to quell a gag, then glanced up to see if we had noticed. Of course we all had. She attempted a bean cake, some cheese, and then a slice of fruit, but nothing was any use.

She nodded at me anyway, and said, "Oh, it's very good." But I was already feeling lost and I put down my plate abruptly, nearly shattering it on the thick glass. There was an ugly pause before my father asked me in a weary, gentle voice if anything was wrong, and I answered that it was nothing, it was the last night of a long year, and we were together, and I was simply relieved. At midnight, I poured out glasses of champagne, even one for my mother, who took a deep sip. Her manner grew playful and light, and I helped her shuffle to her mattress, and she lay down in the place where in a brief week she was dead.

My mother could whip up most anything, but during our first years of living in this country we ate only Korean foods. At my harangue-like behest, my mother set herself to learning how to cook exotic American dishes. Luckily, a kind neighbor, Mrs. Churchill, a tall, florid young woman with flaxen hair, taught my mother her most trusted recipes. Mrs. Churchill's two young sons, palish, weepy boys with identical crew cuts, always accompanied her, and though I liked them well enough, I would slip away from them after a few minutes, for I knew that the real action would be in the kitchen, where their mother was playing guide. Mrs. Churchill hailed from the state of Maine, where the finest Swedish meatballs and tuna casserole and angel food cake in America are made. She readily demonstrated certain techniques—how to layer wet sheets of pasta for a lasagna or whisk up a simple roux, for example. She often brought gift shoeboxes containing curious ingredients like dried oregano, instant yeast, and cream of mushroom soup. The two women, though at ease and jolly with each other, had difficulty communicating, and this was made worse by the often confusing terminology of Western cuisine ("corned beef," "deviled eggs"). Although I was just learning the language myself, I'd gladly play the interlocutor, jumping back and forth between their places at the counter, dipping my fingers into whatever sauce lay about.

I was an insistent child, and, being my mother's firstborn, much too prized. My mother could say no to me, and did often enough, but anyone who knew us—particularly my father and sister—could tell how much the denying pained her. And if I was overconscious of her indulgence even then, and suffered the rushing pangs of guilt that she could inflict upon me with the slightest wounded turn of her lip, I was too happily obtuse and venal to let her cease. She reminded me daily that I was her sole son, her reason for living, and that if she were to lose me, in either body or spirit, she wished that God would mercifully smite her, strike her down like a weak branch.

In the traditional fashion, she was the house accountant, the maid, the launderer, the disciplinarian, the driver, the secretary, and, of course, the cook. She was also my first basketball coach. In South Korea, where girls' high school basketball is a popular spectator sport, she had been a star, the point guard for the national high school team that once won the all-Asia championships. I learned this one Saturday during the summer, when I asked my father if he would go down to the schoolyard and shoot some baskets with me. I had just finished the fifth grade, and wanted desperately to make the middle school team the coming fall. He called for my mother and sister to come along. When we arrived, my sister immediately ran off to the swings, and I recall being annoyed that my mother wasn't following her. I dribbled clumsily around the key, on the verge of losing control of the ball, and flung a flat shot that caromed wildly off the rim. The ball bounced to my father, who took a few not so graceful dribbles and made an easy layup. He dribbled out and then drove to the hoop for a layup on the other side. He rebounded his shot and passed the ball to my mother, who had been watching us from the foul line. She turned from the basket and began heading the other way.

"*Um-mah,*" I cried at her, my exasperation already bubbling over, "the basket's over *here!*"

After a few steps she turned around, and from where the professional three-point line must be now, she effortlessly flipped the ball up in a two-handed set shot, its flight truer and higher than I'd witnessed from any boy or man. The ball arced cleanly into the hoop, stiffly popping the chain-link net. All afternoon, she rained in shot after shot, as my father and I scrambled after her.

When we got home from the playground, my mother showed me the photograph album of her team's championship run. For years I kept it in my room, on the same shelf that housed the scrapbooks I made of basketball stars, with magazine clippings of slick players like Bubbles Hawkins and Pistol Pete and George (the Iceman) Gervin.

It puzzled me how much she considered her own history to be immaterial, and if she never patently diminished herself, she was able to finesse a kind of self-removal by speaking of my father whenever she could. She zealously recounted his excellence as a student in medical school and reminded me, each night before I started my homework, of how hard he drove himself in his work to make a life for us. She said that because of his Asian face and imperfect English, he was "working two times the American doctors." I knew that she was building him up, buttressing him with both genuine admiration and her own brand of anxious braggadocio, and that her overarching concern was that I might fail to see him as she wished me to—in the most dawning light, his pose steadfast and solitary.

In the year before I left for Exeter, I became weary of her oft-repeated accounts of my father's success. I was a teenager, and so ever inclined to be dismissive and bitter toward anything that had to do with family and home. Often enough, my mother was the object of my derision. Suddenly, her life seemed so small to me. She was there, and sometimes, I thought, *always* there, as if she were confined to the four walls of our house. I would even complain about her cooking. Mostly, though, I was getting more and more impatient with the difficulty she encountered in doing everyday things. I was afraid for her. One day, we got into a terrible argument when she asked me to call the bank, to question a discrepancy she had discovered in the monthly statement. I asked her why she couldn't call herself. I was stupid and brutal, and I knew exactly how to wound her.

Chang-Jin Lee *Stories from the East Village Wall*

COMPASSION

It wasn't the conditions of heat and humidity, peculiar to late summer in New York. It wasn't the stench of trash and softening tar that wafted over pedestrians like a sulfurous cloud. It wasn't the dilapidation of the tenement houses on the route she took from subway station to office. The sight of squatters circling dumpsters until nightfall had become, for her, commonplace. She directed them to shelters with the facility of a crossing guard. When a regular had reappeared last week as a gaunt and mottled corpse, she'd stifled the waves of horror and nausea and expertly sidestepped the police barricade. A mugging, botched. *These things happen,* she told herself firmly. The next morning, she was early for work.

But today was another matter; today she'd behaved badly. The boy deserved an explanation. Surely she owed him that.

They were at the community center where she'd been a counselor for about three months. Deep in the bowels of a converted church, the room that functioned as office space for Sandra and an on-site social worker was painted the flickering blue of fluorescent lighting and tiled with linoleum. Makeshift partitions separated their desks, the barest of nods to privacy. The arrangement suited the social worker just fine. Henna-haired and garrulous, she liked to regale Sandra with anecdotes about her relatives in Port of Spain. *The both of us from countries no one could pick off a map. We got to stick together.* Sandra couldn't find it in her heart to agree.

In the common area, assorted paperbacks with their covers torn or pages missing were crammed onto plywood shelves. A pint-sized refrigerator sighed and hummed in one corner. It was the kind stocked with miniature whiskey bottles and beef jerky in motor lodges; here, it held open cans of condensed milk, tomato soup, wizened apples for runaways. The stuffing oozed through a slash in the back of a sofa meant to suggest the center's informality to adolescent visitors. Not that anyone was duped: Sandra's clients remained wary, gravitating instead to the molded plastic chairs arrayed about the conference table in the middle of the room. There, they were forced to hold their spines straight or hunch forward with unwavering stares like green-leafed plants growing into the sun.

The young man Nano was no exception. Affecting a gait between a shuffle and a swagger, he staked out a chair during his first visit and slumped into it extravagantly, all the while darting his head from side to side as if on a reconnaissance mission. His date of birth she remembered because it coincided with the closing of banks and post offices, the gift of a public holiday. When they filled out forms together, she tried to enliven his deadpan expression with banter about hitting twenty-one. He shrugged and replied that a year made no difference since he rarely got carded at bars and preferred Olde English anyway, obtained in brown paper bags from the corner bodega. With a nice, fat blunt, he added, and offered to hook her up with his dealer. She didn't waste time chatting after that; during their subsequent sessions, she listened to him with a tight, fixed smile. The day she left him, the smile wouldn't thaw.

It was an aberrant moment with a not especially aberrant client. Lord knows he wasn't any more of a burden than the others in need of family placement and drug rehab and GED classes. The story in his files was tragic: a father who refused to acknowledge the results of a one-night stand, a mother with full-blown AIDS. Bounced around by Child Welfare until he got too old to be placed with a foster family. Now he lived downtown in a crumbling Section Eight building with a distant uncle who was on disability insurance and prone to issuing ultimatums when funds ran low. Kid had a week, the uncle told Sandra over the phone; any odd job would do. Sandra's ears burned through the morning's conversation, the uncle's grating *haw-haw* the soundtrack for his belittlement of Nano. *Just between us, he don't got a pot to piss in and never will.*

Sitting at one end of the table, Sandra pushed a bag of potato chips toward her client. He dove for a fistful and crammed it into his mouth, his stubby fingers at the corners trapping any stray crumbs. For fear of gawking, she flipped through her legal pad and uncapped her ballpoint pen.

"OK, Nano," she said, "what do you want to do?"

"Get paid," he said.

"I'll rephrase that."

"I heard you."

"Then let's talk about employment options. Given your education—"

"Why can't you understand? I don't want no stupid-ass job at McDonald's. *Punto*."

Sandra breathed. "There are a number of local businesses where we've placed your peers successfully."

"If it ain't fries, it's chicken, right? Or groceries. Shoes. I ain't having it."

"So these are the jobs you've ruled out. Fine. What about cars? A mechanic's assistant. Are you good with your hands?"

Nano threw down his chips. "Listen to you. Sitting up here saying, Go, get your arms and nails all nasty with grease, and you writing it down with your nice clean pen in your nice clean office."

And which office would that be? Sandra thought irritably. Most of her friends had secured entry-level positions at law firms or publishing houses after graduation. Their salaries were no higher, but there was room for advancement. One classmate working in retail even rated a small wardrobe budget. Conversation with her ran to fabrics and new designers and charity fundraisers plugged in the styles section of the *Sunday Times*. Sandra suspected that it appealed to her friends to claim her, to be able to mention to strangers at dinner parties that they knew someone who worked with inner-city teens—still, in this day and age. Our girl, they would think, their pride commingled with a worldly condescension.

Meanwhile, it was Sandra who had to forgive late paychecks from an organization that was perpetually in arrears and could only afford a janitor three days out of the week. Like everyone else at the center, she'd had her share of clogged toilets, faulty wiring, refuse that escaped a perfunctory sweep and mounted, even in sections of the church with continual foot traffic. She'd taught herself to stash a sweater in her bottom desk drawer in case the boiler broke down, to dress in layers that zipped or unzipped at a moment's notice. Sitting up here, she longed to tell Nano, was hardly worth the view.

"What about that?" he said. "An office job."

"Is that what you'd like? Clerical work?"

"A desk to put my feet up. My own phone. A secretary who makes coffee and gives me the mail—special, you know what I'm sayin'?"

"Nano." Sandra tapped her pen against the edge of the table and shook her head. "You'd be lucky to be the secretary."

She watched him shift his weight into the curve of the chair, hitch up his voluminous jeans, considering. How his mind operated, she hadn't the foggiest. Her gaze fell to his white leather hightops, laces untied but accounted for. For weeks he'd taken to wearing them without the strings. A bona fide trend for these kids, said the social worker, one based on the fact that prisoners' laces were confiscated to prevent their use as weapons. Sandra was willing to bet prison had nothing to do with it for Nano. A fashion statement. Looking the part.

"I'm asking you to be realistic," said Sandra.

"So it's like that."

"What do you suppose goes on in an office? Bill Gates, Michael Eisner—these guys fiddle with their beepers all day?"

"*Mira,* I don't even know who you talking about."

"You can barely read. Filing papers would present a challenge."

From the way he tucked his chin into his chest to avoid her scrutiny—as if he was recoiling from a lit stoveburner—she saw she'd gone too far. He tugged on his gold rope of a chain and narrowed his eyes.

"I guess that sounded brusque," she said.

He wouldn't respond.

"I'm trying to help direct you to job opportunities that best utilize your skills. Do you see that?"

"I got no skills."

Observing an Ox, I Reflect

Poem by Kim Yangshik

*Leaving is not simply leaving
and staying is not simply staying.*

*People and beasts and even plants;
each stays as if leaving
and leaves as if staying.*

*There is no heaven without earth,
neither is there earth without heaven.*

*All created as one in the beginning
remain as one endlessly.*

*Likewise
no one stays without leaving
or leaves without staying.*

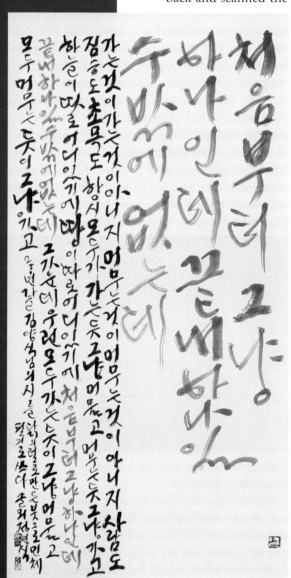

Calligraphy by Jung Hyunsik

wasn't cut out for medical school.

Wearily, she set down the drained tumbler. She knew she should eat. But all she wanted was to lie down on her futon with a wet towel over her face. She tilted her head back and scanned the constellation of gnats and fruit flies that had perished in the etched glass of her light fixtures. She imagined the effort involved in cleaning: hoisting herself onto a footstool, unscrewing the glass, and rinsing it under a faucet until the water ran clear. What she started, she'd feel compelled to finish. She would mop the floor, vacuum the blinds, scour the porcelain planes of the tub until she was loath to use it. Better wait, she decided, and got up to fetch a towel.

Back in Chicago, a woman came on Saturdays to do the housecleaning. She had worked for Sandra's father first, dusting his office, until Sandra's mother complained that it wasn't easy to keep up their ranch house by herself. The cleaning lady was Korean, too, and had a complexion like barley tea and nostrils that fanned out wide. *Chollado,* Sandra's mother said. *Lucky she got off the farm.* Sandra's mother had poreless skin and wore foundation labeled ivory beige. Sometimes she foisted shrink-wrapped packages of candy, left over from Halloween, on the cleaning lady to give to her young son. Sandra couldn't tell what the cleaning lady thought. She would duck her head, reveal her bridgework in a hapless giggle, and protest the giving, but as far as Sandra could tell, there was no greed or unmitigated desire. Sandra's mother was another story. She couldn't have been more convinced of her own largesse if the peanut-butter cups were hundred-dollar bills.

There was her mother. There was her father. They had different motives; did the ends justify the means? Did it count, being kind, when in the process you could savor the petty triumph of parading your big-screen TV and antique celadons before an employee who was obliged to wipe them down? It was a way of queening it over another, cheaply. In all fairness, Sandra had to admit that her mother also gave the cleaning lady a savings bond for her son's education when the boy entered grade school. *Christians share,* Sandra's mother would say, writing generous checks to her church. At least her sanctimony served a purpose.

Sandra wrung her washcloth over the bathroom sink. In the mirror she sucked in her cheeks so that a scar on the left side of her face would show. It became more noticeable when she put on weight or retained water from eating pickled, salted vegetables. The cheek looked sunken where the infection had been—a dent set off by broken capillaries that radiated outward. The skin was swollen there. A few years ago, she had developed an infection in her back gums that manifested itself as an abscess on the outer cheek. She ignored it the first time, and again when it flared up six months later, although she couldn't take big bites or chew her food properly. She was almost proud of weathering the pain, which would dissipate with the blister in a week. Her friends noticed the swelling but didn't know what to say. Was it serious, someone asked; had she gone to a dentist, a dermatologist even? *Why bother?* Sandra responded, and arranged her hair to fall over her cheek. Her body didn't seem hers to own, so she could go about her business oblivious to its needs. As if her body were a squalling infant and the infection merely one in a string of tantrums. But the third time, when a week had come and gone and the abscess had lingered, she could no longer deny the condition or her alarm. The periodontist told her he'd have to pull two teeth because the gums had deteriorated and the sickness spread too far. He added that he'd never seen a case like hers in twenty-eight years of practice. The pronouncement broke her, made her cry. He then lanced the abscess but bungled the job. Incensed, Sandra's father flew her home.

That weekend, he shut his office and operated on her. She sat on the edge of an examining table swaddled with white paper as her father scrubbed down. He dried his arms, then snapped on a pair of latex gloves. A whiff of isopropyl alcohol assailed her. He dampened the end of an extra-long cotton swab with anesthetic and daubed it on her cheek. She crossed her legs at the ankles. The paper underneath her crackled. He brandished a sleek blade; she imagined its terrible precision across a wrist or throat and tried to slow her pulse. Her father didn't have to slow his own. He was intent on making the smallest incision possible, one that would allow the fluids to leach without leaving a permanent mark. As the metal touched her cheek, she shuddered and cried out. The slit was tiny, she later discovered—maybe an eighth of an inch—but at the time, the cutting seemed interminable.

What impressed Sandra most was the detachment her father showed. *This is how he treats his patients,* she thought. Without a surgical mask, his breath was measured, temperate, soothing. He peered at her but was really looking at the affected area, perhaps seeing her as a collection of ill and well areas that he would have to isolate in order to excise the problem. He understood her pain; more important, though, he understood how to assuage it—and without the interference of sentiment. Sandra was reminded of an old brainteaser: *A child is wheeled into an emergency room. The attending*

HOME SPHERES

K.T. was not in bed. I knew where he was; it had happened often enough. Even during the very early months of our marriage, when we lived in a crammed brick building in Cambridge that had no yard or deck, I once found him sitting on the roof in the middle of a breezy autumn night, gazing up at the stars. Because the roof had no railings or side walls, the sight of him on the rough cement at first frightened me. But as I approached him, I could see how completely at ease he was: he had his knees up and his hands locked on top of them, and his black hair waved in the wind. He took my hand and kissed my cold knuckles. "It was such a clear night that I had to come up and take a look," he said. Above us, a waning half-moon hung in the midst of a vast, dark field studded with celestial lights. Things could not have turned out any other way, it seemed. How could I not have fallen in love with this man—gentle, not quite knowable, slender as a doe? When the chill under our feet crawled up into the soft inner folds of our limbs, we retreated down the stairs. And under our light, plush duvet, we warmed each other, the bristling hair on the backs of our necks, goose-bumped buttocks, hardened nipples, round-tipped toes, pale, pink lips.

Now we have a clapboard colonial by the sea, two boys, two cars, and a cat that never seems to be around. K.T. had not wanted a house. He said he didn't want the dark corners that came with space: the creaky basement, the sliver under the staircase, the unfinished attic with yellow, spongy heat filters and crumpled ventilation pipes running along the walls like spilled guts. So he has since become a home-improvement expert, as American as cowboys or astronauts. "There are almost none of them in Korea," he likes to say, "not to mention housekeeping husbands."

He soon filled in the shadowy spots in our home with white sanded shingles and cabinets with ornamental knobs. I guess we owe part of the success of our book-design business to his carpentry skills: without our airy and awesome home office, we might not have found working side by side as pleasurable as we have. Throughout our marriage, we have rarely been apart for more than a day.

The following day, K.T. would be going back to Seoul. For the first time in seventeen years. Only for a week or so—maybe two. The old house he once lived in was going to be torn down.

Here on Marblehead Neck, we live in an insular, well-groomed neighborhood built on a promontory, connected to the Massachusetts shoreline by a narrow, mile-long causeway. But too many nights, my husband sat out on the back porch, at the edge of this huge continent, the tip of this terrestrial world, and let his eyes wander the night sky.

From our bedroom window, I could not see him, but I knew where his eyes were gazing. The night was hazy, the thin crescent moon striped with gray clouds. I spotted twinkles toward the south that I hoped were the constellation Leo, the harbinger of spring, but they kept moving across the sky, eventually turning into blinking blue, red, and white lights. A plane, departing this land, embarking into the night, swift as a feathered dart. But I felt the pull of the earth's gravity on my body, heavy from the weight that I've put on through two births, from the load of K.T.'s unshared memories.

K.T. stood in the check-in line at Logan, his ears attacked by unfamiliar chattering voices. All this Korean conversation baffled him, and he felt as if he should respond even though no one was talking to him.

The uniformed young lady wearing a scarf with the blue, red, and white whirl of *taegeuk* patterns said, "*Myeotgae shijyo?*" K.T. could not understand her right away. How many? How many what? "Your luggage—how many, sir?" she asked again in English. "*Hana, hanaipnida.*" He answered that he had one, then quickly realized he had used a verb form much too formal. She assigned him a seat, giving him the boarding information in kind, slow Korean. "*Gomawoyo,*" he thanked her, this time satisfied with his verb. The woman gave him an impersonal smile.

He turned to look for Melanie and the boys. They were sitting next to a family of grandparents, many kids, and a baby. Passengers from the flight that had arrived from Seoul were pouring out, and Melanie waved, standing up to make herself seen in the crowd. Surrounded by the round, Korean faces, his family suddenly appeared foreign: two beautiful, exotic boys and a broad-shouldered, brunette woman in chinos and an L.L. Bean parka. K.T. realized that what he was wearing was almost identical to Melanie's clothes, but the similarity only seemed to heighten their differences.

K.T.'s eight-year-old son, Garrett, was the one with Asian features—black hair and dark-brown eyes, darker skin—while his younger child, Tyler, definitely looked more Caucasian, his hair brown like his mother's. Once when Garrett was a baby, a cashier at the supermarket had remarked that he was adorable and had asked Melanie, "Where did you get him?" The cashier had assumed that Garrett was adopted from overseas, which was not uncommon in their predominantly white town. But it seemed to K.T. that neither Garrett nor Tyler looked like Melanie or him. He had heard this was often the case with mixed-race children. Rather, each was a darker or lighter version of the other—both possessing deep eyes lined with thick lashes, small but distinct noses, and oval faces with delicate, sharp chins. In K.T.'s eyes, they were the loveliest creations.

It was 9 P.M., way past the boys' bedtime, and K.T. felt bad about having dragged them to the airport. Tyler was tugging at his arm, asking for a ride on the tall escalator that led up to the departure area. K.T. realized that two hours would be too long a wait for the kids.

"Will you be OK?" Melanie asked.

"Don't worry, I'll find my way back," he said, and she smiled a sad, complicated smile. *Back where?* she seemed to be asking. *Back home to Korea? Back home to us?* K.T. pulled her close and kissed her cheeks, lingering for a short while to breathe in the childlike smell of her hair and skin. Her body, ample and fleshy in his arms, calmed his uncertainties. He wouldn't turn away from his old home as he had done before when his father, then his birth mother, the concubine, and just last year, his father's legitimate widow, passed away, one after another, as if they were faithfully taking turns getting hit in a silent, slow game of dodge ball.

K.T. knelt on one knee to hug the boys. Tyler still kissed him, but Garrett only brushed his cheek timidly, and K.T. feigned a punch on his arm, which made him laugh.

"So, you guys decide on a wish list? What do you want me to bring back?" K.T. asked.

"Lots and lots of toys!" Tyler said.

"I want a book," Garrett said softly. "A book with Korean action heroes. Like Superman!"

"OK, I'll give it a try," K.T. said and then stood up, running his hand through the boys' hair.

They left, walking through the sliding doors into the frigid night, and K.T. was alone in a crowd of strangers with strangely familiar faces.

Around midnight a week before, K.T. and I were sitting in front of the computer screen with bloodshot eyes, trying to wrap up a 450-page history book that had taken painfully long to finish, when Ki-hun called about the old house. Ki-hun is K.T.'s only family now, though they have never lived under the same roof. The last time he had called was a year before, with news that their father's wife, the woman who had raised K.T. in the old house, had died. Deaths formed the only occasion for these short, businesslike phone calls from the other side of the northern hemisphere. This time, it was the death of the house, to make room for a high-rise building. And though K.T. was not entitled to any of the inheritance because he had given up his Korean citizenship, Ki-hun said he would preserve his brother's fair share, looking

217

Seasonal Flowers and Birds,
with Chinese Couplets
Chosŏn dynasty
Ink and colors on cotton

K.T. vaguely recalled seeing a CNN report about the demolition of the Japanese Imperial Government-General Building, the most vivid architectural remnant of Korea's colonial years. He wondered how he could not have noticed its absence on the northern tip of Taepyeong-ro—this imposing structure that once blocked from view the palatial grounds of the conquered Joseon dynasty.

Only after they were on the highway did it occur to K.T. that he should have called Melanie at the hotel. By the time he got to Suwŏn, it would be almost midnight at home. Would he be able to make an international call at the restaurant? Indistinct, industrial blocks of concrete and stifling layers of pointed hills made up the scenery outside the window. He felt fatigue closing in on him. Though blurry and uninviting, what he saw seemed much more real than the quaint townscapes of Marblehead, a historical settlement with a proudly and beautifully restored colonial past. The colorful playground, gold sand, and sailboats gliding past rolling rock cliffs—the backdrop of his everyday life—felt removed, like commercial photographs categorized according to a designer's needs. He closed his eyes. His body was still clinging to Eastern Standard Time, but even with his eyes shut, he knew where he was.

Ki-hun was the child that wasn't supposed to be. The same could be said of K.T., but their father's wife, unable to bear a child, formally accepted him as her son. She then forbade his birth mother—his father's concubine—to have anything more to do with the Hahn family. However, even after K.T. came to live in the Hahn household at age five, his father continued his relationship with his mother, a glamorous but uneducated woman twenty years younger, and Ki-hun was born.

K.T. could remember his first night in the old house. Alone in his *sarangbang* quarters and missing terribly his mother's perfumed hair, he somehow realized that he mustn't cry, mustn't make a scene in his father's house. During his years in that dark, majestic house, he made efforts not to stand out. But on the days when the entire Hahn clan gathered at the house for *jesa,* the Confucian ancestral rites, his mere existence would become unbearable. When the worshipping ceremony was about to start and the women were busy with food preparation, his birth mother would come pounding on the gate, wearing one of her many flamboyant flared dresses and carrying Ki-hun as if he were her entry pass. She would claim that the baby had every right to join his father in the main *sarangchae,* but the women of the house would refuse to look at her. In the end, K.T.'s mother would make him carry Ki-hun up the ill-lighted path to the *sarangchae.* K.T. would stand at the very back, behind the men in their black suits and *hanbok* coats, and then put Ki-hun on the floor to do his two head-to-floor bows. After it was over, his mother would leave, carrying a basket full of food from the ritual table: persimmons and pears, slices of pan-fried fish fillet, rice-cake balls rolled in red bean powder. An envelope of glossy new bills was probably stashed underneath.

Afterwards, nobody would talk about her, or Ki-hun.

The lunch now laid before K.T. was as elaborate as the *jesa* food, but everything tasted like sand to his jet-lagged tongue. He was with Ki-hun at a restaurant serving traditional court cuisine. The tall glass windows looked out on a centuries-old fortress. At the table next to them sat a group of elderly tourists with wide-brimmed sun hats and cameras. Their guide was giving them a lecture about the fort and the young and benevolent king who built it to honor his murdered father, a mad crown prince. The guide, a young woman with thick and bright makeup, spoke in an animated tone that made K.T. quiver slightly.

"Construction starts next week," Ki-hun said, wiping the corners of his mouth with his napkin.

Would I have recognized him if I had run into him on the street? K.T. thought. Ki-hun's face was stern and square, bearing no trace of the adolescent acne that had been erupting like volcanoes of discontent the last time K.T. had seen him. And he had turned out to be the son that their father had wanted: surefooted and ambitious, someone like their father himself.

"I owe much to you and your wife," K.T. said. "The funerals and all the family affairs—I have nothing to say for myself." He tried to use all the expressions of polite gratitude that he could summon.

Ki-hun was quiet for a minute, taking a sip of his ice-cold plum tea. "I'll set up an appointment with my lawyer tomorrow afternoon so that you can go over the entire estate," he said conclusively.

"That's not necessary," K.T. stammered. "Really, you don't have to do that."

"No, I'm glad you came. I had a lot of paper work to clear up since the funeral, and now that you're here, we can finally talk actual figures."

"That is not why I came," K.T. said. He put down his chopsticks abruptly.

"When we spoke on the phone, I made it quite clear that I'm going to be fair about sharing the profit from the construction of the new building." Ki-hun looked away from K.T. and toward the stone walls of the fort. "Let's at least try to be honest about this. You don't have to pretend as if you don't care about the money—as if you're too noble for that kind of thing. You're not our father."

Part of K.T. wished Melanie were with him, as a reminder of another sphere of life he had, of the small but safe corner that he inhabited in America. But at the same time, he was relieved his wife and sons were not here to see this. Melanie would still be up, waiting for his call; she was never good at falling asleep by herself. But K.T. could not deny that, for the moment, the distance created by the oceans and continents between them was comforting and inevitable.

"But I don't want that money," he said.

"Then what do you want?" Ki-hun spoke like a jaded lawyer, unafraid to meet K.T.'s gaze across the table. "So why are you here then? Are you here to tell me we should preserve the house as a family treasure? To claim that you are the official heir to the Hahn legacy, the high and proud spirit?" He swiftly folded his napkin and put it on the table, then lifted his hand for the check as if he were leaving his courtroom, declaring the case closed.

"I don't want this," Garrett said, pushing his dinner plate away. I had heated up the leftover sweet-and-sour pork and fried rice.

"Sorry, guys. I promise I'll cook something tomorrow," I said, trying to hide my sigh with a spoonful of rice.

"It's yummy. I like it all the time!" Tyler said, licking his fingers.

"I never want to eat this stuff again," Garrett said. "Can I be excused?"

"But why?" Tyler asked.

"No," I told Garrett. "I said we'll have something else tomorrow. What is this about—you always ask for Chinese takeout."

"No, you don't understand!" Garrett said, kicking the table, and I finally realized that this had nothing to do with dinner.

"Honey, what is it?" I asked, kneeling next to Garrett's chair, my hand on his legs. Garrett had his arms crossed and his head dunked low. I lifted his chin. "Come on, big guy."

"Billy Crowse called Anna and me this word." My heart sank. This was something K.T. and I expected would happen at one point—a rite of passage we'd handle like any other growing pain—but still, my heart sank. Anna was Garrett's classmate: a pretty, porcelain-faced adoptee from China. "*Chinks,* he said. And he told the other kids that we had to come live here because there was no food in our country, and it was horrible, so no one could live there, and now it's like a desert—everything's dead."

I held his hand. "But you know that that's not true, right?" I wanted to pull him into my arms, but did not want to make this incident any more dramatic.

"Yeah, I guess," Garrett said, wiggling his sticky fingers inside my hand. "So you know what I told him?" His face was now beaming. "I said my dad was going to bring me the coolest superhero books and toys from Korea and I'll never let him near them."

"Never?" I said, squeezing his hand.

"Well, maybe if he says he's sorry." I let myself give him a kiss on the cheek.

After three days, K.T. still hadn't called. My initial panic had passed. For me now, it was about what awaited us when he came back. Everything seemed to be in a fog except for my own realization that we would not be the same.

There was a story that K.T. remembered. Among the many Korean legends of goblins, tricksters, dragon slayers, and vicious stepmothers—everyone's story not so different, after all—the tale of Hong Gil-dong was chivalrous and uplifting, surely something Garrett would like. In white *beoseon* and straw-woven shoes, Gil-dong was a master of martial arts, jumping above trees and defeating the enemy with a kick. He could transform himself into anything he wanted to, make a thousand replicas of himself by blowing into a strand of his hair. Like Robin Hood, he was the king of good thieves, stealing from the rich to give to the poor—an ill-fated young man who overcame social stigma. This swashbuckling hero was Korea's most famous bastard son.

In high school, K.T. had studied a chapter of *Hong Gil-dong Jeon,* a seventeenth-century novel written in the style of a fictional biography. This was also when he learned the term *seoja*—sons born to secondary wives. It was in a lecture explaining the social status of these illegitimate sons, to provide a context for the Hong Gil-dong tale. When Gil-dong first set out on the road, he lamented his fate of having lived under the same roof with his noble father, the master of the house, yet having been forbidden to address him as Father; Gil-dong's mother was a servant, a slave.

The year K.T. was preparing to leave for the States, Ki-hun was a high-school sophomore. Constantly in trouble, he assaulted his teacher soon after the spring semester started and was suspended from school for several months. The day K.T. received his admission letter to Tufts, he took Ki-hun out to a pub near his university. Ki-hun seemed pleased at being treated like an adult, but did not lower his shield for the brother he rarely saw. K.T. realized that telling Ki-hun he'd soon be leaving was not going to be easy; instead, he brought up the incident with the teacher.

"*Ssip-saekki.*" Back then, Ki-hun spat out profanities as if they were watermelon seeds. "He knew. That's why he kept getting on my case."

"What do you mean?"

"I got into a fight trying to defend some weaklings, and the guy called me in, slapped my face, and said with this ugly smirk, 'Who do you think you are, Hong Gil-dong or something?'"

SUE KWOCK KIM

Montage with Neon, Bok Choi, Gasoline, Lovers & Strangers

None of the streets here has a name,
but if I'm lost
tonight I'm happy to be lost.

Ten million lanterns light the Seoul avenues
for Buddha's Birthday,
ten million red blue green silver gold moons

burning far as the eye can see in every direction
& beyond,
"one for every spirit,"

voltage sizzling socket to socket

as thought does,
firing & firing the soul.

Lashed by wind, flying up like helium balloons

or hanging still
depending on weather,

they turn each road into an earthly River of
    Heaven
doubling & reversing
the river above,

though not made of much:
colored paper, glue, a few wires,
a constellation of poor facts.

I can't help feeling giddy.
I'm drunk on neon, drunk on air,
drunk on seeing what was made

almost from nothing: if anything's here
it was built
out of ash, out of the skull-rubble of war,

the city rising brick by brick
like a shared dream,
every bridge & pylon & girder & spar a miracle,

when half a century ago
there was nothing
but shrapnel, broken mortar-casings, corpses,

the War Memorial in Itaewon counting
MORE THAN 3 MILLION DEAD, OR MISSING—
still missed by the living, still loved beyond reason,

monument to the fact
no one can hurt you, no one kill you
like your own people.

I'll never understand it.
I wonder about others I see on the sidewalks,
each soul fathomless—

strikers & scabs walking through Kwanghwamoon,
or "Gate of Transformation by Light,"
riot police rapping nightsticks against
    plexiglass-shields,

hawkers haggling over cellphones or silk shirts,
shaking dirt from *chamae* & bok choi,
chanting price after price,

fishermen cleaning tubs of cuttlefish & squid,
stripping copper carp,
lifting eels or green turtles dripping from tanks,

vendors setting up *pojangmachas*
to cook charred silkworms, broiled sparrows,

frying sesame-leaves & mung-bean pancakes,

hanyak peddlars calling out names of cures
for sickness or love—
*crushed bees, snake bile, ground deer antler, chrysanthemum
    root,*

the grocer who calls me "daughter" because I look
    like her,
for she has long since left home,
bus drivers hurtling past in a blast of diesel-fumes,

dispatchers shouting the names of stations,
lovers so tender with each other
I hold my breath,

men with hair the color of scallion root
playing *paduk*, or GO,
old enough to have stolen overcoats & shoes from
    corpses,

whose spirits could not be broken,
whose every breath seems to say:
after things turned to their worst, we began again,

but may you never see what we saw,
may you never do what we've done,
may you never remember & may you never forget.

K.T. could still see Ki-hun's glimmering, intoxicated eyes staring into his beer mug; he looked like a beast waiting for the right moment to attack. K.T. promised himself that he would soon take Ki-hun away with him. But while K.T. struggled to make a living after dropping out of his Ph.D. program, Ki-hun quickly transformed himself into a law student at Seoul National University, lifting, kicking, pulling his bruised life out of the rubble.

Ki-hun sent K.T. the keys to the old house. K.T. had not shown up at the meeting with the lawyer and two days later Kim-*gisa* brought him the keys, with no message attached.

The distance from the hotel to the house was not far, but to get to the other end of Taepyeong-ro, K.T. had to cross several rotaries and intersections. Over the weekend, K.T. had been watching the crowded city from his room, feeling as if he were in a capsule suspended between time zones. From up high, the road to the old neighborhood of Naeja-dong had not seemed too complicated, but once inside the underground walkways, K.T. kept getting lost. He bumped into the throngs of people saturating the labyrinthine tunnels and was confused by the numerous exits. Finally, he made it out to

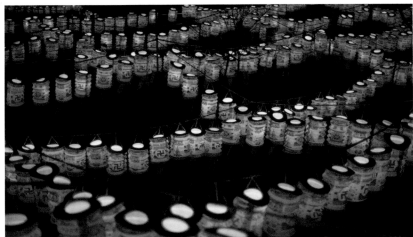

the northern tip of the boulevard and faced the Gwanghwamun Gate. With the Japanese Imperial Government-General Building gone, the view was open all the way to the mountain ridges of Bugak-san; the spiky granite peaks showed off the green grandeur of spring.

Wind slapped K.T.'s face. It scratched his skin and stung his eyes. The weather reports had warned against *hwangsa,* the strong winds that carried yellow sands from China every spring. This year, the winds were terribly severe, the reports said. Many of the pedestrians were wearing scarves or cotton masks over their mouths, which made them appear even more foreign. K.T. recalled the dusty, dry winds of his past. The sharp sensation of grainy sand hitting his skin felt completely alien, the winds barely weakened during their long travel across the Gobi Desert to the Korean peninsula.

Many times, K.T. had imagined being transported back to the old house, unable to escape the grasp of a ghostly hand. But he had never pictured himself making his way back like this: step by step, through wind and dust. Nevertheless, he navigated every crossing and corner without making a single wrong turn, even though all the old neighborhood storefronts—the confectioner's shop, the photo parlor, the public bathhouse—had been replaced with four- or five-story buildings, their facades covered with the competing signs of accountants, courier services, travel agencies, and public notaries.

Karen Hong   *Girls with Guns*

THE LONE NIGHT CANTINA

T he Lone Night Cantina was not a real cowboy bar. In those places, imagined Annie Yung, in those roadside joints outside of Cheyenne or Amarillo, just off a two-lane highway with pickups made in the good ol' U.S. of A. parked in the dirt lot, the men angled their sweat-stained Stetsons over the eyes and were the picture of stoic reserve. They stood leaning the small of their backs against the counter, an elbow crooked behind for support, pelvis swung out, a boot crossed at the ankle to touch the floor with a dusty, permanently curled toe. Once in a while a cowboy removed the Camel dangling from the corner of his mouth, flicked some ashes, and raised his Bud for a slow swig, condensation from the bottle leaving a wet imprint on his jeans, but otherwise there was no movement, no justification for the odd sense of expectancy and danger in the bar, the feeling that with a single misguided look, anything could happen.

"You're dreaming," Annie's sister, Evelyn, had told her. "This lonesome cowboy thing, it's all a myth. It's something straight out of the movies."

At thirty-eight Annie was old enough to know that her sister was right, and although she also knew that the only real cowboy who had ever set foot inside the Lone Night Cantina was its owner, Rob Wilson, and he was too much the gentleman to wear his hat with the big scoop brim indoors, the knowledge had not stopped her from coming here for four nights in a row. Despite its location in Rosarita Bay, which was as suggestive of the American West as a piña colada, despite the fact that the bar was usually dead quiet, lucky to draw the handful of people it had this Friday night, the place possessed, as she had tried to explain to Evelyn, the right feel. The bridles and ropes hanging from the walls, the jukebox stacked with the best of the country and western standards, the long oak bar counter, smoothed down in warps where forearms had rested to cradle drinks, the small framed photograph of Rob during his rodeo days, chasing a calf on his horse, swinging a flat hornloop over his head—everything gave Annie the impression that, at least for a few hours, she was where she thought she belonged, in the cheatin' heart world of Loretta Lynn and Patsy Cline songs, in one of those rotted-wood, corrugated-tin, hole-in-the-wall, spit 'n' sawdust saloons in the desert which had a screen door that banged too hard but no one bothered to fix.

"Look at this face," Rob Wilson said, laying the *Daily World News* on the bar counter so Annie could see. He tapped the picture of Delores Hoots when she was fifteen— beaming with honey-eyed innocence for the high school photographer. The adjacent picture was of an old woman, hair shock-white, eyes ablaze and teeth bared in a demented snarl. The headline read: FATHER LOCKS DAUGHTER IN BASEMENT FOR 30 YEARS FOR NECKING!

"Believe that?" said Rob. "Maybe in a backwoods town, with a Baptist preacher

Bobby Cho was the systems engineer Annie had been living with for the past three years. She had yet to tell Evelyn that Bobby had proposed to her, and that she had turned him down, after which he accepted a long-standing job offer from a company in Bellevue, Washington. "No, Ev, it's not because of Bobby. I told you, I'm not busted up about it."

"Why'd you break up with him all of a sudden? What did he do? I always thought Bobby was so nice."

"You and everyone else." She was sick of hearing how great Bobby was—gentle, sweet, adoring, solvent, not terrible-looking. "Just let me have my fun, OK?" Annie said.

Evelyn regarded her ruefully and said, "Your hair, it looks awful."

She had bleached it blond a week ago, the evening after she had taken Bobby to San Francisco International for his flight to Seattle. The next day, no longer able to stand their empty apartment in San Jose, she had decided to visit Evelyn, and, driving over the hill on Highway 71, she picked up a country station—transmitting weakly from Salinas—on the car radio. They were broadcasting "Crazy" as part of an all Patsy Cline special. Annie had heard country music before, but never with this pure, deep-voiced insistence of truth which, at exactly the right moment, would crack and quaver and break your heart. "Walking After Midnight" came on afterward, then "I Fall to Pieces" and "Lonely Street," and, as Annie listened on through the squawk and static, constantly having to wobble the radio dial, she felt as if she had been hit by religion. There it was, she marveled. There it was. Every bane of life imaginable: dreaming, hurting, leaving, and lying, cheating, missing, drinking, loving, and crying. Mawkish and melodramatic, but the pain was real.

When she arrived in Rosarita Bay, she bought every Patsy Cline CD she could find and mooned around Evelyn's house all day, playing song after song, only going out to get more CDs, her devotion growing to include Emmylou Harris, Kitty Wells, and Hank Williams. Then by chance on Tuesday, trying to park near Tommy's Tunes, she turned off Main Street onto Sutter Road and saw the Lone Night Cantina—its name in red neon tubes designed to look like ropes—and just like that, she had a place in which, she could imagine, lived the soul of those plaintive country songs, a place where losers in love could knock back disappointment with a couple of cold ones, where the unlucky and the forsaken could commiserate in holy, countrified silence. She had found, as Patsy Cline had bidden, a place to sit and weep.

In the old days there was a superstition among sailors: when you crossed the equator for the first time, you pierced your earlobe and stuck a gold ring in the hole. The tradition was gradually abandoned, but Joe Konki, as he traversed the equator off the north shore of Papua New Guinea two years ago, had had his ear pierced anyway, an Aussie named

Mary Long *Circus Cowboy*

Shank ministering to him with two ice cubes and a needle sterilized by a Zippo lighter. The inside of the gold earring was engraved later with the longitude, 147° E.

Annie didn't learn any of this for a few hours, but she did notice the earring when Joe first walked into the Lone Night Cantina. She liked it. She liked everything about him, in fact. He was rangy, a lean six-two with straight brown hair parted somewhere near the middle and swept back casually, as if he had run his hand through it for so long, his hair just grew that way now. He had a tanned, narrow face, the evidence of about forty hard-worn years beginning to line the skin, recessed sockets making the eyes seem dry and black, and a square chin you couldn't chisel any better. To Annie, he was perfect. With his leather jacket, black T-shirt, bandy-legged jeans, and scuffed cowboy boots, he was the lonesome stranger personified, a living testament to when men were men.

Flapping the rain off his jacket, he surveyed the bar from where he stood beside the door, glancing at the only other customers, two young couples at a table. Then Joe looked straight at Annie, who was straddling a stool and looking straight at him, but his gaze passed right over her to Rob Wilson. As Joe strode up to him, Rob, wiping the suds from his hands with a towel, said, "What can I get you?"

"You serve any food here?" His voice was granular and had a trace of a drawl she couldn't quite finger.

"Sorry. All I got for you is Beer Nuts."

"OK, a bag of those and a Corona." He took off his jacket. There was a tattoo of a dragon, once indigo and now faded to a kind of smalt blue, on his right forearm, and a Rolex watch on his left wrist. No ring.

"Howdy," Annie said sprightly.

He turned to her slowly, as if he wasn't sure she was speaking to him, studied her with curiosity, and said, very flatly, "Hi." He turned back, tugged several crumpled dollar bills out of his jeans pocket to pay Rob, and moved across the room to a table in the corner. Annie watched him prop a boot on a chair, take a swallow of his beer, and open the bag of nuts.

The song on the jukebox, "Pancho and Lefty," ended, and Annie lifted two quarters from her pile of change on the counter and crossed the room to the machine. She took her time picking a song. Finally she dropped one of the quarters into the slot and punched the buttons for Kris Kristofferson's "Help Me Make It Through the Night." She waited for the record to begin, flipping the second quarter in the air, then, with the coin held loosely in her palm, she lazily twirled around as if to go back to her stool.

Mary Long *Circus Cowboy*

Shank ministering to him with two ice cubes and a needle sterilized by a Zippo lighter. The inside of the gold earring was engraved later with the longitude, 147° E.

Annie didn't learn any of this for a few hours, but she did notice the earring when Joe first walked into the Lone Night Cantina. She liked it. She liked everything about him, in fact. He was rangy, a lean six-two with straight brown hair parted somewhere near the middle and swept back casually, as if he had run his hand through it for so long, his hair just grew that way now. He had a tanned, narrow face, the evidence of about forty hard-worn years beginning to line the skin, recessed sockets making the eyes seem dry and black, and a square chin you couldn't chisel any better. To Annie, he was perfect. With his leather jacket, black T-shirt, bandy-legged jeans, and scuffed cowboy boots, he was the lonesome stranger personified, a living testament to when men were men.

Flapping the rain off his jacket, he surveyed the bar from where he stood beside the door, glancing at the only other customers, two young couples at a table. Then Joe looked straight at Annie, who was straddling a stool and looking straight at him, but his gaze passed right over her to Rob Wilson. As Joe strode up to him, Rob, wiping the suds from his hands with a towel, said, "What can I get you?"

"You serve any food here?" His voice was granular and had a trace of a drawl she couldn't quite finger.

"Sorry. All I got for you is Beer Nuts."

"OK, a bag of those and a Corona." He took off his jacket. There was a tattoo of a dragon, once indigo and now faded to a kind of smalt blue, on his right forearm, and a Rolex watch on his left wrist. No ring.

"Howdy," Annie said sprightly.

He turned to her slowly, as if he wasn't sure she was speaking to him, studied her with curiosity, and said, very flatly, "Hi." He turned back, tugged several crumpled dollar bills out of his jeans pocket to pay Rob, and moved across the room to a table in the corner. Annie watched him prop a boot on a chair, take a swallow of his beer, and open the bag of nuts.

The song on the jukebox, "Pancho and Lefty," ended, and Annie lifted two quarters from her pile of change on the counter and crossed the room to the machine. She took her time picking a song. Finally she dropped one of the quarters into the slot and punched the buttons for Kris Kristofferson's "Help Me Make It Through the Night." She waited for the record to begin, flipping the second quarter in the air, then, with the coin held loosely in her palm, she lazily twirled around as if to go back to her stool.

The quarter flew out of her hand and pinged, bounced, and slid until it came to a stop not more than three feet from Joe's table in the corner, exactly where she had planned.

Sheepishly Annie walked over and retrieved the quarter and, as she was straightening up, said to him, "I've got butter for hands." He regarded her blankly. He popped a nut into his mouth and crunched down on it. She touched the back of the chair occupied by his boot and asked, "Mind if I sit down?"

"Huh?"

"Use some company?" she asked in her best cowgirl lilt.

He stared at her expressionlessly. Perhaps five full seconds passed before he lifted his foot and let her take the seat.

She extended her hand. "My name's Annie Yung."

He gave her a limp shake. "Joe."

"Joe what?"

"Konki."

"Pleased to meet you, Joe Konki." In her nervousness, she forgot the trick of using her tongue and flashed a big, toothy, salmon-pink gum smile. "Where you from? You ain't from around here, are you?"

He shook a Newport from his pack and lit the cigarette with a match. He blew out smoke, and said, "Florida, originally."

"Yeah? What parts?"

"Gainesville."

"So you're just passing through Rosarita Bay or something?"

He nodded. "Had some business to take care of here. Heading to San Diego in the morning."

"San Diego. That where you living now? Or you going back to Gainesville?"

"I don't know. I just got back to the States a couple of nights ago. I was overseas, in Indonesia, for the last two years."

"Yeah? Doing what?"

He drank from his Corona. "I worked boats in the Molucca Islands."

Annie fancied the idea: it was exotic and adventuresome; he had found the frontier exhausted but had kept going west. "Must've been humid as hell down there," she said to him.

He tilted his head back. "Why are you talking like that?"

"Like what?"

"Like some yahoo." He leaned across the table and brandished his watch. "That accent's about as real as this Rolex."

"Listen, let's just forget it," Annie said, standing up.

"Hey, sit down, sit down," he said. He ran his hand through his hair. "I wouldn't mind talking to you, but let's be straight with each other, all right?"

She remained standing. She didn't know what she had expected from him, but she certainly had not thought he would confront her like this.

He was smiling at her now.

Grudgingly, she said in her normal voice, "All right."

"Let's start over," he said. "My name's Joe Konki."

She settled back down in the chair. "My name's Annie Yung."

They sat in the Lone Night Cantina and talked for close to three hours. He told her about his short-lived boxing career out of high school, traveling the club circuit in Florida until he fought a southpaw and didn't keep his right up to protect his chin. After the jawbone healed, he enlisted in the Navy, making ports of call in the Philippines, where he had the dragon tattoo drawn on his arm, in Japan, and even in Korea.

"Han'gŭl mal chokum aro?" Annie asked. Do you know a little Korean?

"Uh, *kamsa-hamnida,*" Joe said. Thank you.

After his tour was up, he returned to Gainesville, where he worked construction for ten years. Then he moved to Louisiana, Morgan City, and got a job offshore on the rigs. He enjoyed the life, seven days on and seven days off, the hurricanes and Cajun food and whipping chains, but he had this hankering to go somewhere, and on a whim he took off to Southeast Asia, tramp-steaming between Menado, Amboina, and Banjermasin.

"One time," he said, "we heard on the radio that a cargo ship lost three containers in the water, and we raced over there, thinking VCRs, oh, man, fur coats, and what do we find when we open them up? Cocoa Puffs. Three containers—forty-footers each—of Cocoa Puffs."

"It almost sounds like you were a pirate on the high seas."

"No, mostly it was smuggling," Joe said.

Annie raised her eyebrows.

"Joking," he said.

"Sure you are," she said. "You know, Rosarita Bay has an outlaw history. My sister told me during Prohibition the town was filthy with rumrunners and bordellos."

"You'd never know it, looking at it now."

"You got that right."

He said he didn't have a clue where he'd go from here. He had recently come into an unexpected windfall—he alluded to some sort of an inheritance—and would use the money to travel. He'd go to San Diego to visit some old naval buddies, then Vegas, then Houston to see his mother, then maybe Europe.

Annie told him that in comparison to his life, hers had been fairly dull. Strikingly normal, actually. Grew up across the Bay in Walnut Creek, went to Caltech, and had worked for a series of software companies in the Silicon Valley. Now, like everyone else, she was on the Internet bandwagon. "It's not as glamorous as you might think," she said. "I'm going blind, looking at all those lines of code."

She had been married twice in her twenties. Her first husband had left her for another woman, her second had left her for another man.

"You're kidding," Joe said.

"Sadly, no."

The first marriage—right after she graduated from Caltech—had lasted all of a year. Phillip Han had been her roommate's brother, and he was like no Korean she had ever met. He taught *hapkido,* wore a ponytail, rode a Harley, and wanted to be a movie star, the next Bruce Lee. He was wild, fun, and very, very cool. He was also terrible with money, squandering all of hers since he didn't make any, and he was an inveterate philanderer. Annie came home one night to find him in bed with two coked-out starlets, and Phillip was unrepentant, telling her, "Man, you are such a drag. Get the fuck out of here, you fat cow."

Her second husband, Nils Sigridsson, was a middle-aged Swedish architect with a gorgeous house in Sunnyvale. He had impeccable taste and manners, and they spent summers antiquing up and down the coast and winters skiing in Tahoe, where he patiently tutored her on the bunny slopes. All was perfect, until he became impotent. They began trying things, benign attempts at being risqué escalating to porn videos and rape fantasies, anal sex and bondage. They entered couples therapy, and Nils fell in love with another husband in the group, a lapsed Mormon podiatrist.

Annie told none of this to Joe—it wasn't her favorite subject—instead asking, "You been married?"

"Once."

"What happened?"

"Let's just say it ended badly, too."

They got on the topic of bad dates, and Annie had plenty to recount—a lot of them with white men afflicted with AHF, Asian Hottie Fetish, wanting her to titter with high-cheeked China-doll timidity, or vamp it up as a wanton Suzie Wong, a dirty little yum-yum girl. "You've spent a lot of time in Asia," she said to Joe. "You're not like that, are you?"

"No," he said, blushing.

Then there was the guy she met at a party who asked her out, and who, on their date, said, "You know, I usually only go out with beautiful women, but you're so *funny*."

And she couldn't forget Juan Pablo Sevilla from Chile. He had whispered endearments to her in bed, *querida mía, niña bonita, linda,* his baritone a fluttering seduction, corny but nonetheless effective, making her squirm whenever she heard it. His gift, his great secret as a man and a lover, he told people, was this: the simple knowledge that to want to please a woman was enough; it showed he cared, whether he did or not. Annie was beginning to fall for his machismo, but his friends, whenever she was introduced to them, kept asking her if she'd met Juan Pablo's sister, Gabriela. It was very mysterious. Even more so when Gabriela visited from Santiago, and she was all over Juan Pablo. It was unnatural, their affection for each other. Annie finally asked Juan Pablo, "Is there something going on between you and your sister?" and he admitted that there was: they

were lovers. Had been for many, many years. "It is sex, but not sex," he said. "It is brother-sister. It is—how you say?—chaste, yes?" "No," she said. "Not chaste."

"I'm glad you can laugh about all this," Joe told her.

"Believe me, I cry about it, too."

"Was your last boyfriend some sort of cowboy?" Joe asked. "I've been meaning to ask you about the honky-tonk outfit."

"No, he wasn't," Annie giggled, thinking of roly-poly Bobby Cho as a cowboy. "I'm just having your everyday nervous breakdown."

"I can respect that."

She glanced up at Joe, liking him enormously for saying that.

"Looks like we're closing the place down," he said. The two young couples across the room were putting on their coats to leave.

"Maybe we should go soon," Annie told him. "Let Rob go home."

He nodded.

"Where you staying? Need a ride?" she asked.

"I'm around the corner at the Goose Inn."

Annie chewed on a cuticle, then asked shyly, "You want to continue this conversation? Maybe in your room?"

"You sure?"

"Just give me a minute," she said.

She went to the back of the bar and used her cell phone to call her sister.

"Hello?" Evelyn answered.

"I got lucky tonight, sis."

"Annie? Where are you?"

"I hooked me a sailor," she said. "I ain't gonna be home tonight, honey."

"Are you going to be OK?" Evelyn asked. "Do you know what you're doing?"

"I'm a big girl," Annie said, not hiding her annoyance. "You know, we used to be so close. When'd it get like this?"

"Don't drive if you've been drinking," Evelyn told her, and hung up.

In the Goose Inn, he lay on top of her, face buried in her hair. "I can't do this," he said.

"Tell me what to do," Annie said.

"No, it's not that." He rolled away and swung his legs off the bed. "Listen, you mind if we get dressed?"

Annie went to the bathroom to put on her clothes. As she fastened the hooks and eyelets on her bra, she peered at herself in the mirror. She looked a mess. Black roots were showing at the part on her hair, her makeup was smudged, there were bags under her eyes. She planned to say goodbye and leave quickly, saving them both further embarrassment, but when she came out of the bathroom, she hesitated, seeing Joe in the chair beside the desk, holding a folded piece of paper between his fingers, sunk into himself, lost. She took a seat on the edge of the bed.

"There's a bridge outside of town, in the marsh, where Highway 1 crosses a canal," he said. He handed her the folded piece of paper. "Take a look at this."

It was an Allstate Insurance check, made out to Joe in the amount of $50,000. She gave it back to him.

"This is the reason I was in town today," he told her. "To pick this up. Last winter, Kathy was driving on that bridge. There was an accident, somebody trying to pass a truck, coming right at her. She swerved, went off the bridge, drowned trapped in the car. I didn't even know she'd been living here. I didn't know where the hell she was, and I didn't care. I hadn't seen her since we were twenty-seven. I don't know, it came out of the blue. I never understood it. One day she just took off. I didn't know what'd

242

happened to her. I was worried sick, I thought maybe she'd been in a wreck or kidnapped by some maniac. Put out a missing person's report, but the police said she wasn't in any of the hospitals or the morgue. I was going out of my mind. Then, a week later, I came home from work, and there she was, drunker than piss on the couch, and over there at the dining table was her boyfriend, scared shitless, looking at me and swearing he didn't know she was married. I yanked the son of a bitch up, ready to whale on him, and he could barely stand, he was so fucking wasted. I could tell from his breath he'd just puked, and he said to me, 'Listen, it wasn't my doing, understand? If you're going to beat the shit out of someone, beat the shit out of her.'

"Later, I found out about it, I found out the facts. She'd gone to Fort Lauderdale and picked the guy up. He was a welder or something, just some guy in a bar. They shacked up in the Ramada Inn for the entire week. Never left the room. Just stayed in there and fucked and drank tequila like it was a honeymoon. They got kicked out of the hotel, and she told him to come back with her to Gainesville. It was deliberate. She'd planned it. She wanted me to see what she'd done, so she brought the son of a bitch to our house. I didn't know any of that. I didn't find all that out until later, but right then, I knew the guy was telling the truth. I knew he was right about Kathy, about who was to blame, and I should've let him go and said to hell with it, but I looked down at her passed out on the couch, her tit hanging out of her dress, and I went crazy. I broke the guy's face in, busted two ribs. I nearly killed him.

"I got put in jail for six months, and around the second month, Kathy came to visit me. I wouldn't see her, told the guard to tell her to go to hell. She didn't come back. When I got out, I heard she'd left town. Never saw or heard from her again. Then here it is, almost fifteen years later, and I'm in Indonesia, and I get this telegram saying she'd been in an accident. It took them over a year to track me down."

For a moment, he was speechless, shaking his head. "She'd made me her beneficiary. Fifteen years I hadn't seen her, and she made me her beneficiary. I don't get it." He stared at the Allstate check. "What am I supposed to think now? Did she still love me? The only way I could get through the last fifteen years was to blame her, to think she hated me for God knows what reason. Why else would she've brought that guy to the house? I think to myself, maybe she left me the money so I'll always wonder, maybe it's part of her hate. But I don't know anymore. Maybe I was wrong. Maybe she still loved me."

They sat silently in the room. There was nothing Annie could tell him.

Joe said, "I just wanted you to know, it had nothing to do with you. You're a pretty woman."

It was raining hard, the wiper blades squeaking muddy arcs across the windshield. Offshore, sheet lightning flared, illuminating the sky for a suspended second, then leaving Annie in the dark of her car.

She flicked on the radio. Linda Ronstadt singing "Long, Long Time." She turned it off. After waiting for a Chevron truck to clear the intersection, its wheels shaving through the water on the road, she swung into the parking lot of an all-night drugstore on the corner. She ran from her car into the store, where a woman in her sixties with coarse white hair stood behind the counter, reading a magazine. Annie was momentarily spooked, thinking the clerk resembled the woman in the tabloid photo, the one hidden in the basement, Delores Hoots.

"Nasty out, huh?" the clerk asked.

Annie realized she had been wrong, there was no likeness at all. The magnifying effect of the lady's thick eyeglasses had made her appear, in that moment, frightened and lunatic.

Annie walked down the aisles to the hair coloring section. She carefully studied the samples, then picked out a box of Number 36 Midnight, Neutral Black—the closest to her original color she could find.

The clerk, as she was ringing up the purchase, gave out an enormous yawn. "Sorry," she said.

"Long night?" Annie asked.

"Sometimes it feels like a long life," the woman said.

Annie got back in her car and pulled onto Highway 1. She leaned over to the dashboard and raised the heat. Light flickered in the distance. More lightning, she thought, flaring down somewhere far behind her. When she glanced in the rearview mirror, though, she saw a pair of headlights—flashing from low to high beam—rapidly gaining on her, blinding her. Before she knew it, the truck had loomed abreast, the coupling between its two trailers bouncing and rattling, and then it hurtled past her, slapping water on her windshield and barreling down the highway in a contrail of spray and tailights.

She stopped her car on the shoulder of the road, dug her cell phone out of her purse, and called Evelyn.

"Please don't tell me you've been in an accident," her sister said.

"No. I'm just calling so you won't worry. I'm taking a little drive."

"In this weather?"

Annie stared through the windshield at the rain. "Ev?" she said.

"What?"

She wanted to tell her sister what she was feeling—that she hadn't been living, she had been hiding, that she'd only been with Bobby because she had been afraid of getting hurt, and he had been safe, he would have never cheated on her, or lied to her, or left her, yet she hadn't loved him—but it was so hard for Annie to talk to Evelyn, who at thirty-four had never been married, who, as far as Annie knew, hadn't had a boyfriend in years.

"I'll be home soon," she told Evelyn. "I want to drive some more."

She rooted through the glove box and found a CD by Emmylou Harris, *Bluebird.* She cued the song "A River for Him," then resumed down the road, following the yel-

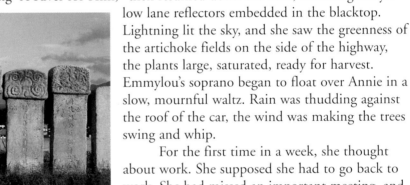

low lane reflectors embedded in the blacktop. Lightning lit the sky, and she saw the greenness of the artichoke fields on the side of the highway, the plants large, saturated, ready for harvest. Emmylou's soprano began to float over Annie in a slow, mournful waltz. Rain was thudding against the roof of the car, the wind was making the trees swing and whip.

For the first time in a week, she thought about work. She supposed she had to go back to work. She had missed an important meeting, and she was behind on a beta test. She had to buy some furniture, a new bed. The queen with the

bird's-eye maple frame had been Bobby's, and he had taken it with him to Seattle. Annie wished she could keep driving instead. It'd be so much easier to keep driving. She had money; she was vested. She could drive forever.

Celebrating the Tiger

Finally, a note about the title of this book. Tigers were present many thousands of years ago when the first Koreans—through the benevolence of a divine spirit—were created in a country they named Chosŏn. In fact, the Tiger who was present at the creation was so jealous of this ideal land of harmony and calm that he longed to be a human—and would have succeeded except that his impatient nature got the best of him at the last moment.

Ever afterwards, Koreans have held Tiger close to their hearts, in folk tales, legends, and rituals, and they've come to know him in all his contradictory, paradoxical manifestations. Tiger became the companion of the Mountain Spirit who founded Korea, and so acts as a messenger between humans and the divine. Tiger is ferocious, but his special affection for Koreans makes him their guardian against invaders. By nature, he is a man eater, but in folk tales he eats only the wicked, unmasks hypocrites, and protects the Golden Thread that binds all Koreans together. But Tiger endears himself not least of all because he is a playful trickster, and at the same time one who is easily tricked. He is a source of humor, and is often portrayed grinning—though we know what a good joke it must take to make a cat smile.

Because of their long association with Tiger, Koreans are like their beloved friend in many ways. Otherwise, how could they have made Tiger into a pet and a member of their family? When Koreans have their claws out, it is often in protection of their independence, their family, and their homeland. But like Tiger they also love to laugh and to celebrate. The twentieth century has tested the Korean character, especially through the decades of foreign occupations, war, and other hardships. Korean heritage and pride, however, are still strong. As a result of Korean immigration, that incomparable heritage combines with and invigorates the best qualities of America's national character. We trust that the next century will bring more reasons for Koreans and Korean Americans to celebrate the Tiger.

About the Contributors

Esther Kwon Arinaga is a retired attorney, writer, and community worker. Her father was among the first wave of immigrants from Korea to the United States and her mother was an early picture bride. Both parents were active in the Korean independence movement. Arinaga is coeditor of *Allan Saunders: The Man and His Legacy* and a contributor and consultant to many other books, including *Montage: An Ethnic History of Women in Hawai'i*.

Heinz Insu Fenkl was born in Inch'ŏn, Korea, in 1960 and came to America with his parents when he was twelve. A writer, translator, and former Fulbright scholar, he directs the creative writing program at the State University of New York in New Paltz. His autobiographical novel, *Memories of My Ghost Brother,* is about the coming-of-age of an Amerasian in Korea.

Jenny Ryun Foster was adopted from Korea in 1974. She has studied Korean literature, shamanism, and folklore in the United States and Korea. A fiction writer, she works as a librarian in Honolulu.

Ok-Koo Kang Grosjean was a poet, essayist, and translator who was born in Korea and came to the United States in the sixties. She translated into Korean the works of Krishnamurti, His Holiness the Dalai Lama, Thich Nhat Hanh, Czeslaw Milosz, and Gary Snyder. With her American husband, she translated into English the Korean poet Pak Nam-Su. Her poem in this volume is from *A Hummingbird's Dance* (Parallax Press, 1994), which renders a life suffused with Buddhist spirituality and deep compassion. In 2000, Ok-Koo passed away after a long illness.

Tom Haar was born in Japan in 1941 and moved to Hawai'i in 1959 with his family. After receiving his masters' degree in visual design from the University of Hawai'i, he spent fifteen years in New York as a freelance photographer. He has had solo exhibitions in Budapest, New York, Honolulu, Japan, and Seoul. In 1983, he was invited to teach photography at the Seoul Institute of the Arts, during which time he traveled around the South Korean countryside. In 2001, he completed a book on the photographic career of his father entitled *Francis Haar: A Lifetime of Images*.

Karen Hong is a painter whose work has been shown at various galleries and museums, including Salon 5, the Pegge Hopper Gallery, and the Honolulu Academy of Arts. In 1996, she graduated with a degree in fine arts from the University of Hawai'i.

Ezekiel Chihye Hwang was born in 1975 in Korea and moved to the United States in 1991. Her paintings and prints have been exhibited at Honolulu City Hall as part of the Korean Artist Association of Hawai'i's yearly showcase and at the Commons Gallery of the University of Hawai'i. She is currently pursuing a degree in fine arts at the university.

Hwang Sun-wŏn (1915–2000) was born in Taedong, in northern Korea; his family escaped to the south in 1946. He graduated from Waseda University in 1939 and taught at Kyŏnghŭi University in Seoul until 1993. In an exceptionally long literary career, he published seven novels and more than one hundred stories.

Ha-yun Jung was born in Seoul, where she lived most of her life before coming to the United States in 1996. She is at work on a novel as a fellow at the Radcliffe Institute for Advanced Study. She was previously the Carol Houck Smith fiction fellow at the University of Wisconsin–Madison and has received a grant from the Korea Literature Translation Institute.

K. Connie Kang was born in 1942 in Tanch'on county, northern Korea. At the age of nine, she fled war-torn Korea for Japan with her family. She did not return to her homeland until 1967, after spending nine years studying in the United States. She returned to the States in 1970. She is a journalist for the *Los Angeles Times* and a columnist for the *Korean Times*.

Kloe Sookhee Kang studied clothing and textile art at Seoul National University in Korea and painting at the University of Hawai'i, where she now teaches. She has exhibited at the Koa Gallery, Honolulu Academy of Arts, and the Contemporary Museum. Among her awards are best-of-show from the Association of Hawai'i Artists and award-of-the-year from the Korean Artist Association of Hawai'i.

Younghill Kang (1899–1972) escaped to America from Korea in 1921, having participated in the March 1, 1919, demonstration and come to the attention of Japanese police. He studied in Canada, then earned an undergraduate degree from Boston University and a graduate degree from Harvard. In 1931, while teaching at New York University, he published *The Grass Roof,* the first Korean American novel, to critical acclaim. A Guggenheim fellowship allowed him time to write *East Goes West.* He later worked as a curator at the Metropolitan Museum of Art and, during World War II, served as an Asian expert for the U.S. government in Korea.

Caroline Jeong-Mee Kim was born in Pusan, South Korea, in 1969 and immigrated to the United States when she was six. She grew up in a former mill town forty miles outside Boston, Massachusetts. She is a graduate of Tufts University, the University of Michigan at Ann Arbor, and the University of Texas at Austin. She has taught creative writing at the University of Michigan and Asian American literature at San Francisco State University. She lives in San Francisco.

Diane Chongmin Kim is pursuing a master's degree in painting at the University of Hawai'i. Born in 1965 in Seoul, Korea, she has exhibited her paintings at the Honolulu Academy of Arts, the Atherton Gallery, and the Coffeeline Gallery. In 2002, she received a Honolulu Academy of Arts purchasing award.

Grace Kim was born in 1967 in Korea and graduated with a degree in fine arts from Sungshin Women's University. Her paintings were exhibited in Korea as part of the sixteenth Independent Exhibition at the National Museum of Modern Art, the seventh Nan Wŏn Exhibition at Gallery Total, and the Kyung-in Museum exhibition, for which she received an honorable mention. Since 1991, Kim has been living in the United States.

Jinja Kim received her degree in painting from Ewha Women's University in Seoul, Korea, in 1965 and a master's degree in printmaking from the University of Hawai'i in 1975. In addition, she has studied at the Pratt Institute of Art and at the Atelier 17 in Paris, France. Her work has been shown in galleries and museums in Korea, Japan, France, Germany, Italy, Finland, and the United States.

Richard E. Kim was born in Korea in 1932. After fighting for the South during the Korean War, he immigrated to the United States. His first novel, *The Martyred,* published in 1964, became a phenomenal best seller as well as a critical success. His other works of fiction include *The Innocent* (1968) and *Lost Names: Scenes from a Korean Boyhood,* published in 1988 and excerpted here.

Kim Ronyoung (1926–1987) was born in Los Angeles as Gloria Hahn. Her mother, Haeran (Helen) Kim, was a poet and activist in the Korean independence movement, and her father was an immigrant laborer. Her novel, *Clay Walls,* was published in 1987.

Sue Kwock Kim has had poetry in the *Nation,* the *New Republic,* the *Paris Review,* and other publications. *Notes from the Divided Country,* her first poetry collection, won the 2002 Walt Whitman award.

Colleen Kimura has been designing and producing screen-printed fabric for clothing, home furnishings, interior wall hangings, and outdoor banners since 1980. She lived in Fiji for two years and traveled through other parts of the Pacific. Under the label Tutúvi, she produces colors and images that reflect the natural environment and cultures of the Pacific Islands.

Chang-Jin Lee was born in 1939 in Korea. Exhibited widely in both Korea and the United States, he has had one-man photography shows in Seoul, New York, Los Angeles, and Honolulu. He is a six-time recipient of the best-image award from the Image Exhibition, held annually in Hawai'i, and has organized exhibitions commemorating Korean immigration to the United States.

Chang-Rae Lee was born in Seoul in 1965 and immigrated to the United States with his family when he was three years old. His first novel, *Native Speaker* (1995), won the PEN/Hemingway Award and the American Book Award. In 1999, he published his second novel, *A Gesture Life,* also critically acclaimed.

Don Lee was born in 1959. The son of a State Department officer, he spent the majority of his childhood in Tokyo and Seoul. His short-story collection, *Yellow,* was published in 2001. He lives in Boston, where he edits the literary journal *Ploughshares.*

Mary Paik Lee was born Paik Kuang Sun in 1900 and immigrated with her family to the United States in 1905. Her autobiography, *Quiet Odyssey: A Pioneer Korean Woman in America,* is one of the few accounts by a first-wave Korean immigrant and is perhaps the only account by a woman.

Peter H. Lee is a professor of Korean and comparative literature in the department of East Asian languages and cultures at University of California–Los Angeles. An influential scholar and prolific translator, he has edited numerous collections of Korean poetry and fiction.

Sandra Sunnyo Lee studied American and English literature at Ehwa Women's University in Seoul, Korea. After moving to the United States, she received her bachelor's and master's degrees in fine art from the San Francisco Art Institute. Her multimedia artwork has been exhibited in Los Angeles, San Francisco, Chicago, New York City, and Frankfurt, Germany.

Walter K. Lew has recently published *Treadwinds: Poems and Intermedia Texts*; *Kŏri: The Beacon Anthology of Korean American Fiction,* coedited with Heinz Insu Fenkl; and *Crazy Melon and Chinese Apple: The Poems of Frances Chung,* which he compiled. He is the author of a "critical collage" on the work of Theresa Hak Kyung Cha, *Excerpts from: ΔIKTH DIKTE, for* DICTEE *(1982).* Lew is currently translating the works of Yi Sang (1910–1937) and writing a biography of Younghill Kang, about whom he has published several essays.

Mary Long was born in San Francisco, California, in 1977 and moved with her family to Hawai'i in 1979. Her paintings and dioramas were exhibited at Hesham's Studio in Honolulu as part of a group show and at the University of Hawai'i Commons Gallery. She now lives in Seattle.

Naomi Long was born in 1974 in Korea and moved to the United States shortly after. Her photographs are forthcoming in *OKAYBOOK (Overseas Korean Artist Yearbook).* She is currently writing a book of poetry.

Richard J. Lynn is a professor and chair of the department of East Asian studies at the University of Alberta. His books of translation include *The Classic of Changes: A New Translation of the I Ching As Interpreted by Wang Bi* (1994) and *The Classic of the Way and Virtue: A New Translation of the Tao-Te Ching of Laozi As Interpreted by Wang Bi* (1999).

Michael E. Macmillan is a publications specialist with the Center for Korean Studies at the University of Hawai'i at Mānoa.

David R. McCann is the Korean Foundation professor of Korean literature in the department of East Asian languages and civilizations at Harvard University. His publications include *Selected Poems of Sŏ Chŏnju, Form and Freedom in Korean Poetry,* and *Early Korean Literature: Selections and Introductions.*

Chris McKinney was born in 1973 and is of Korean, Japanese, and Scottish descent. He is the author of the novels *The Tattoo* and *The Queen of Tears* and has received the Ka Palapala Poʻokela Award for Excellence in Literature and the Elliott Cades Award for Literature. He received his bachelor's and master's degrees at the University of Hawaiʻi and teaches English at Honolulu Community College.

Margaret K. Pai was born in 1914. Her father arrived in Hawaiʻi as a sugar-plantation worker and became a successful furniture and bamboo-drapery manufacturer; her mother was one of the first picture brides and an activist in the independence movement. After teaching English at several high schools on Oʻahu, Pai began writing short Hawaiian legends, poems, and personal reminiscences.

Gary Pak was born in 1952 and grew up in Hawaiʻi. His grandparents were among the first Koreans to immigrate to Hawaiʻi. He is the author of *A Ricepaper Airplane* and *The Watcher of Waipuna and Other Stories*, which won the 1993 National Book Award for Literature from the Association for Asian American Studies. His forthcoming novel is *Children of a Fireland*.

Morris Pang was the youngest of seven children born to a Korean couple who immigrated to Hawaiʻi. He taught for eight years at secondary public schools in Hawaiʻi and for thirty-one years at the University of Hawaiʻi at Mānoa, retiring in 1989.

Ishle Yi Park was born to Korean immigrant parents in New York in 1977. After abandoning business school, she received a degree from Sarah Lawrence College. A recipient of a fiction grant from the New York Foundation for the Arts and currently a writer-in-residence for the program Youth Speaks, she has been published widely. Her first book is *The Temperature of This Water* (Kaya Press, 2003).

Edward J. Shultz is a professor of history and director of the Center for Korean Studies at the University of Hawaiʻi. He has published extensively on medieval Korean history and is a recipient of fellowships and grants from the East-West Center, Fulbright-Hays, and the National Endowment for the Humanities.

Frank Stewart is the editor of *Mānoa: A Pacific Journal of International Writing* and the recipient of a Whiting Writer's Award and an Elliott Cades Award for Literature for his poetry.

June Unjoo Yang is the 2002 winner of the *Chicago Tribune*'s Nelson Algren award for short fiction. At the University of Houston, she received a Michener fellowship while pursuing her master's degree. She recently received a grant from the Cultural Arts Council of Houston and Harris County and full fellowships for residencies at Hedgebrook and the Vermont Studio Center.

Kwang Kyu Yi was born in 1947 in Korea and studied metal crafts at Seoul National Polytech University. An award-winning jewelry designer as well as photographer, Yi has exhibited at the Honolulu Academy of Arts, Center for Korean Studies at the University of Hawaiʻi, and Honolulu City Hall.

PERMISSIONS AND CREDITS

"Would You Go?" by Anonymous. Translated by David R. McCann. From *Early Korean Literature*, edited by David R. McCann, © 2000 Columbia University Press. Reprinted by permission of the publisher.

"The First Wave Pioneers" and "The Struggle for Independence" by Esther Kwon Arinaga from "Contributions of Korean Immigrant Women" in *Montage: An Ethnic History of Women in Hawaii*, General Assistance Center for the Pacific College of Educational Foundation, University of Hawai'i, 1977. Reprinted by permission of the author.

"On the Road" by Ch'oe Ch'i-wŏn. Translated by Peter H. Lee. From *Anthology of Korean Literature: From Early Times to the Nineteenth Century*, edited by Peter H. Lee, University of Hawai'i Press, © 1981. Reprinted by permission of the publisher.

"The Autumn Sky," "Cotton Flowers," and "Looking Up the Oregon Coast" by Ok-Koo Kang Grosjean. Reprinted from *A Hummingbird's Dance,* © 1993 by Ok-Koo Kang Grosjean with permission of Parallax Press, Berkeley, California, www.parallax.org.

"Sending Off" by Hŏ Nansŏrhŏn. Translated by David R. McCann. From *Early Korean Literature*, edited by David R. McCann, © 2000 Columbia University Press. Reprinted by permission of the publisher.

"Cranes" by Hwang Sun-wŏn, "When That Day Comes" by Sim Hun, and "Does Spring Come to Stolen Fields?" by Yi Sanghwa. Translated by Peter H. Lee. From *Modern Korean Literature: An Anthology*, compiled and edited by Peter H. Lee, © 1990 University of Hawai'i Press. Reprinted by permission of the publisher.

"The Resistance" and "Escaping the Oncoming Communists" by K. Connie Kang from *Home Was the Land of Morning Calm: A Saga of a Korean-American Family*. Reprinted by permission of Perseus Books Publishers, a member of Perseus Books, L.L.C. © 1995 K. Connie Kang.

"The Valley of Utopia" and "Doomsday" from *The Grass Roof*, and "East Goes West" from *East Goes West: The Making of an Oriental Yankee*, by Younghill Kang. Reprinted by permission of the Kang estate.

"Lost Names" from *Lost Names: Scenes from a Korean Boyhood* by Richard E. Kim. Reprinted by permission of University of California Press.

"Haesu" and "Faye" by Kim Ronyoung. Reprinted by permission of the publisher from *Clay Walls*, The Permanent Press, Sag Harbor, NY 11963.

"Azaleas" by Kim Sowŏl. Translated by David R. McCann. From *Modern Korean Literature: An Anthology*, compiled and edited by Peter H. Lee, © 1990 University of Hawai'i Press. Reprinted by permission of the publisher.

"Coming Home Again" by Chang-Rae Lee. Reprinted by permission of International Creative Management, Inc. © 1995 Chang-Rae Lee.

"The Lone Night Cantina" by Don Lee. Reprinted from *Yellow: Stories by Don Lee*, © 2001 by Don Lee, by permission of the publisher, W. W. Norton & Company, Inc.

"Oahu and Riverside" from *Quiet Odyssey: A Pioneer Korean Woman in America* by Mary Paik Lee, University of Washington Press, © 1990. Reprinted by permission of the publisher.

"Isan Kajok Spora," from *Treadwinds: Poems and Intermedia Texts,* © 2002 by Walter K. Lew, reprinted by permission of Wesleyan University Press.

"The Death of Kwang Ja" from *The Queen of Tears* by Chris McKinney. Reprinted by permission of Mutual Publishing. © 2002 Chris McKinney.

"The Tragic Split" and "Poinciana" from *The Dreams of Two Yi-Min* by Margaret K. Pai, © 1989 University of Hawai'i Press. Reprinted by permission of the publisher.

"Abŏji's Story: An Interview with My Father" by Morris Pang. Reprinted by permission of the author.

"Dora Moon" sidebar adapted from *Notable Women of Hawaii,* edited by Barbara Bennett Peterson, University of Hawai'i Press, © 1984.

All color photographs in *Century of the Tiger* are by **Tom Haar**, except as noted.

Honolulu Academy of Arts: Celadon bowl, 6; Scroll, 9; Ewer, 20; Celadon bowl, 38; Painting, 40; Scroll, 42–43; Scholar's screen (detail), 74; Wine bottle, 95; Wrapping cloth *(pojagi)*, 132; Cup stand, 165; Bridal robe, 176–177; Scroll, 209; Scroll, 231.

Sajin ŭro ponun tongnip undong: Imjŏng kwa kwangbok **(The Independence Movement through Photographs), annotated by Yi Kyu-hŏn. Seoul: Sŏmundang,** 1987: Student, 6; Demonstration, 67; Firing squad, 83; March First Demonstration, 96; Student, 98; Provisional government, 98.

Sajin ŭro pon paengnyŏn chŏn ui Han'guk: Kundae Han'guk **(Korea 100 Years Ago in Photographs) edited by Kim Wŏn-mo and Chŏng Sŏng-gil. Seoul: Kat'ollik Ch'ulp'ansa,** 1986: Portrait, 27; Flag, 56; Queen Min, 62.

Han'gŭl Calligraphy: Reflection of the Spirit of Korea. **Honolulu: The Korean Society of Calligraphic Arts and the Center for Korean Studies University of Hawai'i,** 2001: 22, 36, 50, 73, 78, 92, 111, 129, 147, 158, 206.

Hal Lum: Collection of Joan Namkoong: Chest, 30; Brazier, 42; Basket, 52; Brushes, 86–87; Large bag, 130; Fan, 144; Hairpin, 166; Octagonal lacquer box, 190; Gold chopsticks and spoon, 193. **Collection of Ai Young Higuchi:** Wooden figures, 173, 189. **Collection of Elsa Carl Lee:** Wedding ducks, 229.

Clarence Lee: Poinciana, 115. **Collection of Waipahu Plantation Village Korean House:** Straw shoes, 45; Child's dress, 70–71, Basket, 127; Shoes, 143; Gong, 238. **Collection of Ai Young Higuchi:** Bed warmer, 69; Lacquer box, 172. **Collection of Naomi Long:** Small bag, 157.

Collection of Ryun Namkoong: 76, 84, 181, 203, 243, 246.

Independence Hall of Korea: Korean National Association, Kook Min Hur, 6 and 79; Buttons, 101 and 119.

National Museum of Korea: Tiger, Frontispiece and cover.

Collection of Elsa Carl Lee: Detail of passport, 28; Family portraits, 31.

Collection of Alice Yun Chai: Picture brides, 46.

A Pictorial History of the Japanese in Hawaii (1885–1924) **by Franklin Odo and Kazuko Sinoto. Honolulu: Bishop Museum Press,** 1985: Laborer's identification tags, 47.

Collection of Duk Hee Lee Murabayashi: Poster, 58; Portrait of Pak Yong-man, 81; Portrait of Syngman Rhee, 81; Portrait of Moses Lee, 102.

Collection of Esther Kwon Arinaga: Award, 115.

Collection of Jenny Ryun Foster: Children, 156.

Collection of Yong-Ho Choe: Pak Yong-man and Korean Military Corporation, 61.

Dosan Memorial Foundation: Korean Provisional Government, 61; Portrait of An Ch'ang-ho, 81.

Courtesy of Dante Hahn: Movable type, 24; Nails, 53; Medals, 103 and 117; Manzanar plaque, 109.

Collection of Sun Il Yee Family: Makaweli Methodist Church, 79.

Han'guk ui ko chido **(Old Maps of Korea) by Yi Ch'an (Lee Chan). Seoul: Pomusa,** 1991: Map 98.

Collection of Young Oak Kim: Portrait, 102.

A NOTE ON THE SPELLING OF KOREAN WORDS

Korean is a difficult language to romanize. In general, the editors have retained the romanization as it originally appeared in each previously published work. Otherwise, they have tried to use the McCune-Reischauer system wherever possible. This has not always eliminated inconsistencies, especially in personal names. The proliferation of romanization systems and, in some instances, the changing preferences of the authors have resulted in a variety of spellings.

Diane Chongmin Kim   *Mute*

ACKNOWLEDGEMENTS

Producing *Century of the Tiger* has been a community effort. For making it possible, the editors would like first to thank those individuals who made generous monetary gifts, many of whom also gave generously of their time, energy, and moral support:

In memory of Pyung Chan Chun
    and Shin Ai Park Chun
Arthur and Patricia Park
Frank and Elaine Min
Helen Pyo Park
Gayle Park Ishima
Ruth Kiehm
Evelyn Choi Shon
Clifford and Esther Arinaga
Dr. Edmund S. M. Whang
Stephen T. Sawyer
Dr. Timothy Y. C. Choy
In memory of Dora Moon,
    Wihla Chung, and
    Ai Young Chung Higuchi
Barbara Choi Takashige and Family

Robert and May Kim
Roberta W. S. Chang
Estate of Timothy I. Wee Sr.
Estate of Miriam K. Wee
George Hong
Elizabeth W. Takahashi
In honor of Mary Hong Park
Melvia Kawashima
Dr. Rosie Kim Chang
Jan Tamura
Lester and Pearl Kim
Hon. Herbert Y. C. Choy
Elizabeth McCutcheon
Esther Mookini
Rachel Lee

The editors also thank the leadership of the Centennial Committee of Korean Immigration to the United States, General Chairperson Donald Kim, Vice General Chairperson Duk Hee Lee Murabayashi, and Academic Committee Chairman Professor Edward J. Shultz, who is also Director of the University of Hawai'i Center for Korean Studies. They thank Elsa Carl and Clarence Lee for the book's design, and photographer Tom Haar for sharing his incomparable work. Julia White, Asian Art Curator at the Honolulu Academy of Arts, generously helped by providing access to the Academy's fine collection of Korean art. Many excellent Korean American artists also offered their work—more excellent pieces than could be used. Among other individuals who were very helpful to this project were Dr. Kyungmi Chun, Henry Ahn, Clifford Arinaga, Charles Park, Roberta Chang, Joan Namkoong, Evelyn Choi Shon, Joan Yanagihara, and a generous donor in Austin, Texas, who wishes to remain anonymous. The editors would like to thank the staff of *Mānoa:* managing editor Pat Matsueda; production editor Liana Holmberg; associate production editor Lavonne Leong; assistant editors Naomi Long, Kathleen Matsueda, and Amber Stierli; Abernethy fellows Celeste McCarthy, Brent Fujinaka, and Georganne Nordstrom; intern Eryn Nakamura; and volunteers Phyllis Young and Lisa Ottiger. The editors would also like to acknowledge the University of Hawai'i College of Languages, Linguistics, and Literature for its continuing support of the cross-cultural and international Asia-Pacific projects of *Mānoa,* which in 2003 is celebrating its fifteenth anniversary.

ABOUT THE KOREAN CENTENNIAL FOUNDATION

The Centennial Committee of Korean Immigration to the United States is building upon the success of the 2003 celebration to establish the Korean Centennial Foundation. The Foundation will initiate projects to further encourage cross-cultural understanding and harmony among Koreans and non-Koreans, and to nurture young leaders committed to the development of both the Korean American community and American society as a whole. The first Korean immigrants understood the power of combining many small contributions to achieve a greater goal, and the Korean Centennial Foundation is requesting donations, no matter how small, to foster its mission. Donations or requests for information may be sent to the Korean Centennial Foundation, Center for Korean Studies, University of Hawai'i at Mānoa, 1881 East-West Road, Honolulu, Hawai'i 96822.

ABOUT MĀNOA

Century of the Tiger is a production of *Mānoa: A Pacific Journal of International Writing,* a non-profit, semiannual publication of the University of Hawai'i Press since 1989. *Mānoa*'s mission is to foster understanding among peoples and cultures of Asia, the Pacific, and the Americas; to encourage tolerance and respect by creating transnational communities and conversations; and to make Americans aware that our shared heritage includes significant contributions from peoples whose origins are in Asia or the Pacific.

To do this, *Mānoa* presents outstanding contemporary writing—often in translations commissioned by the journal—including fiction, essays, poetry, interviews, and plays. Works in *Mānoa* have been cited for excellence and reprinted in such prize anthologies as *Best American Short Stories, Best American Poetry, Best American Essays, Prize Stories: The O. Henry Awards,* and the *Pushcart Prize. Mānoa* has also received national awards for its design excellence.

In addition to publishing, *Mānoa* works in partnership with other organizations to sponsor readings, conferences, exhibitions, and performances. *Mānoa* is also engaged in projects to create curricular materials for secondary schools in order to promote teaching and learning about Asia and the Pacific. For example, *Mānoa* recently joined with educators in Hawai'i and Viet Nam to facilitate face-to-face contact among students and teachers in order to exchange perspectives. Future projects include developing programming for public radio appropriate for student audiences as well as the general public.

Mānoa encourages you to support our many initiatives by subscribing to the journal and by buying gift subscriptions for your friends. And we invite you to become a *Mānoa* Partner through a tax-deductible gift to the University of Hawai'i Foundation, Bachman Hall, 2444 Dole Street, Honolulu, Hawai'i 96822. Please specify that your gift is for account 121-6060-4.

Subscriptions to *Mānoa* for individuals in the U.S. and Canada are $22 for one year and $40 for two years. For individuals in other countries, subscriptions are $25 for one year and $45 for two years. To subscribe by telephone, call (808)956-8833 or 1-888-UHPRESS (toll free). Orders can be placed online at www.hawaii.edu/mjournal/text/order.html. For a free brochure or more information, write to us at *Mānoa* Journal, University of Hawai'i English Department, 1733 Donaghho Street, Honolulu, Hawai'i 96822 or mjournal-l@hawaii.edu.